IN-SERVICE CASEWORK TRAINING

IN-SERVICE CASEWORK

TRAINING

Elizabeth Nicholds

COLUMBIA UNIVERSITY PRESS
New York and London, 1966

Mrs. Elizabeth Nicholds is Chief of Staff Development, State Welfare Department, Hartford, Connecticut, and author of A PRIMER OF SOCIAL CASEWORK (1960).

To E.M.

CONTENTS

Contents

PREFACE

Because so much of my experience has been with the public welfare agencies and because I have for so many years been obliged to struggle with their problems in staffing, this book is written with the public agencies in mind. They are chronically understaffed. Private agencies as well as a number of related professions have no difficulty in outbidding the tax-supported agencies on salaries and fringe benefits. A public welfare agency can expect each year a staff turnover of at least 25 percent, with the largest exodus from the group of most recent arrivals. Here we have young married girls who work for a while and then leave to raise their own families; newly fledged college graduates who find that the grim realities of work with the disturbed and the underprivileged are somewhat less glamorous than they had expected; young men looking forward to marriage who need to find a better paying position before they will feel ready to support a wife; individuals of either sex who discover that half-forgotten problems from their own early lives flare up now to interfere with their functioning in a demanding job of relating to and helping disturbed, unhappy people.

The high staff turnover poses a problem for in-service training since a great deal of teaching time must necessarily go into offering basic material to inexperienced caseworkers who then leave the agency before they have had time to give adequate return, and the whole program must be started over with a new batch of young innocents.

Caseworkers in public assistance as well as in child welfare need to be helped toward a deeper self-awareness than they are likely to reach without guidance. Ner Littner[1] points out that many of the stresses are realistic, and of a kind which the worker recognizes and can deal with consciously; many more stem from the worker's unconscious feelings about events and relationships in his own early life. An untrained worker, or even a trained one, for that matter, may take out on a foster mother his unresolved resentments toward his own mother, or may identify unrealistically with a child who complains crossly about the discipline he is getting from his parents. Supervisors must help the workers know themselves, and must help them grasp the deep-lying motivations behind the clients' contradictory and sometimes bewildering behavior.

Caseworkers, even the newest, the youngest, the least prepared, find themselves working directly with confused, unhappy children who may express their bewilderment by withdrawing behind a cold façade of apparent indifference, or by scrappily preparing to fight the world in whose good intentions they have had no reason to believe. Caseworkers must have some understanding of what is going on inside these disturbed youngsters, and be able to interpret the frequently aggravating behavior to the well-meaning but puzzled foster parents. The workers must provide emotional support when the foster parents are tried almost beyond endurance and are growing understandably discouraged. The caseworker must make every effort to rehabilitate the disrupted home so that someday the child may go back to his family and feel that again he is with his own. The workers must have a sympathetic grasp of the effects on families of financial stress, chronic unemployment, marital discord, the

[1]Ner Littner, *The Strains and Stresses on the Child Welfare Worker, pp. 2ff.*

birth of a defective child, the illegitimate pregnancy of a fifteen-year-old daughter, inadequate housing, racial discrimination. They must have an understanding of ethnic differences and contrasting social cultures.

This is a great deal to ask of young people brought up for the most part in protected middle-class homes. It is an impossible demand to make of a twenty-year-old fresh out of college with no experience of the seamier side of life. All these young workers need help as they make the plunge; help to withstand the onslaught of other people's troubles, to face up to hostile uncooperative clients, to get a sufficient grasp of human motivations so that they can have some confidence in their ability to help and to avoid blunders which might result in further and possibly irretrievable damage to some already damaged client.

Without exception these inexperienced, untried workers come to their new responsibilities eager to do a good job. This is so whether or not they realize what a good job entails, whether or not they remain to make social work a life career. This very eagerness, along with the agency's need to ask new workers quickly to carry a varied and difficult caseload, presents one of the major problems to supervisors and to the inservice training program. The new caseworkers yearn to run before they can walk, and supervisors are tempted to stimulate them to efforts beyond their capacity, to give them a standard of performance which the workers gradually realize they cannot meet. Inexperienced workers cannot do skillful counseling, but they sometimes try, and find themselves in far over their head. They cannot handle play therapy, but they fumble their way into it and do not know how to set limits nor how to interpret what they observe. They attempt to conduct a family interview, and stagger back to the office battered by the cross currents of hostility they did not foresee and could not direct. It is not improbable that some

of the high turnover can be explained by the feelings of
inadequacy and discouragement that new caseworkers experience when they recognize that a standard has been set for
them higher than they can attain.

So the delicate task of the supervisor and the in-service
training program is to keep young staff members always
reaching for deeper understanding and improved techniques
while at the same time saving them from thinking of themselves as useless because clients need and could use more than
the workers are yet equipped to give. They must be helped
to see that it is enough at first to listen sympathetically while a
distressed mother tells her troubles or an outraged father
complains about the younger generation of today. Talking
will help the client. Listening will provide the caseworker with
data from which he and the supervisor together can reach
a diagnosis and a plan of help. The inexperienced caseworker
needs reassurance that listening may be a sizable part of casework, and gradually he will learn to listen with deeper awareness, greater sensitivity. That is why the early classes in our
in-service training programs must deal with communication
and with the techniques of interviewing.

Although these chapters were written for the most part
while I was employed in the staff-development unit of a large
child-care agency, I have never doubted that casework is
generic; understanding is needed by all. In a child-oriented
agency the professional staff must work quite as much with
adults as with children. All social workers, whether they
specialize in child care, old age assistance, family counseling,
or some other area, must see each client as a separate human
being, must be able to relate to all ages with understanding
and acceptance. They must see children as themselves today
and also as the adults they will be tomorrow, twisted and
distorted in personality if they are not helped now. They
should be keenly aware of the physical and emotional needs

of the child at each stage of his growth, as infant, as toddler, as gradester, as adolescent. Equally, caseworkers in the adult program will benefit from a knowledge of the specific deprivations which his client endured as he stumbled along the road toward maturation. They must see the adults as people who are what they are today because of yesterday's childhood, many of them suffering a pressing emotional hunger, in great need of help tardily though it may come. Gradually, as inexperienced, untrained caseworkers begin to see why people behave as they do, begin to understand the needs which make them grope and blunder, the techniques will come, and with the techniques the assurance that they can supply at least some small bit of what is needed.

I hope this book can help. The case material which is included in these chapters was drawn with permission from records of several agencies, with names, dates, and identifying circumstances disguised, of course. I can only hope that the theoretical discussions and the case situations can be helpful to caseworkers whether they are new or experienced, and to supervisors who are trying to help the workers help the needful clients.

I am deeply grateful to Mrs. Rose Savoca for the chapter on work with the families of retarded children. Mrs. Savoca, Assistant Director, Retarded Children's Program, a function of the Division of Child Welfare in the Cuyahoga County Department of Welfare in Cleveland, has worked intimately with these children, has supervised the classroom teachers, and has directed the staff of home visitors who go to the families of retarded children who are either too young to attend classes or are homebound due to a physical as well as a mental handicap. Her chapter adds value to this book.

ELIZABETH NICHOLDS

August, 1965

I

WHY A NEW CASEWORKER
NEEDS TO STUDY

When a person enters upon his first casework position, he finds that he has a great deal to learn. This is true even if he has recently completed a graduate course in social work and arrives at his agency with the ink not yet dry on his master's diploma. He, as well as the new worker who has a bachelor's degree in sociology or psychology, or the little case aide who has only a high school education, must learn about the agency with which he has affiliated.

All organizations of help, whether in child care, public assistance, family service, or any other field, must operate within the limits set by national and state laws, and by the established policies of the individual agency. Every new worker must learn the law as it applies to his agency, must become acquainted with the agency's policies and procedures, must know what services his agency is equipped to offer, what kinds it cannot give. For example, many public welfare agencies may not enter a situation even when there is clear evidence of an emotional problem unless there is also a proved financial need. Some child-care agencies supply no financial aid to families, yet they can give protective services to children who are living with their own parents, or can support the children apart from their families in foster homes or institutions.

Since no agency can be all things to all men, the novice must acquaint himself, not only with the limitations of his own agency, but also with the resources of his community. He must know to whom he can refer a client whose needs his own agency cannot meet. If there are gaps in coverage, as there frequently are, especially in rural areas, the caseworker must find an acceptable substitute—and also be prepared to help with a publicity campaign that will stir the community to an awareness of the need.

Laws differ from one state to another. Policies vary from area to area. Even within one locality procedures change as needs and situations change. Economic stresses, job-training facilities, racial problems, availability of psychiatric consultation, all vary from place to place, from urban to rural, from North to South, from East to Middle West, to Far West. So each worker must know his own community and learn to meet as best he can the needs peculiar to his locality, making the most of whatever resources are at hand.

For this a worker must depend on his own ingenuity and on his supervisor. Many agencies have a more or less formalized orientation program to introduce new staff members to the job. There are usually books, pamphlets, and brochures describing the area, and almost always somebody at some time has written a history of the place. Even if the history is an old one, even if the brochures stress only the local tourist attractions and omit all mention of the grim realities that welfare agencies encounter, still it is well worth the beginner's time to read anything pertinent that he can find. Only thus can he get the tone of his community, the image which the community would like to present to the world. Even if the self-made picture glosses over such shadowy spots as poor housing, unemployment, racial difficulties, that false optimism is something of which a caseworker should be aware since it is an attitude he must face if he is to be of any help in broadening the scope of services in the community.

He must be aware, not only of what may be lacking, but of what is present in the way of need coverage, and that means getting acquainted with other agencies. Many counties have welfare federations from which the tyro can learn about other agencies and their work. The federation may publish a directory, which should be available to all social workers in the community. There are often welfare council luncheons which provide a worker with the opportunity to talk with the personnel from agencies to which he may be referring clients or with which he may be cooperating on a case. Conferences with other agencies or with other units within his own agency, if it is a sizable organizaton, help to give him a valuable over-all picture of resources. A face-to-face discussion of a common problem is far more useful than any number of letters or telephone calls. It is probable that there is a branch of the National Association of Social Workers in the community. Even though membership would be denied the untrained worker, there are often open meetings well worth attending for the insight they provide of the direction the profession is taking.

A new social worker should use every means to acquaint himself with other agencies and other professional people. It is not fair that clients should be deprived of help because of a caseworker's ignorance or misinterpretation of other services in a community. In such matters, a book like this one can be of very limited help. There is not too much that can be said about resources, about legal or procedural matters, that would apply to every agency in every state of the union. However, there are aspects of a caseworker's job that are generic, common to all agencies and to all communities.

Every agency, for example, must have some kind of intake procedure in the course of which determination is made of the nature of the prospective client's need and whether or not he is eligible for assistance from that particular agency. If the need is real and he is for any reason not eligible for acceptance, then he must be referred to another source of help. In all agencies this initial determination of eligibility must be formalized to a certain extent and recorded in some manner. The concept of the intake procedure as a service in its own right as well as an investigation of eligibility is important enough and general enough to be well worth discussing here.

All clients who turn to an agency for help have feelings in common—diffidence, insecurity, fear of rejection, humiliation at their own inadequacy, anger that someone has the power to give or withhold help, bitterness because they are in need, resentment at the circumstances which have made the application necessary. These are feelings which any caseworker in any agency must learn to recognize and to help the client resolve.

All human beings, client and caseworker alike, have certain feelings in common—a desire to win approval, a yearning to be loved, a need for some autonomy to enable them to make their own decisions. The proportionate strength of each of these feelings in different individuals, the sort of circumstances which deprive people of normal satisfactions, the things that happen to them along the way which leave them unable to accept or use gratifications no matter how deep their need—these are matters which a caseworker must learn through training, reading, and experience.

What compulsion makes a man get drunk repeatedly even if he knows that the next day will bring an uncomfortable hangover and deep humiliation?

Why does a client persist in behaving with rudeness and hostility toward the worker who is trying to help him?

Why does a woman avoid employment, although it is evident that she could earn enough to buy comforts she will never have on relief?

When a child is rescued from an abusive mother and placed with foster parents who want only to love him, why does he often behave in an aggressive, exasperating fashion that makes it difficult to love him at all?

Why do children so often remain obstinately loyal to rejecting parents who never wanted them in the first place?

Why does an unmarried woman have one out-of-wedlock child after another when she cannot take care of those she already has?

Why do marriage mates act toward one another in destructive, hostile ways and yet never manage to separate?

We still are not sure how much we really know about what makes people behave in such illogical and self-damaging ways, and we are even less certain how an individual can be helped to change. Sometimes all we can do is provide a better environment and hope that our client is able to make use of it. But sometimes we do catch shadowy glimpses of the half-hidden feelings, the submerged impulses, the subterranean emotions which send people off into unreasonable and unreasoning tangents. Then we, the caseworkers, must be ready to recognize the emotions and the needs for which they are, no matter how distorted, the expression. In this diagnosis and evaluation, graduate training helps greatly. But for those who plunge into social work without the graduate degree, perhaps a book of this kind can be useful.

II

THE INTAKE PROCESS

The first impressions which a prospective client receives of the feeling tone of an agency may well make all the difference to his ability to trust, to establish any relationship with a case-worker, to accept or use constructively the help which the agency is equipped to provide. A client, almost by definition, is upset at the moment of his first contact with a welfare agency. He is in some sort of need about which he may have feelings of uneasy guilt. He has come to ask for help which he knows the agency has the power to refuse. There must be within him an echo of the emotions he experienced as a small child when he asked his father for something he very much wanted. Will father give—or won't he? The need creates a feeling of uncertainty. The memory of the kind of father he had will influence his reaction. Some clients creep in, abject and apologetic. Some bluster, covering their trepidation with brash defiances. Very few can come in calmly, present their situation in a straightforward manner, and face the possibility of rejection without either collapse or blowup.

It is probably doubly difficult if the client has come to the agency, not of his own volition, but because pressure has been applied by another agency, such as the school, which says that his children are not behaving as they should; the visiting nurse, who insists that he must provide better care for an aged relative; or the court, which has ordered him to place his children in foster care. Then the client feels less like a child asking a favor of a parent than like a schoolboy sent to the principal's office for scolding and punishment.

When any client comes for the first time to a welfare agency he is sure to be feeling a highly uncomfortable combination of guilt, insecurity, resentment of authority, and a panic fear of what may happen to him if he does not get the help he seeks. The first person he encounters is likely to be the receptionist, and right then and there he gets his first impression of the agency. The task of the caseworker can be made easier, or more difficult, or next to impossible, according to the attitude which the client is helped to assume at the beginning of his contact.

The receptionist must ask enough questions to obtain necessary information—the prospective client's name, whether he was referred by someone else or has come of his own volition, and a bit about his problem. The receptionist need not and should not get too much involved with the client's situation. Nevertheless, he must learn enough to know with which worker an appointment should be made and, moreover, to recognize an emergency that calls for fast action.

If the receptionist shows by the tone of his voice, the expression of his face, or the phrasing of his greeting and his questions that he thinks the client is a nuisance, or a fool for getting himself into whatever trouble he is in, or that he is just one more of an endless chain of undifferentiated blank faces, then the client will surely react in ways which will make it more difficult to carry out plans for helping him. A client who senses scorn or indifference may try to avoid telling the whole truth about his situation because he shrinks from the expected criticism; he may erect an elaborate defense of excuses and alibis; or he may become belligerent, making angry demands that he would not make if he were given a better impression of the agency's concern for him and his needs. Tact and courtesy will not transform a disgruntled client into a cooperative one, but rudeness and hauteur will inevitably stir up the worst behavior in anyone.

The job of the receptionist demands skill, tact, a nice judgment, and a certain agility in walking a verbal tightrope. Coldness, indifference, a brush-off, an air of scorn, may set a client's teeth so on edge that it will be months before he can accept anyone from that agency as a truly helping person. So the receptionist must remain courteous and concerned. At the same time, he cannot give the impression that he is in a position to make promises or any final decisions. Yet, he must show the client that he is sufficiently interested so that the client will talk freely enough about himself to indicate whether he has come to the right agency, and if he has not, whether he can accept redirecting without feeling abashed or rejected.

A skillful receptionist will sense whether a client needs to talk to a caseworker before he can accept referral elsewhere, but the receptionist should not encourage the client to pour out a mass of intimate material which will only have to be repeated later to the worker. The extent of the receptionist's responsibilities will differ from one agency to another, but the role should be well and clearly defined, understood by all staff members, especially by the receptionist himself and by the caseworker who will next interview the client.

It is vital that the intake procedure be conceived as a service, never merely as a mechanism for testing eligibility. This concept is important for the receptionist as well as for the caseworker who conducts subsequent interviews. Never let the client feel that he has made a mistake or revealed a weakness in coming for help. It is his strength that he is aware of a need and that he feels himself able to use help. A reapplication from a client whose case was previously closed is not an indication of failure, neither the client's nor the caseworker's. People have different rates of growth, and a reapplication shows that the client had grown as much as he was able at the time. Now he is aware that he needs help before he can make further progress.

A good intake worker must have the ability to establish an easy, comfortable relationship quickly. He must have sensitivity to be as alert as is humanly possible to the feelings and attitude of the client, whether openly expressed, consciously distorted, or hidden deep in the client's subconscious mind. He must have skill in making an accurate diagnosis: is the client's situation truly emergent, as he is saying, or is the client in a panic and chiefly in need of reassurance, interpretation, and counseling to help him plan his own solution? The intake worker, as well as the worker carrying the ongoing relationship, must know the resources and the policies of his own agency and the resources available in the community.

Some agencies have one unit, or perhaps one specific worker, assigned to handle intake, while a smaller agency may have less specialization of responsibility so that the prospective client moves directly to the person who will implement the casework plan if the case is to be carried in that agency. In either event there is a caution to be observed here. The warmth that is so important in these initial contacts must be tempered by skill in avoiding too close an involvement. This applies both to the worker whose full-time job is intake and to the worker who may conduct the intake interviews and also be responsible for the continuing contacts if the case is accepted.

The full-time intake worker must certainly relinquish the relationship to someone else when the case is accepted. The worker who does both intake and long-term planning may find that the situation should be referred to another agency, and he will therefore be ending his contacts when he arranges for the referral. To establish a close relationship only to break it off is damaging to the client. An undue holding on is no service to the client and comes from the caseworker's own need. Only when the worker is sure that he is the one who will continue with the help and the planning should he permit himself to move into a close relationship.

Again it is a matter for judgment. During the intake process there are certain questions to which answers must be found without making the client feel that information about his birth place or his previous addresses or his last salary is more important than his present predicament. If the intake worker is skillful, and if his own emotional needs are under control, he will establish an atmosphere that is comfortable for the client without encouraging a closeness that would be hurtful to break later.

Books and articles have been written on interviewing techniques, but most of the instructions can be condensed to a few basic rules:

1. The worker should be courteous.

2. The worker should be interested.

3. The worker should let the client know that he is seen as an individual, not merely as a type or a category.

4. The worker should listen to the client—really listen, both to what he is saying and to what he needs to convey but dare not put into words.

5. The worker should let the client express his emotions without feeling that he disapproves of people who react as the client does. If the client is angry or resentful, the worker should give him a chance to bring it all out. The worker should not argue or try to justify himself or his agency. Once the air is cleared, there will be a much better chance to get behind the client's façade to the real person and his troubles.

The intake worker must be willing to hear the client's story through, and he must be able to see the client often enough, both in the office and in the client's home, to reach an accurate diagnosis. The next move must be either to provide the counseling which will enable the client to find his own solution to his problem, or to start a plan of help with the agency, or to refer him to an agency equipped to provide the needed help. If the agency cannot help him, this fact should be explained, pleasantly and in as much detail as the client can grasp. The intake policy must be flexible, adjusting itself to referral, counseling, or moving into further help as the need and the circumstances dictate.

The type of help the client needs and other factors of his situation — health, age, residence, and so on — indicate which agency can provide what he needs. The Federal Social Security Act and its various amendments have set up basic eligibility requirements for the categorical types of assistance (those which share in Federal funds, such as Aid to the Aged, Aid to Families with Dependent Children (AFDC), Aid to the Disabled, Aid to the Blind). The local units often set up such additional requirements as are permitted within the structure of the Federal law. In some states a certain period of residence is required. Some limit the amount of insurance a recipient may carry, or the amount of property he may own. The eligibility requirements for general relief (home relief) and for medical care for children living apart from their families are set within each state.

If the client has been referred by another agency, some of these eligibility factors will probably be made known through the referring letter or conference, but if he comes in voluntarily, they must all be learned in the first few interviews. However, questions must never be permitted to block the client from telling what he thinks his trouble is, how he feels about it, what he has already done about it, if anything, and what he himself plans or what he hopes can be done. Even if all the external factors are known to the intake worker through the referral letter, still the client must have an opportunity to talk about his situation and what he hopes the agency can do to help him. Listening to the client's troubles is a part of the service which intake can give, and by no means the least important part.

Some agencies by policy will enter a situation only if there is an established financial need, but this does not release the intake worker of such an agency from the obligation to provide the service of counseling or of referral to another agency if the person is not eligible for help from the agency he has chosen.

Whatever the legal requirements may be, if an application for help is accepted, somewhere in the agency's record there must appear a clear indication of the evidences of the client's eligibility. Most agencies prefer that this material appear compactly in outline form on a single sheet well toward the front of the record. This must not be taken to mean that the intake worker secured the facts all at once in a rapid-fire series of questions. Not at all. The information may have emerged gradually over a series of interviews, perhaps coming spontaneously from the client, perhaps in response to tactfully inserted inquiries which did not block the client from explaining his troubles as he saw them. The speed with which an intake worker can secure the necessary statistics depends on the attitude of the client. Some arrive expecting to be questioned and ready to give the answers. Others are so full of their emotional problems that it takes several interviews before they are sufficiently relaxed to put their minds on giving their age, their birth date, address, occupation, and similar data which seem to them unrelated to their immediate pressing need. The intake worker must be in this, as in all other areas, flexible.

Let us look at the "face sheet" of one case in one agency, bearing in mind that while the facts are condensed into an outline for the record they were secured piecemeal over a series of contacts between the intake worker and the referring organization (in this case, the hospital), the parents, and the child himself, whose physical condition precipitated the referral. Other agencies might set up their face sheet differently, but in any agency the sheet can give in compact, easily accessible form the facts necessary to indicate eligibility and the vital statistics which must be known before an agency can formulate its plan of help. In most agencies the face sheet would also indicate what other organizations had known the family.

FACE SHEET

Surname: Carlton
Referred by: General Hospital 5/29/59
Date of present marriage: 6/1/50

Place of marriage: New York City

Family
  Adults
    Father: David, born 2/8/24, Mobile, Ala.; white, Protestant
    Mother: Vivian Burke, born 1/15/33, New York City; white, Protestant
  Children

Ray	born	1/10/51	Mobile, Ala.
Alice	,,	5/19/53	Cleveland, Ohio
Vernon	,,	7/31/54	,,
Ronnie	,,	5/25/55	,,
Barbie	,,	9/12/56	,,
Steve	,,	7/7/57	,,
Susan	,,	10/1/59	,,
Chester	,,	2/10/61	,,
Tommy	,,	12/10/62	,,

Address: 215 Liberty Street, Cleveland
Relatives: None in Ohio
Social Service Clearinghouse

General Hospital	2/18/59
Visiting Nurse Asso.	7/17/57
County Welfare Dept.	3/12/56
Women's Bureau	8/20/55
Juvenile Court	11/20/53

Previous marriages: None
Citizenship: American
Insurance: None
Institutional care: None
Social Security number: Man — 115–23–3541

It will be observed that while this face sheet must have been drawn up in May of 1959, when the agency first received the referral from the hospital and began the intake process, some new information has been added since that date, namely, the birth of Susan in October of 1959, of Chester in 1961, and of Tommy in 1962. Changes of address, divorces or separations, or deaths would also have been added so that current vital statistics would be available to anyone who picked up the case record.

It might be interesting to pause here and see what deductions we might feel justified in drawing about this family from the factual material presented on the face sheet, keeping always aware that the deductions are not final, that we may need additional verification, that perhaps some of the deductions are of no importance in our work with the family.

First of all, we note that the man was twenty-six years old and the woman seventeen at the time of the marriage. Her youth may well be important to keep in mind, especially in view of the number of children she now has to care for. After the birth of the first one there was a lapse of two years, and then five children arrived within five years and two months. This must indeed have been a drain on the woman's health and on her emotional resources. In 1957, at the birth of her sixth child, Mrs. Carlton was only twenty-four, younger than many of the social workers who will be trying to help her.

Almost certainly the mother was pregnant at the time of her marriage, since the first child was born seven months after the marriage. This may or may not be significant, depending on the social standards in the culture of the young couple, but it is something to keep in mind (not, of course, to talk about unless one or the other of the parents wishes to bring it up). If this was a forced marriage, that fact may now be affecting the relationship between the two partners. Also there is a possibility that their attitude toward each other or toward their first-born might have accounted for the two-year lapse after the birth of the first child before the others began arriving so rapidly. This is not a matter on which we would act unless we had far more evidence that it is or was important to the intrafamily relationships; but, being aware of the facts, we would be alert for signs in the attitudes of either parent that it was important to them.

The man came from the South; the woman, from the North. They were married in New York, the woman's birthplace, but must have moved shortly afterward to Mobile, the man's home town. The face sheet offers no explanation of the various moves. We do not know how long the man was in New York before meeting and marrying his wife, but it is worth note that he took her back to Mobile so soon. It is also worthy of note that not long after this the couple moved North again, but not back to New York. Whatever this means, it does indicate that the couple are now removed from any close contact with their own relatives. The face sheet tells us that there are no relatives in Ohio, and our guess would be that the man's relatives are in Alabama and the woman's in New York. How do the couple feel about this?

At the time that this case was referred there were six children, four boys and two girls. When we learn, subsequently, that the hospital referred the Carltons to the agency because of a hemophiliac condition in the family, from which boys suffer but not girls, we are inclined to wonder if the preponderance of male children is not a cause for worry. Later, when two more boys are born, we wonder again.

The report from the Social Service Clearinghouse is not to be overlooked. It suggests the degree to which a family has been able to handle its problems without outside help, or, if the report lists several helping agencies, it shows where we can turn for additional information.

We observe that Mr. Carlton, in spite of his rapidly increasing family, was apparently able to carry his financial responsibilities for a time without asking for assistance. The County Welfare Department reports that their first contact was in 1956, after the Carltons had been in Cleveland for at least three years. The Social Service Clearinghouse report does not specify the extent of the help given to the Carltons, or even whether any help was given. We see only that they must have applied, or been referred in 1956. We must read the welfare agency record to know more.

We see that things had not been all plain sailing even before the contact with the welfare agency. Juvenile Court had a record in November of 1953 when the second child was six months old and the first-born was going on two. A record in Juvenile Court sometimes means a charge of delinquency, but this would be fantastic with the oldest child not yet two. It may mean a charge of nonsupport against the wage earner, or a charge of neglect or abuse against either parent. It will be necessary to read the court record in order to know what happened.

The Women's Bureau in this city is the female branch of the police department. Their report lists a contact in something less than two years after the Juvenile Court record. So we certainly must find out what the Women's Bureau knew of the family.

By studying the face sheet we have learned a good deal about the Carlton family, we have surmised more, and we have seen that there is much more to be learned. So let us turn now to the intake recording, reading it as though we were a caseworker to whom this case is about to be assigned.

III

RECORDING THE INTAKE
PROCESS

Agencies differ widely in their systems for recording information secured during the intake process. Some prefer detailed reports on every interview which has taken place with the prospective client, with every member of the client's family, with every collateral informant. Agencies may copy or file in the record every letter received — those which first referred a client, and those that came in response to agency inquiries. Other agencies, in an effort to cut down recording time and to keep records compact, put all necessary information in outline form. A few attempt to get it all on sheets comparable to the face sheet but set up to include proof of eligibility, the work plan, and other details.

A worker, of course, must follow the policy of his agency, but my own feeling is that a combination of systems is best. The individual interviews may well produce evidence of emotional problems, or patterns of relationships, or methods which the client has developed for coping, that could not well be conveyed in any outline, but which would be important in determining the case planning. At the same time, detailed process recording can become so verbose that records are clumsy and the necessary factual information is buried in a mass of minutiae. There is information which we have a right to find readily in any recording of the intake — proof of eligibility; names of family members and their birth dates; names and addresses of relatives; main problems; the decision regarding disposition of the application.

Somewhere in the record, preferably well toward the front, there should be on one sheet in easily available form this information to which any subsequent worker will want to refer. Perhaps this would be set up like a face sheet. Perhaps it would be more detailed, in outline form, stating the basic as well as the emergent problems and listing the intellectual, physical, and emotional strengths or weaknesses which must be taken into consideration in formulating a plan. My own feeling is that such a data sheet or outline should appear in the record whether or not the interviews are recorded in detail.

Let us go back to the Carlton family. We saw the face sheet for this case in the last chapter. We remember that at the time of the first contact with the Division of Child Welfare there were six children in the home, living with both parents. We recall also that the referral was made by the hospital. So we turn now to what would always be the first entry in the intake outline — a report of the agency's first contact, either a note as to why the client came to the office or, as in this case, a summary of the facts given in the referral letter.

CARLTON CASE

Referral.
5/29/59. General Hospital referred the Carlton family for our consideration because of the inability of the parents to meet the cost of current hospital care for Vernon and Ronnie who are both bleeders and bruise easily. Vernon is presently in the hospital for the second time in three months. He was first admitted 2/18/59 following an injury to his head which caused severe internal bleeding. Surgery was required — right partial craniotomy and removal of the fossa hemotoma, removal of bone flap. Bleeding was difficult to control. The boy was discharged to his home on 3/5/59. He was readmitted 5/15/59 because of further bruising of the head close to the scars of the surgery. It was even more difficult to control the internal bleeding. The doctors feel that the mother is insufficiently impressed with the need for extreme care and the great need for prompt medical attention if the boy is bruised. It seems impossible

that any woman with so many children could supervise to the extent that this boy requires. Three children sleep in one bed, and an accidental blow or kick during the night might have serious effects for Vernon. The boy is now ready for discharge, but the doctors are reluctant to permit him to go to his home. It is hoped by the hospital authorities that a foster home placement might be arranged where Vernon would be the only child and could receive the constant undivided attention of the foster mother. Another boy in this family, Ronnie, is also hemophiliac but his condition is less serious than Vernon's. Ronnie is more tractable than Vernon, whose personality and perhaps his intellectual capacity have been adversely affected by the brain surgery.

Not all referral letters are as explicit as this one, nor do they usually make definite suggestions as to what plan would be considered desirable. The fact that this one does outline a plan of foster home care for Vernon poses a problem for the child-care agency. Any welfare agency will follow the recommendations of medical advisers as far as possible; but good foster homes are in short supply, and it would certainly be difficult to find one in which the foster parents would be willing to assume the care of a willful, five-year-old hemophiliac boy who might bleed to death while their backs were turned. Moreover, even if the perfect foster home could be found, it is not legally permissible for an agency to remove a child from his home without the consent of the parents or a court order. Nothing in the referral letter indicates that foster home placement has been suggested to Mrs. Carlton, and we do not yet know what she thinks about it. Part of the intake worker's job will be to discover how the parents feel about things, to see whether court action is necessary or justified, as well as to determine whether foster home placement is possible if it proves an acceptable plan to the parents.

Since we have already studied the face sheet for this family, we have the advantage of knowing that almost certainly the family is eligible for help from the agency. There is a deficit in the family's budget, small but still enough to show that the family would have difficulty in meeting additional medical costs, such as would be involved in prolonged hospitalization for either of the hemophiliac boys. We know also that the family appears to have lived in this city for almost six years, and therefore more than meets the residence requirement for eligibility. These facts, however, were not known to the agency when the referral letter first arrived. The intake worker must uncover them, as well as learn how the parents feel about the children and the suggested plan for placement.

In this case the full intake process took almost a month, part of which was spent in verifying statements concerning eligibility, but most of which was probably occupied in working with the parents to find a plan acceptable to them which would safeguard as much as possible the health of the hemophiliac boys. The record starts off with the face sheet. This is followed by a summary under topical headings of the information needed to establish eligibility and present a casework plan. Detailed recording of each interview follows the intake summary, but we shall confine ourselves here to the summary, presenting it as one possible method of getting important facts into a concise and easily accessible form:

CARLTON CASE:

Intake Summary

Contacts

5/29/59.   Miss Walsh, social worker, General Hospital, phoned this office.
6/2/59.   Visited Mr. and Mrs. Carlton in their home.
6/3/59.   Letter received from Miss Walsh, General Hospital.
6/4/59.   Telephone call received from Miss Walsh.
6/8/59.   Visited Mrs. Carlton in her home.
6/10/59.   Visited Vernon in the hospital.
6/11/59.   Conference in the office with the Home Finding Unit.
6/15/59.   Visited Mr. and Mrs. Carlton in their home.

6/18/59.   Visited in the Carlton home.
6/20/59.   Visited in the Carlton home.
6/21/59.   Met Mr. and Mrs. Carlton and Vernon in the clinic, General Hospital.

Clearinghouse Reports

11/20/53: Juvenile Court. Mrs. Carlton brought charges against Mr. Carlton for nonsupport. He was ordered to supply necessities or apply for general assistance from the Division of Public Assistance.

8/20/55. Neighbors reported that the Carlton children were left alone and crying. Women's Bureau checked and found Ray, eight years old, in charge of three siblings, age two, one, and three months. When located, Mrs. Carlton claimed that she had gone to the store to buy groceries. She was warned about leaving such small children alone.

3/12/56. Mr. Carlton applied for and received general assistance for four months during a temporary layoff.

7/17/57: Visiting Nurse Association. Called at home after birth of Steve, the sixth child. Found home disordered and confused. Vernon and Ronnie both known to be hemophiliac, but their activities are not controlled in the home. Both boys active.

2/18/59: General Hospital. Vernon admitted to hospital following a bad head wound. Surgery. (See referral letter.)

Statement of Financial Situation

Income and place of employment. Mr. Carlton is employed by American Agricultural Company. His take-home pay is $78 a week (confirmed by three pay envelopes).

Real estate. Mrs. Carlton states that they own no real estate and never have. At present they are renting a five-room apartment on the second floor of a two-family house for which they pay $80 a month including heat but not utilities (confirmed by landlord).

Insurance. Mr. Carlton carries life insurance through the company for which he works. Paid by payroll deduction. The family carries Blue Cross for Mrs. Carlton and all the children. The policy, however, did not cover all the cost of Vernon's recent hospitalization.

Indebtedness. The Carltons list an outstanding debt with Ever Ready Finance Company where they still owe $100 on their car, a secondhand 1954 Chevrolet. Mr. Carlton pays $23 a month on this debt. They also owe the Standard Loan Company a balance slightly over $150 for a loan to pay a hospital bill. They are paying $23 a month on this.

Home Conditions and Neighborhood

The Carltons live in a rather overcrowded neighborhood where there is limited play space for the children. The exterior of the house is in poor condition. There are two bedrooms in the apartment. Steve, the youngest child, sleeps in the room with his parents. Alice and Barbie share a day bed in the living room. Ray, Vernon, and Ronnie sleep together in one bed in the second bedroom. Mrs. Carlton is again pregnant and worrying about the possibility of having another boy who may be hemophiliac, and about how to arrange sleeping space for another child of either sex. Both bedrooms are small and overcrowded with the furniture now present.

Mrs. Carlton seems to make some effort to keep the apartment straight, but she complains that the children quickly have everything cluttered no matter what she does. The family needs larger quarters, especially more bedrooms and a larger yard for play space.

Verification of legal settlement

Mr. Carlton has been living in Cleveland since 1951 (verified by his work record, supplied by the employer). Mrs. Carlton came to Cleveland with her husband in 1951 (verified by hospital records for Mrs. Carlton and the children). The family had previously lived in Alabama, and according to Mr. Carlton, left because Mrs. Carlton did not like the South and felt that her health suffered in the warm climate.

Religion

Mr. and Mrs. Carlton say that they are both Protestant. They do not have any church affiliation.

Marriage

Mr. and Mrs. Carlton were married in New York City (verified by marriage certificate). Mr. Carlton says that he had always lived in the South but went to New York City for a vacation trip, met Mrs. Carlton and married her there.

Relatives

Paternal. Mr. Carlton's parents live in Mobile, Ala. They are reported to be in good health. His father has steady employment and has always been able to maintain his family. They have never visited Cleveland, and the Carltons have never been back to Mobile since moving away. Mr. Carlton regards himself as on good terms with his parents, but he is "a poor letter writer" and has never had money enough for the long trip back South and so has had very little direct contact with his parents since leaving them. He has one brother, married, living in Mobile not far from his parents. There were no other children.

Maternal. Mrs. Carlton's father has been dead for a number of years. She does not know the cause of his death. Her mother is living in New York City. There were seven children in the family, four boys and three girls. One brother and the sisters are still living and in good health. Three of the brothers died in childhood. Mrs. Carlton did not know the cause of their death, but recognizes now that they might have been hemophiliac.

Mrs. Carlton keeps in touch with her family by letter. She would like to visit them but feels she will never be able to do so because the trip would be expensive with so many children. She would enjoy having some of her relatives visit her, but she has never lived in a place that had room enough for an overnight guest.

Parents

Father. Mr. Carlton is of medium height and build. He was rather sloppily dressed when I met him, having just come from work. He is not very verbal and spoke briefly in answer to direct questions. He finished grade school in Mobile. He has not had military service. He seems to think that both Ronnie and Vernon are spoiled and want their own way about everything. He feels that Vernon has behaved worse since his recent hospitalization. He was surprised when the doctors explained the nature of the boys' condition and feels upset by it. He thinks they will never be taught to behave since he is afraid now to use the strap on them. He believes that strapping is the only way to get a child to mind. I suggested ways in which the children might be disciplined by withdrawing privileges, but he did not seem much impressed.

Mother. Mrs. Carlton is a short, plump woman with very attractive features. She was at first most reticent in discussing her situation but talked more freely after the first few contacts. Mrs. Carlton went as far as ninth grade in the New York City schools.

She seems quite overwhelmed by the responsibility of raising such a large family and is concerned because she is again pregnant. Mrs. Carlton said she had not been aware of the medical problem of Vernon and Ronnie until the occasion of Vernon's surgery when the doctors explained it to her. She seemed to have the impression that the doctors blamed her for the boys' condition. She thought they had said that the boys got it from her, and this she could not understand. I am not at all certain that she understood much better after I had attempted to explain that hemophilia is inherited through the female line. She said that she had no idea that any such disease existed or that the two boys were any different from the other children. She had recognized that they bruised easily but she had not thought this was serious. The doctors have now explained the nature of the disease and that only boys have it. That is why she is so upset to find herself pregnant again. She is dreading the possibility of having another boy who may also be hemophiliac.

She was emphatic in saying that she did not want any of the children to leave home. She wants them all together and with her. She says that she will try to take better care of them now that she knows what the trouble is. She had been in the habit of letting them play as they pleased without trying to supervise but now she will watch them, although she does not know how she can prevent them from being bumped and knocked about. They are all active and likely to get into mock fist fights which are never very serious but could mean blows. She feels that Vernon's condition is worse than Ronnie's. Also, Vernon's behavior prior to his surgery was better than it has been since. He is now more disobedient and willful and he sometimes has temper tantrums when he flings himself down and whacks his head against the floor. She would not know how to stop him when he has a spell like that. But she does not want him to leave home. Now that she knows what is required she will try to take better care of all of them, especially Vernon.

This woman impressed me as being limited in her ability to plan for such a large family and in any ability to set consistent controls for the behavior of the children. She may never give voluntary consent to the placement of either Ronnie or Vernon, even if a foster home could be found. However, she is now alert to the need for prompt medical attention in the event that either boy is bruised or cut.

Children

All of the children except Ronnie and Vernon seem to be in good physical health. Ray, the oldest boy, and Steve, the youngest, have not been affected by the hemophilia. All the children are friendly and outgoing, but none of them is well disciplined nor able to accept their mother's somewhat disorganized efforts at control.

Ronnie. This is a four-year-old youngster who has a hemophiliac condition. His mother describes him as having a mild case since he does not seem to bruise as easily as Vernon, and has not had as much difficulty with health problems. He is attractive in appearance, friendly and outgoing, and apparently a happy child. He was hospitalized 3/26/59 for a leg injury and discharged 4/9/59.

Vernon. This boy also has a hemophiliac condition. He was admitted to General Hospital on 2/18/59 where he underwent extensive surgery on his head. (See referral letter.) There is a possibility that either the original wound which necessitated the surgery, or the surgery itself, has resulted in brain damage. The boy seems less controlled and more disorganized since this time. The second hospitalization was because of a second head wound brought about, according to the mother, by a temper tantrum during which Vernon banged his head repeatedly on the floor. The doctors are most reluctant to discharge this boy to his home. They feel that the overcrowded conditions and the mother's inability to handle her children will inevitably bring further serious damage to this boy.

IV

COMMUNICATION

One of the qualities most needed for good casework is sensitivity in communication, and that means sensitivity both in sending and receiving. This has little or no relationship to versatility in the use of language. Frequently, the best communication is accomplished with no word spoken, and even more often it can be accomplished only if the caseworker ignores the dictionary meaning of the words which the client uses, and listens with a "third ear"[1] to the feeling and the need behind the groping words.

Dr. Selma Fraiberg[2] gives a good illustration of a caseworker responding to the true questions behind the words rather than to the literal words. Jimmie, aged seven, has been referred to the therapist because of his reluctance to go to school and his inability to read even though he possesses average intelligence. The therapist introduces herself and conducts Jimmie to her office, suggesting that he might like to look around. This is a good beginning since it does not push the boy but gives him a chance to move into a relationship at his own pace.

Jimmie examines the room and a few of the toys scattered around, and looks at a few of the children's drawings pinned on the wall. "Who drew those lousy pictures?" he demands.

[1] Theodor Reik, *Listening with the Third Ear*. Dr. Reik borrowed the phrase from Nietzsche's *Beyond Good and Evil*, Part VIII. He is referring to the perceptiveness which makes a listener aware of emotions that are not verbalized.
[2] Selma H Fraiberg, *Psychoanalytic Principles in Casework with Children*, p. 3.

The therapist might have answered literally, "Mary Smith did this one, and a boy named Stanley Jones did that one." But that was not what our Jimmie was really asking. He could not care less *who* drew the pictures since he did not know any of the children who come to this office. What he really needed to find out was the attitude of this lady toward drawings made by children, and possibly also he wanted to know how this lady would react if he drew pictures that were not very good. Remember, Jimmie is here because of a school problem. Is he going to be judged on performance as he is in school? The answer to that unspoken question will make all the difference in the time it will take for him to feel comfortable here.

Wisely, the therapist responds to the boy's inner question. She says, "Oh, we all draw pictures here when we feel like it. We don't care whether we draw good or bad. We don't have to be artists. We draw just for fun. This isn't school, you know."

So Jimmie has found out one thing he needed to know. This is not like school, and one is not judged on the perfection of his performance. He is reassured. He moves on to another indirect question. "Jeez," he says with some effort at indignation, "who broke your fire engine?"

Again Jimmie cannot really care who broke it, but, as Dr. Fraiberg points out, this is really a very good question to test the reaction of adults under stress. What the boy really wants to know is what happened to the guy who broke the fire engine. Once more, the therapist responds to the unspoken question: "Oh, one of the kids broke it accidentally, but I didn't get mad."

Following this point neatly, Jimmie says, "If he did it on purpose, would you get mad?"

Now this is truly a poser. Jimmie is really asking just what the words say: Do you get mad at children who break things on purpose? It would be all too easy to make the wrong answer. If the therapist says yes, she would be angry, it would seem to Jimmie that she is now in the same category with all the other adults of his life who scold and criticize him. He would probably do what he has done before with unpleasant adults, withdraw into his shell. On the other hand, if the therapist, anxious to maintain a friendly relationship, tries to reassure the boy by saying she would not be angry, it would appear to him that she is giving permission for open and destructive expression of an anger he knows very well should be controlled.

What the therapist does say in response to this really tricky question is, "I wouldn't like it, but I don't get mad at children."

Children have a need for help in controlling their own hostile impulses which they fear might get out of hand. Frequently, they ask in roundabout terms that somebody older and wiser and stronger set limits for them. This came out very clearly in an interview with a ten-year-old boy who announced abruptly that he wanted to become a Catholic. Now this boy had very little religious background of any kind and could have had only the haziest notion of Catholicism, but he had fastened onto one aspect that seemed to him to fill a need. When the caseworker asked why he wanted to become a Catholic, he said, "You know—you tell the priest things and he stops you. He tells you how to behave."

There are many emotions, many needs, of which an individual may not be completely aware with his conscious mind, or which he is afraid to express because of the punishment or disapprobation he might be bringing down on his head. Or possibly there are things about himself that he cannot easily face. Often the only therapy a caseworker can provide is to help this individual put into words the feelings he dreads to admit. Maybe they are not so horrific after all. Maybe emotional health can be reached only if the client faces what has to be faced, talks through his fears, his self-doubts, his guilt. To give this kind of help wisely takes sensitive timing on the part of the caseworker, and courage in facing with the client something that hurts. The following interview with Conrad shows a needful boy and a kindly caseworker who could not look bravely at the child's pain and thus tried to turn the boy's face away.

Conrad was eight years old at the time of the interview, an attractive boy with an awkward, plunging gait caused by an unidentified neurological difficulty. He is the fifth child in a family of seven. His mother died when Conrad was five. All seven children lived with an aunt during the mother's last illness and for a short time after her death. Then the three oldest were taken back into the father's home; the fourth remained with the aunt; the youngest was placed in an adoptive home; and Conrad and one sister went to a foster home. The boy's propensity for stumbling into things and for breaking delicate articles so distressed the foster mother that she insisted that he be removed. His sister remained in that home.

So here we have a boy who must be quite convinced of his own lack of worth. From his point of view, and despite all reasonable explanations, his mother has deserted him. His father does not want him — did he not take back three brothers but leave Conrad out? The aunt kept another but did not offer to keep Conrad. Somebody wanted his baby brother enough to adopt him, but nobody adopted Conrad. The foster mother kept his sister but put Conrad out. Of course Conrad feels rejected.

The interview took place in the caseworker's car as they drove toward the clinic for another physical examination. Conrad said, "I wish I had a horse. I'd be a cowboy on a ranch."

Now this was almost certainly a television inspired daydream in which Conrad saw himself as swift and powerful (symbolized by the horse) and doing active things like his heroes.

The worker said, "Well, it's pretty unusual for little boys to ride horses."

He meant well, and was probably attempting to reassure Conrad that he is just as good as other boys, but all he actually accomplished was to shatter the dream and bring Conrad back to reality with a bump. Conrad had no reason to think that he was in actuality as good as other boys.

They drove in silence for a while, and then Conrad said, "I had a cowboy hat when I was at Aunt Lily's, but they've probably thrown it away now."

Sensitively translated, this would mean, "Once I had what other boys have, but it got thrown out and I got thrown out too."

Again the caseworker missed his cue. He replied, "Well, you're probably too big a boy for that hat now."

This, Conrad would translate to mean, "You think I ought to get along without needing anybody." His verbal response was, "I don't feel much like a big boy. I feel like just a little boy." ("I know I'm not so big or as strong as other kids.")

The importance of a sensitive alertness to a need which a client can express only indirectly applies to working with adults just as much as with children. Sometimes the client is reaching for evidence of acceptance, of understanding of what he is going through. Sometimes he is almost ready to face up to his own inadequacy but needs help to take the last step into self-awareness. Then the courage of the caseworker must supplement the client's. When a client has reached this point, it is not sympathy or reassurance he needs, but strength to look directly into the grim reality of his own situation or his own deficiencies.

A man had placed his nine-year-old son Peter in the care of an agency following the death of his wife. The loss of his home life was more than this man could face. He began drinking, lost the job he had held for years, lost other jobs, missed appointments to visit Peter, avoided contacts with the case-worker. Things were going from bad to worse until he met a woman who became fond of him and was interested in helping him make a home for Peter once more. The couple married, and Peter went to live with them. Then fate dealt another blow. Four days after Peter's return, the stepmother died very suddenly of a heart attack. The man moved with Peter into the home of his mother, an elderly woman completely unable to handle the badly upset boy. She was nagging-ly critical of the father, who was giving no real help in the boy's discipline and was slipping back once more into the escape of drinking. Once more he avoided every effort the caseworker made to get in touch with him, absenting himself from the home and consistently missing appointments. Finally, after several weeks the worker did manage to find the man at home. The worker's record of the interview follows:

I visited the home after talking with Mr. S. on the telephone the previous evening. He was present when I arrived. He was overly courteous but a little uneasy. He offered me a cigarette twice in less than five minutes. He tried to give excuses for not being at home on the date of the last scheduled visit but became badly tangled in contradictions and finally gave up.

I told him that I had been wanting to contact him because I was interested in talking about Peter and in learning how things were going.

He said in a rather testing manner that he supposed his mother had already told me everything there was to tell.

I said that she had mentioned some things. However, I had been unable to get a clear picture of how things had been with him.

He began to recall the difficult time he had had, and to bemoan the fact that there had been so many changes in his plans. He spoke of the death of his second wife and how shaken he had been over this and how he felt that Peter also had been much affected. He asked if I thought he had done a poor job as a father to Peter.

I said that I gathered plans had not been fully worked out for Peter and that I could realize how difficult everything was in view of the things that had happened. I said that I was aware that he had

made plans for Peter but they could not be carried out because of
the death of his second wife.

He said that he felt he had done the best he could for Peter. He
felt unhappy over having Peter live with the grandmother because
of her age and poor health but he did not know any other place to
turn. He wanted to do the right thing but felt overwhelmed by the
difficulties.

Here is a man who has twice faced a tragic loss. But other
men have faced equally severe losses without coming apart,
without resorting, as this man did, to escape from responsibilities. The worker in the early part of the interview shows
good observation: "He was overly courteous, but a little uneasy. He offered me a cigarette twice in less than five minutes."
This is clearly the behavior of an uncomfortable man, half
inclined to propitiate the caller whom he had tried to avoid
and who may, now that they are face to face, be about to
criticize.

The worker sees this. He does not criticize but says simply
that he had been wanting to talk about how things were going
with Peter. It was good technique on the part of the worker to
let bygones be bygones, and to pick up with the present
situation.

The man's uneasiness is not completely soothed. He suspects that his mother has been complaining.

The worker does not deny anything but puts no emphasis
on it. He opens the way for the man to express his own feelings about his situation. So far, the worker has handled the
interview very well. He has been keenly aware of the man as
an individual—not a case or a category or a type. He has
neither directly nor indirectly punished the man for his past
behavior but has indicated a readiness to start moving from
the present. He has not denied the reality of the nagging,
critical grandmother, but has not put any great stress on it.
He has said by implication, "Your mother does nag, and
maybe that is not too easy to live with, but it is not the most
important thing in the world."

It is not surprising that the man is ready now to talk more freely. He takes the opportunity to parade his difficulties, to bring out excuses for his inadequacies as a parent. The fact that he is unhappy and somewhat guilty comes out clearly when he asks if the worker thinks he has done a poor job as a father to Peter.

But now the worker's sympathy for Peter's father clouds his awareness of what the man is trying to say. The worker's sudden spate of verbalization is enough to prove that he is relieving his own feelings about the man's misfortunes rather than keeping alert to the client himself. The fact that the man speaks as he does about doing a poor job as a father should have been clear evidence to the worker that guilt was very close to the surface. Guilt is never assuaged by a pouring out of blame and criticism—that serves only to strengthen rationalizations—but neither is it resolved by ignoring reality or by smoothing over events with excuses. That only provides additional rationalizations and leaves the festering guilt untouched.

The caseworker in this situation might better have opened the door a little wider, perhaps by saying, "Where would *you* think you have done a poor job?" From the father's response the worker would be able to see how the man sees himself, to what extent he thinks of himself as a failure, how reality-based his impressions are of himself and his situation, how deep his self-awareness, what he believes he should do differently and how well prepared he is to act. The caseworker was right in not trying to tell the man what he ought to do with his life. That would have been worse than futile. What the worker should have done was to help the man himself tell what he should and can do. That would have been the first step toward rehabilitation.

In casual, friendly, nonprofessional conversation one's responses are very likely to be evaluative, to respond to any expression of opinion with agreement or disagreement, approval or disapproval, shifting to a judgment from one's own frame of reference. If someone says, "I don't like what that man said," one will probably respond by saying, "I don't either. I thought he was terrible." Or one will say, "Oh, I don't know. He wasn't so bad."

That is all right. Evaluative and judgmental responses are expected and accepted in day-by-day communication. But in a professional interview they are to be avoided. If a caseworker too clearly indicates his own opinion, he is likely never to find out what the client himself actually thinks or what he wants to do about his situation.

If a small boy bursts out, "I hate my father. He picks on me all the time," a teacher overhearing him may produce one of the following rejoinders. "I'm sure your father is doing what is right for you"; or, "Well, maybe your father is tired and you do too many things to annoy him"; or, "Oh, Tommy, you're mistaken; your father wouldn't do that"; or, "Why don't you try to be a better boy at home?"

Every one of these responses defends the father and puts blame on the boy. All of them evaluate, pass judgment on the boy's statement and, by implication, on the boy himself. Nobody, child or adult, will talk freely to someone from whom he has reason to expect a negative evaluation. Since in social work communication is important, both for conveying an impression of acceptance and willingness to listen to both sides and also for listening to what the client really feels, it is vital that nothing should be permitted to block the free back-and-forth expression. So the social worker must avoid an evaluative response which might dampen the client's spontaneity.

In the situation just described, a social worker would not defend the father, nor the boy either. Instead, he might say, "You feel he doesn't understand you?" or, "You feel that's not right?"

There are solid, practical reasons for acquiring skill in this type of communication, both verbal and nonverbal. Of course, it is probably possible to secure enough factual information by the question-and-literal-answer type of interview to be reasonably certain of the client's financial situation, to figure a workable budget, and to authorize a fair grant of assistance. But that is not casework, or only a small part of it. On some few occasions, temporary financial need is the only need, and delving further would be a waste of agency time and an irritation to the client. But this is unusual. Far more often, financial stress is closely associated with other and deeper problems, either as cause or as result. Then a cash grant of assistance will help only as long as the cash lasts, or perhaps not even that long. Casework help is needed to make it possible for the client to meet and solve his inner conflicts. To provide that sort of help we surely need more than a question-and-literal-answer sort of interview can provide. Before we undertake any long-term planning of rehabilitation we must know the client's emotional strengths and weaknesses; we must know in what light he sees his problems and himself, how realistic his view may be, to what extent he will be able and willing to involve himself in a plan of help. But no client will reveal himself until he has some assurance that he will be understood, that he will not be criticized or punished for past failures or current attitudes. An individual will reveal himself to another only when such communication promises release from tension, and this cannot happen until a good relationship has been established. Relationship depends on mutual respect and confidence. So we are right back to the need for both verbal and nonverbal communication.

V

CONCISE RECORDING

In any welfare agency, a record must be kept of every service provided in any case:

1. To indicate from the point of intake until termination of services the basis for agency participation, the extent of agency responsibility, the manner in which the responsibility was carried out, and the effectiveness of the services.

2. To make it possible for the supervisor and the worker to base an individual treatment plan on the diagnosis of the problem, to maintain continuity of service, and to evaluate the quality of the service given.

3. To provide a learning tool for the caseworker, since in the very act of rethinking an interview, or organizing material for the record, the worker must evaluate the results of his activities, the effectiveness of each interview, the kind of relationship he has established with the client.

This third purpose, and perhaps to some extent the second, might be achieved by handwritten reports, not to be entered in the permanent record but to be discussed in supervisory conferences. In some agencies this is done, but it has seemed to me that several important values are sacrificed. The report will not be available for comparison later when the worker might benefit from looking back to study the line of his own progress. Also, cut-down reports often omit details that could be most enlightening to any future worker to whom the case might be transferred. The very fact that an earlier worker had been inexperienced or inept may provide the explanation of a client's attitude today.

It must be admitted, however, that case records in welfare agencies have a tendency to grow to unmanageable proportions. The clerical time demanded for transcribing repetitious records and the exasperation generated when a reader attempts to locate vital data in a hundred pages of verbosity have put the running record in disrepute in some agencies. Experiments have been tried with the "data-sheet" type of record which lists vital statistics, medical reports, financial reports, and perhaps the dates of client-agency contacts with no details added. There is certainly some value in keeping this information in a separate and easily accessible section of the record, but for any agency that provides casework services as well as financial assistance this record is hardly sufficient. Especially is it insufficient as a learning tool for new caseworkers who want to help people with their marital or their emotional problems as well as with their money difficulties. Any caseworker needs to be able to look back and observe how a situation was handled last month or last year in order to see how the helping techniques can be improved today.

A running record of interviews need not be confused or verbose. Here are a few practical hints:

Description of the person.—Height, weight, coloring, and so on, should be included *only* if these details are unusual, or if they furnish a clear indication of health, potential for employment, or probable reaction of others toward the individual, as in the case of conspicuous blemish or physical malformation.

Description of dress.—Description of the way a person is dressed may be included as part of the narrative if it indicates an individual's attitude toward himself (fastidious or slovenly) or if the clothing of a child shows how he has been cared for.

An extreme of style might be worth mentioning if it suggests the person's self-image. But these details should be included only when they offer clues to an understanding of a client's problem, situation, or personality.

Description of the home. — Select a few typical details. Poor housekeeping standards or extremes of poverty can be shown by a few vivid details. Long descriptions of the whole house room by room only blur the impression.

Description of facial expressions. — Description of facial expressions should be used with the greatest caution. It is easy to fall into the error of using generalized tag phrases, such as "sulky," "resentful," "dull," when actually the expression may be caused by the facial musculature rather than by mood or emotion. Probably an expression should be mentioned only when the worker observes that it has changed in response to a stimulus, or when he sees that it is very different now from what it had been on previous occasions.

Mention of motions and gestures. — Where these suggest medical problems, as do the large, uncoordinated movements of a chorea patient, they must be remarked. An habitual tic should also be mentioned since it provides a clue to the source of inner tensions, especially if it becomes more exaggerated in some situations. Certain other mannerisms, such as frequent sighing, a strong expelling of the breath, nail biting, stammering, chewing on hair or beads, have psychiatric implications and are worth recording once, but not in every interview unless the mannerism changes, ceases, or becomes more pronounced. A rigid, overcontrolled carriage or a very limp, sprawled posture would be worth recording, as would an agressiveness of manner or a self-depreciatory way of speaking. However, it must always be remembered that the manner of speech or gait or stance may be imitative, or assumed for one occasion only. Perhaps these details should be mentioned once for the record and then tabled until more evidence appears to reveal the true basic attitude of the individual.

End of interview.—Since every interview should close with a clear understanding on the part of everyone concerned as to just what will happen next, this should be explicit in the record: "I said I would come to see him next Tuesday"; "I explained that I would call for her at nine o'clock to drive her to the clinic."

The value of recording these arrangements is partly that it emphasizes plans in the worker's mind, and partly that it affords the supervisor or another worker an idea of what the client expects in case a question should arise during the worker's absence.

Even with these rules in mind, records are often voluminous and cumbersome. Let us see if there is a way to make them briefer without loss of content. Kathryn Bork lists four causes for unnecessary verbosity in records:

1. Repetitious and unnecessary words, such as: that; I said that; he said that; however; I said to her that (in conversation with only one other person); also; this; these; those.

2. Minute, lengthy descriptions of office "mechanics" such as searching for a record; detailed recording of attempts to reach a client by phone; common courtesies which can be taken for granted.

3. Lengthy descriptions of client when description is seemingly without other significance to record.

4. "Verbatim" recording—the chronological conversation between worker and client; too often each sentence starting with *"I said to her that"; "she said to me that."*[1]

With these comments in mind, examine the following bit of recording:

Caseworker received a phone call from foster mother today asking for permission to take Chris with them to California. Caseworker was somewhat surprised by foster mother's phone call as I just did

[1]Kathryn Bork, "A Staff Examination of Recording Skill: Part 1," *Child Welfare,* XXXII, No. 3 (1953), 4.

not expect them to be leaving for California at this time of year.
So I question why are they going now, and she says they had wanted
to make the trip during the Christmas holidays but just couldn't
seem to get started. She said that since they are now between terms
at school they felt that this would be a good time to go since foster
father had some time off so they decided that they would leave
tonight. She told me that they expect to drive to California in five
days and visit with a sister-in-law and brother-in-law and they will be
back by the 12th of February. Foster mother told me that she con-
tacted the school and had got permission to take Chris out for the
time they would be gone. Caseworker explained to foster mother
that I had been planning to call her because I had wanted to come
out to see her since I would be leaving the agency soon. I told her
that since they would not be back until the 12th of February I did
not think I would be able to get out to see them and I asked her if
she would say good-by to Chris for me. Foster mother questioned
me as to why I was leaving, and I told her I was leaving to have a
baby. She was quite pleased and said that she wished me the best of
everything, and I told her in return that it had been nice working
with her and I wished them a safe journey. Foster mother also told
me that their son and his girl friend were also making the trip.
Foster mother gave me the address where they would be staying
at 1265 Glenville Parkway, San Francisco. I thanked the foster
mother for calling me and I told her that I was sorry she had not let
me know sooner so that I could get to see Chris once more. She said
that they had been having so much excitement planning the trip
that she had forgotten to contact me sooner.

This is woefully bad recording. There is a sloppy use of
language in the way the report shifts from third person to
first. The recorder starts off, "Caseworker received a phone
call" and in the very next sentence says, "I did not expect
them." Later she goes back to the third person with, "Caseworker explained to foster mother." Either first person or
third would be acceptable, but the use should be consistent.
The worker is equally inconsistent in her use of tenses. She
starts with the past tense ("Caseworker received"), shifts to
the present ("I question why they are going now and she

says"), and back to the past tense in the sentence immediately following. The past tense is easier to use consistently and usually makes for smoother reading. The present tense is used chiefly in recording a continuing situation.

The recording has used many more words than are necessary. Ten times the worker has used variations of the phrase, "she said that" or "I told her that." Four times she mentioned common courtesies that surely could be taken for granted: "I thanked the foster mother for calling me"; "She was quite pleased and wished me the best of everything."

Moreover, the recording includes unimportant details that would seem to have no bearing on case planning. Let us review the paragraph to see which details are of importance for an understanding of what is happening:

1. The foster mother initiates the call.

2. She asks to take Chris the foster child with her family on a trip to California, starting today.

3. They will be back February 12.

4. The foster mother has already made arrangements with the school for Chris to be absent.

5. The caseworker is leaving the agency before the family will be back from their trip.

6. The feeling between foster mother and caseworker is cordial.

Surely these facts can be presented in fewer words than the nearly four hundred the caseworker has used:

Foster mother telephoned that her family is starting tonight on a trip to California and want to include Chris. Their address will be 1265 Glenville Parkway, San Francisco. They will be back by February 12, and have received permission from the school for Chris to be absent for this period. Worker said she would be leaving the agency before the family's return. Would foster mother say goodbye to Chris for her. Worker and foster mother parted on very friendly terms.

Here we have only eighty words, and nothing of importance has been omitted.

This condensation has been achieved largely by concise terminology, but there are also omissions of items that are unimportant for diagnosis or for future case planning. This kind of organization of material takes thought so that nothing of importance to the case as a whole will be omitted. Unless the worker evaluates with care, significant details may be overlooked and nonessentials will clutter the record. Actually, the sorting and selecting of details will probably take the worker longer than it would to dictate three times as many words, but the time is well spent, both for the sake of anyone who consults the report in the future and for the sake of the worker who, in the process of organization and selection, is also doing some diagnostic thinking.

It is wise to omit material from the record because it is useless or redundant. Such omissions depend on the worker's conscious selection, but there are sometimes other omissions of which the worker may be less aware. Charlotte Wilke points out some of these:

1. The omission of the client's statements of his own feelings that though not unfamiliar to the worker may be particularly unbearable at this time.
2. Omission of feelings and attitudes of the client that are less familiar to the worker because of their complexity and are, therefore, confusing, with special attention to the omission of data that resulted in a real impairment of the worker's understanding of the client's problems.[2]

The first might happen if a client expressed hostility toward her husband at a time when the worker was going through marital difficulties in his own life, or if he had seen hostility between his parents and had found it especially

[2]Charlotte H. Wilke, "A Study of Distortions in Recording Interviews," *Social Casework,* VIII, No. 3 (1963), 33.

painful. It is understandable that he might wish to avoid working with this particular problem now. But if a worker remains alert to his own feelings and the basis for them, he can usually handle them. It is a failure of self-awareness that makes the difficulty.

Miss Wilke says about recording:

Reviewing a difficult interview by writing it down generally clarifies it. Having prepared a diagnostic summary, the worker knows more about the problems of the client and is better able to focus his assessment or to generalize on trends of behavior that repeat themselves. Writing it down helps to achieve a sort of logical order. It serves to emphasize a particular assessment and brings out facts that either confirm or modify the worker's thinking in the light of additional material gleaned from the client.[3]

Gordon Hamilton, whose book on social case recording remains basic, makes this statement:

The record is for use, which means that within an orderly, well-organized framework workers must be able to find significant facts easily. One need not be "literary" to write a clear, brief, accurate, objective, usable record, but one must be a professionally disciplined person to do so. Format, structure, arrangement and style should be conducive to readability.[4]

[3]*Ibid.*, pp. 32ff.
[4]Gordon Hamilton, *Principles of Social Case Recording*, p. 19.

VI

RECORDING THE INTERVIEW
IN DEPTH

Correct, concise use of language and thoughtful selection of the details are important to good recording, as we saw in the last chapter. An effort to achieve these qualities will tighten the worker's thinking, and the resultant recording will be far easier for the supervisor to read or for the worker to use later for reference.

However, although these qualities are helpful, they are not the most important considerations in the production of meaningful records—any more than agile fingering is the most important requisite for rendering a piano concerto. Recording in depth needs more than that. It must show what happened during the course of the interview, what shifts occurred in feeling or attitude, what the relationship was between the persons participating, what effects this relationship had on attitude and behavior.

Good recording and good interviewing are so closely interwoven that it is impossible to discuss one without bringing in the other. So we shall review now a few of the qualities of a good interview.

Every professional interview initiated by the social worker should have a clear purpose of which the worker remains aware and which is either expressed or implied when the interview is recorded. The purpose may be to secure information from or about the client: "What luck did you have when you applied for that job we were discussing last week?";

"Was Annabelle promoted to fifth grade this year?" It may be to hand on information from the agency or to discuss plans for the near future. "I have been able to make an appointment for you at the ear, nose, and throat clinic for tomorrow at eleven"; "Eddie's camp closes on Thursday, and I shall be bringing him home in time for dinner."

The purpose may be neither to secure information nor to give it, but something more subtle. Perhaps a new worker calls to introduce himself and to make a start toward establishing a good relationship with a client. Perhaps the call is to further a relationship already begun. Perhaps it is to observe and assess the attitudes and emotions which a client may have toward his situation. In the case of a family interview, it might be to get the feeling of the intrafamily relationships. There are dozens of other possible purposes any one or any several of which might be in the caseworker's mind as he sets out to see a client and which he will hold in the back of his mind throughout the contact — though, of course, not to the extent that he is unable to listen if the client shows a need to bring in extraneous material. Having the purpose in mind will help a caseworker give some direction and control to an interview, but purpose, like all else pertaining to interviewing, must be flexible, adaptable to the individual client and the particular situation, capable of shifting if the situation changes during the course of the contact.

An interview must have some sort of advance plan, the nature of which depends on the purpose. A plan will be flexible, capable, like the purpose, of shifting if the situation seems to make a change advisable. The plan as such is almost never verbalized during the interview, and it may not be explicitly indicated in the recording. Nevertheless, the caseworker must start out with some sort of structure in mind and will be able to see as he arranges his notes for recording whether the plan remained intact or changed greatly, and this of itself will help him assess what happened during the interview.

Let me describe what I mean.

The caseworker knows why he is undertaking the interview. He plans where the interview shall take place and he arranges as far as possible that the setting shall be appropriate to the purpose. His purpose might be to edge the client gently toward some desirable activity. "When are you planning to start Danny in school? He's old enough now to go." If this is a matter in which the client has been slow to act but concerning which she has not verbalized resistance, the worker will probably try to arrange for a setting in which Danny's mother will be comfortable and at ease. On the other hand, the purpose of the interview may be to apply a little pressure toward taking action about which the client has shown resistance. "You must get Danny started in school this year. He is already over school age, and it will be easier for him if you take him on the first day of school rather than waiting for the matter to be brought before Juvenile Court." Perhaps in this situation the worker may feel that an atmosphere that conveys authority might be advisable, and he may arrange for the interview to take place in the office rather than in the client's home. The recording must show the setting of the interview, and it must show the manner in which the subject was presented to the client. The place, the words, and the tone which the caseworker uses, would all have some effect on the client's attitude and response. Later, in reviewing the interview we can assess it accurately only if we know these things.

If any part of the interview is conducted by question and answer, the worker should be careful to give the client opportunity to respond in his own way, at his own speed. If the client is slow or confused or not very articulate, there is always some temptation for the worker to put words in his mouth. Here is an example of an interviewer asking the questions and then answering them himself:

Doctor: How many cigarettes do you smoke?
Patient: Oh, this package I have had pretty near . . . golly, almost . . .
Doctor: About a pack a week perhaps?
Patient: Yeah, I guess about that. I'm a pipe smoker. . . . I have cigarettes here but I smoke a pipe probably more than I ought to .
Doctor: A pipeful a day?
Patient: Well, yes.[1]

We do not really know what the patient would have said if he had been given time to get his words out. The doctor guessed what the patient was about to say, and possibly he guessed accurately. But possibly the patient let the answer go without correction because he did not think accuracy was important, or because he was too shy to correct the doctor, or because he was afraid of being scolded if he admitted to excessive smoking. The caseworker, like the doctor, is in a position of some power. He can help, or refuse to help; he can give assistance or withdraw it. If the caseworker shows too obviously what he expects the client to say, or what he hopes the client will say, the response may not be what it would have been had the client been left free to take his time and select his own responses.

Almost certainly, this would be bad management of any casework interview where one of the purposes always is to discover all we can of how the client feels about himself and his situation. But however the interview was handled, the worker's participation should be evident in the recording. If a client started to present material that was rather intimate and then abruptly withdrew, it is important to understand the worker–client interchange. Was the confidence started spontaneously and then halted as the client began to realize

---

[1]Robert L. Kahn and Charles F. Cannel, *The Dynamics of Interviewing*, p. 4.

the direction in which he was heading? Or did he begin the
confidence in response to a question from the worker and
then stop because something in the worker's expression gave
him reason to fear criticism? What the client says and why
he says it is important. But what he does not say and his
reasons for refraining are also highly significant. To assess
this the caseworker's participation in the interview must be
clearly evident in the recording.

Throughout an interview, in fact throughout a client–
worker contact, the relationship between the two is of vital
importance. The client may fear the worker's position of
authority with the possibility it provides for punishment,
or withdrawal of favor. The client may resent the worker
because he represents a hated father figure. The client may
show excessive dependence on the worker, as on a good
father who will give and give and give. The caseworker should
be alert to what the relationship means to the client, and in
recording any contact with the client he should be able to
select the details which make the relationship evident.

In most planned interviews there will be some movement.
Perhaps during the course of the interview there has been a
shift in the worker–client relationship. The client has relaxed,
has now for the first time been able to reveal himself. Or
perhaps the movement has been a negative one, and instead
of opening up the client has figuratively slammed the door
in the worker's face. The worker should be able in reviewing
the contact to see what might have caused the change. Was
it something which he, the worker, said? Some tone of his
voice? Some expression or posture that made the client open
up or withdraw? Or possibly it was something said or done by
a third person present during the interview? Or had the
client moved too close to painful material which he was not yet
quite prepared to bring into the open? If the caseworker is
aware of these questions as he organizes his notes, he will be
able to select the significant details for the record.

The following is a tape recording of an interview between a foster mother and a caseworker newly assigned to the case who was meeting the foster mother for the first time. The interview took place in the office at the instigation of the foster mother, who asked for an appointment. The caseworker went to the reception room to meet her:

CW: How do you do? You are Mrs. Todd? I am Miss Green, the new caseworker for Johnny. I was planning to call on you later this week, but you have saved me a trip by coming in.

FM: *(smiles slightly but does not speak)*.

CW: Come into my office where we can talk comfortably.

FM   *(follows caseworker to the office but still seems reluctant to speak)*.

CW: Sit down. How are things going at your house?

FM: Well, okay, I guess.

CW: Has Johnny been keeping well?

FM: Oh, yes. He's a real healthy kid. No trouble about *that*.

CW: But there has been other trouble?

FM: Well *(hesitates, and then in a burst)*, I've come to ask you to move Johnny to some other foster home.

CW: I'm very sorry to hear that. What's wrong?

FM: It's too much for me. I can't do it.

CW   *(says nothing, but waits receptively)*.

FM: I'm not sick. I don't have time to be sick. But I can't keep on this way.

CW: It is quite a job taking care of a family, I know. You have two of your own in addition to Johnny, haven't you?

FM: Yes, Marta and Ginny. And my sister's three kids are staying with me now while she's in the hospital. All three boys.

CW: Well, that is a lot of children. Six of them. How old are your sister's boys?

FM: Gerald is four, Donald is two and a half, and little Tommy is fourteen months. And now she's having another. Born day before yesterday. Another boy.

CW: And yours are only four and six, and Johnny is just five. You certainly have your hands full. I don't see how you do it. How does Johnny work into the group? Does he get along with the three new ones? The boys?

FM: Not too well. He's always been more babyish than Ginny, who's a year younger than he is. He claims he can't do things for himself that she's been doing for months, like tying his shoelaces. I thought that was just because nobody ever bothered to teach him maybe. But since these three others came he's been really impossible. You'd think he'd never been toilet trained even. He hadn't wet the bed for a long time and now he's doing it every night. He messes his pants in the daytime too. Just won't be bothered to come inside to the bathroom. And he whines about his food. He used to eat anything I set before him but now all of a sudden he doesn't want this or he won't eat that and he doesn't like the other. He always wants something different. I told him he better cut that out. He's a pretty lucky little boy to be where he gets good food and plenty of it. It wasn't like that in his mother's house let me tell you. But next time he was worse than ever, and when I told him he had to eat up what was on his plate he threw up all over the table.

CW: Well! You do have troubles. What did you do then?

FM: I cleaned up the mess, of course. And sent Johnny to his room.

CW: How did Johnny react to that?

FM: He just sulked. I let him sulk. I had to feed little Tommy and take care of the other kids too. I couldn't be bothered with a lot of notions from a big boy like Johnny. But I guess maybe I was pretty hard on him. He couldn't have thrown up on purpose.

CW: Well, the way he's behaving does make it hard on you. But you can see what's happening to him. Most children get upset and a little jealous when a new baby arrives in the family, and here Johnny is suddenly faced with not one but three new ones who take up a lot of your attention. I expect he's jealous and is trying in all the naughty ways he can think of to make you pay more attention to him. It might even have been his feelings about wanting your attention that made him throw up.

FM: Well, I do have to give most of my time to my sister's two youngest ones. But Marta and Ginny don't act like that. They enjoy having their cousins there.

CW: They know their cousins, don't they? They have all been together on previous occasions, at your house or at your sister's?

FM: Oh, sure. I had Gerald and Donald over for two weeks when little Tommy was born, and I've had the three of them visiting for an afternoon often.

CW: Since Johnny has been with you?

FM: Not overnight. But they've been here for an afternoon half a dozen times.

CW: So your two children know this is just temporary. A visit. It's happened before. But Johnny may not understand. To him it may seem as though they have moved in just when he was beginning to feel secure for the first time in his life. He was with his grandmother for a short time after his mother left, and then in Receiving Home for a while, and this is the first place where he really got as much attention and loving as he needed. His mother was never able to give him much and neither was his grandmother. He's probably been a little afraid all the time that it couldn't last, and now it looks as though his worst suspicions were confirmed. You have been having to pay attention to these other children when he wants you so badly for himself. Maybe he doesn't understand why they are there, or how long they are going to stay. Forever, as far as he can see, probably.

FM: Well, yes, maybe so. But I can't keep this up, extra washing because he wets the bed and messes his clothes and throws up all over the tablecloth. And it wears me out listening to him whine day in and day out.

CW: I can see that it would be aggravating.

FM: Besides, he's getting as much attention as he ever did, and just exactly as much as my own two girls get. I'm not neglecting him.

CW: I'm sure you're not. But Johnny was really starved for affection all through the first three years of his life. He hasn't caught up yet. He needs extra assurance—more, just for a while, than your two girls need.

FM: That's what my husband says. The girls know I love them. Johnny needs to have it proved to him.

CW: That's it exactly. Your husband must be very understanding.

FM: Yes, he is. He was tickled silly when Johnny came. He always wanted a boy. He loves our two girls, but I think that secretly he was a little disappointed when Ginny was born and wasn't a boy. So he was specially pleased about Johnny. He likes having my sister's boys over to the house, too. He's home with all of them right this minute, taking care of all six so I can come here.

CW: Does he know that you were thinking of asking to have Johnny moved?

FM: Well, no. He'd be upset. I'd hate myself to see him leave. But I was so worn out that I just couldn't take it.

CW: I can see that you would be worn out. I think you are remarkable to take on such a lot of work to help out your sister. How much longer will her boys be with you?

FM: Well, not long, I guess. Maybe a couple more days. I could probably hang on for that time.

CW: That would be good. Maybe if you took Johnny aside all by himself and explained it all to him he would try to help you. Could you make him feel important? Have him fetch diapers or safety pins or something when you change the baby? Or ask him ahead of mealtime what he would specially like that day. Just so he feels he's getting special attention.

FM: Well, maybe. It makes me feel better to talk to you, and after all I am getting paid for taking care of Johnny. I ought not to let him feel slighted for my sister's kids.

CW: I'm sure things will come right for you when you don't have so many youngsters to take care of all at once. I'll come over to see you next week after your sister's children have left and see how you and Johnny are making out. He should stage a pretty good comeback as soon as he is sure that you think he is pretty important. But let me know if things get any worse. I can come over before next week if you want me.

Let us analyze this interview to observe its purpose, the planning, management, shifts in attitudes, and movement.

Since the foster mother, not the caseworker, initiates the interview, the purpose is for the foster mother to clarify. She does not do this at once, and her manner shows that it is not easy to put it into words to the worker whom she is meeting now for the first time.

The worker has had little opportunity to do any planning, but she invites the foster mother into her own office for the sake of comfort and privacy. Her initial handling of the interview indicates that her only purpose at the beginning is to put Mrs. Todd at ease and help her express herself. She does this by asking rather generalized questions—how are things going?—has Johnny been keeping well? This is often an effective technique for starting a reluctant client talking. It succeeds here.

The foster mother is able to tell why she has asked for the

interview — she wants the agency to move the foster child out of her home.

The caseworker does not protest, nor does she at this point express the concern she must be feeling for Johnny, who is facing another rejection. Instead, the worker turns her full attention on Mrs. Todd and her difficulties. She sympathizes with the very realistic problems with which the woman has been struggling.

Free now to talk about herself, Mrs. Todd bursts out with details of what she has been going through in attempting to take care of six preschool children. In the course of presenting this material Mrs. Todd reveals a few emotional undercurrents. She believes that her husband longs for a son, which she has failed to give him ("He was tickled silly when Johnny came. He always wanted a boy"). Her emphasis on the fact that her sister's children are all boys suggests some jealousy. The fact that the foster child is a boy must have made his unpleasant behavior harder to accept.

The caseworker probably recognizes this but does not mention it. A sensitive caseworker always sees a good many undercurrents that she does not talk about to the client.

The foster mother's discouraged mood begins to lighten in response to the worker's sympathetic recognition of the reality of her problem: "I guess maybe I was pretty hard on him."

Then, when the foster mother is ready to accept it, the worker offers some interpretation of the dynamics of Johnny's regressive behavior.

The foster mother is not yet quite prepared to act on the interpretation: "But I can't keep this up," and, defensively, "I'm not neglecting him."

The caseworker gives her support — and does not exact pressure to keep Johnny in the home, although it has certainly now become the worker's purpose to hold this foster home for the boy if possible. She has seen that Mrs. Todd is understandably worn out just now but that she is basically good mother and well intentioned toward the foster child. The caseworker also sees that the foster father is supportive toward his wife and understanding of the boy's problems.

By the end of the interview the foster mother's resentment of Johnny has been dissipated by the chance to talk it out to a sympathetic listener who gives full support for all she has done for the child and who never once criticizes her for suggesting that she give up.

During the course of the interview the foster mother's purpose shifts from her first determination to have Johnny removed from her home to a readiness to go back and try again with the help of the worker's interpretation and suggestions. The caseworker's purpose, unformulated at first, crystallizes into a hope that the home can be maintained. The interview ends with the worker's promise to come over in a week or so to see how Johnny is responding.

This is the material from which we must select the important items and which we must organize into a meaningful but compact form. As Gordon Hamilton points out: "It is an error to think that because an interview has followed a certain course the recording should follow the same order."[2] And again:

Organizing material is a discipline in analyzing; it helps us to formulate trends. [We must nevertheless] remind ourselves of the danger in the tendency toward oversimplification, toward oversharp outlines when the life process is fluid and shapeless, the danger of obscuring sequences and possibly of blurring the emotional overtones in behavior and verbalizing.[3]

In the recording of an interview as long as this one, in which situations have been described and feelings that are important to understanding and planning have emerged, it

[2]Hamilton, *Principles of Social Case Recording,* p. 47.
[3]*Ibid.,* p. 64.

is helpful to use marginal notes to pinpoint precise content and to serve as a ready index for future reference. Such marginal notes also help the worker to organize her notes:

Request made for Johnny's removal.	*8/27/64.* Mrs. Todd called at the office to request that Johnny be moved from her home. She has recently been caring for
Mrs. T. is overwhelmed by care of nephews.	her sister's three small boys and has found the task overwhelming. From her report it is evident that Johnny is reacting
J. is regressing as other children occupy Mrs. T.'s time.	badly to the need to share the foster mother's attention. Mrs. Todd seems unaware of the cause of the child's regression, but Mr. Todd has been more
Mrs. T. lacks awareness of dynamics.	understanding. Worker sympathized with the problems in the home, and Mrs.
Mr. T. has more understanding.	Todd was able to accept the interpretation of Johnny's behavior. By the end of the interview she was ready to say she
Mrs. T. is able to accept worker's interpretation.	was fond of the child and would keep him.
Mrs. T. decides to keep J. in her home.	

VII

TERMINATION OF A CASE

Mrs. Atkins, an attractive woman of thirty-two, was a widow with four children, all girls, aged fifteen, thirteen, eleven, and ten. For nine years she had been receiving a grant from AFDC At the time of her husband's death her oldest girl was in the first grade and the others were preschoolers. She was left with no resources and had no relatives to help her.

Mrs. Atkins lost both her parents when she was six, and from that time until her marriage she had lived in an institution run by the Sisters of Charity. When she was sixteen she had left school to marry Mr. Atkins, the gardener and handy man at the institution. He was eighteen years older than she, a kindly, protective husband, fond of his family, but never able to earn much. The first baby arrived eleven months after the marriage, and from that time Mrs. Atkins was kept busy with her husband and her home. Those were happy years for her.

Mr. Atkins died after a two-weeks' illness, and Mrs. Atkins, lost and grief-stricken, turned again to the Sisters of Charity with whom she had lived as a child. They referred her at once to the Welfare Department for AFDC help.

She was then twenty-three — younger possibly than some of the caseworkers were when they were still in college and being supported by their parents. Mrs. Atkins had been well and carefully trained by the Sisters in the art of homemaking, in the care of small children, and in the economical handling of limited funds. She adjusted in time to the management of her small fatherless family on the AFDC budget. In the nine years she had been receiving the grant she had had three different caseworkers, all of whom liked her and regarded her as a good mother and a cooperative client. There had been minor health problems, a few not too serious behavior problems with the children. In general, Mrs. Atkins was looked upon by the agency as an ideal client, unlikely to give anyone a moment's worry.

Now, with all the children doing well in school, and the fifteen-year-old girl capable and willing, it occurred to the caseworker that Mrs. Atkins could move out of the narrow confines of her home and family. She should be able to find employment. The worker knew that she had never had a job, but she was personable and intelligent. Surely there were things she could do even without experience. How about being a waitress? Or a hospital ward maid or maybe a nurses' aide? Or perhaps she could train to be a telephone operator? Full of enthusiasm, he broached the subject to Mrs. Atkins, who looked startled but agreed that with the help of her daughters she could probably manage her home and still have time to carry a job. At his urging she agreed to register with the employment bureau.

It was more than three weeks before Mrs. Atkins kept that promise, but almost at once she was referred to a position as part-time housekeeper and companion for an elderly woman whose son was worried about leaving his mother alone while he was at work. Mrs. Atkins's duties would include light housework, preparing lunch, perhaps doing a bit of shopping, but mostly she was expected to be company for the old lady, read to her, keep her comfortable and amused. She would be free to go home at five and would not be needed Saturdays or Sundays. The pay was generous — more than she had been receiving on the AFDC grant.

This sounded ideal, and the caseworker was enthusiastic. To his astonishment, Mrs. Atkins was less eager. She wasn't well enough educated to read aloud. The house was too grand, she wouldn't know how to take care of it. Suppose the old lady got sick? She had never had any experience taking care of sick people. She had never shopped for people like that. What if one of her daughters came home from school not feeling well? There would be nobody there to take care of her. The caseworker reassured her, told her she would not fail, she had to take such an ideal position. But three times in succession Mrs. Atkins failed to keep the appointments he made for an interview with the prospective employer who, of course, then decided that he did not care to take a chance on a woman so unreliable. The caseworker was disappointed. Mrs. Atkins had never seemed unreliable before. He urged her to go back to the employment bureau.

The next opening was for a waitress in a good restaurant where she would be trained for a week without pay. The wages would not be high, but the tips might add up to something worth while. The caseworker reminded Mrs. Atkins that she had lost the other position because she failed to appear for the interview and urged her to do better this time. Wouldn't it be fine, the caseworker said, to be independent, earning her own money, no longer on relief? Mrs. Atkins agreed without enthusiasm, did apply for the job, and was taken on for the week's training. Three days later, Mrs. Atkins left the job. Baffled, the worker asked her why. The trays were too heavy, she complained. One had tipped as she carried it, and some desserts had slid off on the floor. Her back hurt. She could never learn how to remember orders. She got excited and confused in the rush and uproar of the dinner hour. She couldn't do it. She wept when she told the caseworker about it, but she remained firm in her determination not to go back.

The caseworker was puzzled. His prize client, who had always been so cooperative, was reacting badly. Worse, Mrs. Atkins began to be, in some subtle way, much less agreeable to work with. Previously, she had always been happy to see the caseworker. She had talked freely about the various small daily problems. She had accepted suggestions and advice. But now she seemed not to want to see the caseworker at all. She was sometimes absent from home when he called, or she received him silently, almost sullenly. Even worse, the school reported that the eleven-year-old girl was for the first time failing in some of her subjects. Twice the caseworker met the thirteen-year-old on the street in the company of older boys whose activities were known to verge on delinquency.

The caseworker was upset. What had happened? Was Mrs. Atkins going into the menopause? It was the only explanation he could think of for the change of mood, but thirty-two was young for the menopause. Was she not feeling well? When the caseworker opened the way for a discussion of health, Mrs. Atkins mentioned a series of minor aches and pains, but a physical examination disclosed nothing to account for the symptoms. Why, then, was this small family which had been so successful for nine difficult years suddenly falling apart, just when things ought to be getting easier?

It was Tessa, the fifteen-year-old, who provided the clue. She came to the office without an appointment, and in the caseworker's absence was seen by the supervisor.

Tessa started by saying that she wanted to leave school and get a job. Since she was still of an age when school attendance was compulsory, this was not possible, but the supervisor wanted to know the girl's reasons. She had been doing well and would graduate from high school in another year and a half.

"I want to go away," said Tessa. "Everything is so awful at home. Mom jumps on us for every little thing. She used to be different, laughing and nice. But now she cries a lot, and scolds us all the time, and won't let us do anything. Everything we want to do she says we can't afford. We used to afford things. Why can't we now? She used to make a kind of game about saving for special fun things and making the money stretch. But there isn't any game about anything now. I want to get away."

The supervisor was catching a glimpse of the trouble in the Atkins home. He explained to Tessa that the law required her to remain in school at least one more year, and he encouraged her to plan on staying to graduate. He pointed out that adults responsible for families sometimes had worries that they tried to keep from the younger members. He asked Tessa to be tolerant and wait for things to improve.

When the caseworker returned, the supervisor called him in for a conference. Together they reviewed Mrs. Atkins's background. Here was a woman with considerable native intelligence and many strengths of personality. Yet when had she ever been completely independent? She had moved from the warm security of loving parents to the sheltered life with the Sisters of Charity, and from that to the protection of a husband almost old enough to be her father. His death had been a grief and a deep pain, but there had been the Welfare Department and the caseworkers to depend on. She had never had much money, but always, all her life, she had been able to count on that little reaching her regularly. She could be sure of it. She had also been able to count on approval—from her parents, from the Sisters, from a doting husband, from caseworkers who found her cooperative and showed their approval.

Now, suddenly, her security was threatened. She was asked to take a job—which she might lose; to work for an employer who might not like her at all; to be a waitress on small wages with the chance that the tips would not amount to quite enough. She was asked to leave security and take a chance. The result for her was uneasiness, tension, a feeling of guilt for not doing what the caseworker so clearly wanted her to do, fear of the future if she ventured out on her own and failed.

"Whose idea was it," asked the supervisor, "that she should register with the employment bureau and look for a job?"

"Well, mine, of course," said the caseworker. "I don't think it ever occurred to her to do anything of the sort."

"That's what I thought. You simply told her to register?"

"I explained how good it would be for her to be off relief and independent."

"Did you talk over with her the kind of job she thought she might like and be able to do?"

"No. I didn't know what would come up. But the first one that was offered would have been just about perfect for her. Good pay, short hours, easy work. What else could she possibly want? But she didn't even apply for it."

"Maybe she was frightened of a life so different from any she had ever known, and afraid of what would happen if she failed to satisfy the employer."

"But," protested the caseworker, "if she lost her job, she could apply for AFDC and get it again right away."

"Did you tell her that?" asked the supervisor. "Did she know she could get the grant quickly and that you would not be critical if she failed? You told me you talked to her about being independent and not on relief any more."

The caseworker had done just that. But independence had not meant the same to this protected woman that it had to the caseworker with his education, his experience, and a family to fall back on in an emergency. To Mrs. Atkins, "independence" meant leaving all security, taking a chance on the unknown, with nothing at all to fall back on in case of failure. It scared her. And when she lacked the courage to take the plunge, she was overwhelmed with guilt, and with anger against the agency whose demands created the guilt.

The next time there was a job available for Mrs. Atkins the caseworker did not mention her going off relief. Instead he talked at some length about the job and what it entailed, the parts that he was sure she could handle without difficulty, the parts that might be more troublesome for her. He re-assured Mrs. Atkins that the AFDC grant would continue until she got her first pay check. He reminded her that the wages would mean more money than she was getting on AFDC and that with the higher income she could do more for Tessa during the girl's last year in school. What did Mrs. Atkins think about the opening? If she decided to tackle it, he would be interested in hearing how she made out. He would be happy to see her any time she wanted to drop in the office, and if anything went wrong, the AFDC grant could be resumed promptly.

Mrs. Atkins got the job, and kept it. She came to the office a few times, not for help, but to report that she liked the work and thought her boss liked her. The children, no longer up-set by tension in the home, were doing better, and a year and a half later both the caseworker and the supervisor were invited to attend Tessa's high school graduation.

It takes sensitivity on the part of a caseworker to feel when a client is ready to "go it on his own." It is, of course, a serious mistake to encourage dependency when a client is physically and emotionally ready for independence. Never-theless, if, like Mrs. Atkins, the client has never been in a situation where he must depend on his own skills to earn enough for maintenance, to plan his own days without direc-tion, or if perhaps he is a client for whom the welfare grant is providing the first security he has ever known, then we can hardly blame him for being fearful, for clinging to the safe way. Mrs. Atkins could not bring herself to say that she really dreaded giving up the assurance of a regular AFDC check. Perhaps she could not admit it even to herself. But fear made it impossible for her to create the happy family atmosphere that had existed while she felt secure.

The caseworker had failed to see the situation as Mrs. Atkins saw it. He looked at the prospect of "independence" with his own eyes, in the light of his own background and experience. It would have been far better if he had discussed plans with her instead of springing the idea of a job on her without giving her any chance to talk out her trepidation and fears. He made so evident what he thought she ought to do that she could not tell him how frightened she was of possible failure. Once she knew that the door was open for her to come back to the shelter of the agency, her tension evaporated, she no longer hesitated, and she was able to "go it on her own."

The mere threat of possible insecurity had paralyzed Mrs. Atkins, a woman who was successful in her own sphere. If the threat of failure and insecurity could do that to a woman like Mrs. Atkins, how much more terrifying must be a threat of withdrawal of help to clients who have never tasted success in any sphere, for whom the agency means the first security they have ever known. It is small wonder that they find excuses to avoid taking chances on their untried and untrusted abilities. When a man does not take an available job, the reason may seem to be laziness. But perhaps it is pure terror of the unknown, a panic fear of failure, a deep-rooted dread of having to make decisions, to plan his own budget, to arrange his own life, to assume responsibilities. Planning must be done *with* the client, not altogether *for* him. And he must have every opportunity to talk out his fears, with awareness on the part of the worker that the client himself may not be completely conscious of the fears. None of us enjoys admitting inadequacy to himself; projecting it on someone else is more comfortable.

It is not always a fear of financial inadequacy that makes

a client want to hold to the security of agency help. A child-care agency returned a fifteen-year-old boy from a foster home to the home of his widower father and maintained supervision for some months. Things went well, but when the caseworker suggested that the agency close the case, the father protested. What if he couldn't make the boy mind him? What if the boy got into bad company? What if he tangled with the law? What if . . . one dreadful possibility after another. So the caseworker did the only thing he could do. He gave the father full credit for the way he had handled things since the boy had been back with him, reassured him, and told him that the agency would always be interested in him and the boy, would always be there, and could step in at a moment's notice if the father really needed help.

In another situation, a mother had been coming to the agency for counseling about the behavior problems of her adolescent daughter. When the caseworker suggested that the mother was now quite able to carry on without help, the woman showed signs of panic. "Couldn't you fix it so I could come in just once in a while to talk to you?" she asked. "I used to get so nervous and upset before I was coming here, and I'm afraid I'll get that way again." So she was told that her regular counseling hour would be kept open for her for two months. After that she need only telephone if she wanted another appointment. The mother was reassured— and she never used the hour that was kept available for her although she telephoned several times to report that all was well and that she was surprised and pleased to find that she really was able to handle her daughter without getting upset.

If a case is to be closed, either because the worker feels that the client is now ready for independence, or because he no longer meets eligibilty requirements, or because the case is to be transferred to another agency, the worker must be very certain that the client understands what is happening and why, that he is given a chance to talk about his feelings regarding the closing or the transfer of his case, and that he is given ample assurance that the agency is still there, that the door will remain open. He is not being thrown into deep water to sink or swim. Somebody will stand on the shore watching, ready to throw out the lifeline if one is required.

VIII

MEASUREMENT OF CASE
MOVEMENT

Every caseworker has need of some sort of tool by which he can from time to time measure the results of his efforts. He should be able to determine how far and in what direction a case situation has moved. He should be able to measure with considerable exactness the degree of movement between the opening and the closing of a case. How far did the situation advance toward the original casework goal? Possibly there has been no discernible movement in any direction; possibly there has been retrogression. Or possibly the improvement has gone beyond the worker's wildest expectations. But whatever the situation, a clear presentation in a closing summary will be useful in the event that the case is ever reopened. Perhaps of equal importance is the fact that every time a worker evaluates a case he has an opportunity to learn. Were the original plans realistic? What mistakes prevented the plan from arriving at its goal? What need existed but was ignored, so that no help was offered and no movement made in that area? Can these mistakes be avoided in the next case to be considered?

Even better than the application of a scale of movement at the closing of a case is the periodic review, and application of the scale while work is still being done on a case and there is an opportunity to correct mistakes, change direction, note ways of helping which were overlooked at the beginning.

How frequently a case should be reevaluated depends, not

only on the nature of the case, but also on the size of the worker's load and the demands on his time. My own feeling is that
while every case should be reviewed at least once a year, more
frequent reviews would be even better. It is easy to overlook
the forest as we lose our way among the trees. There is always
a temptation for a worker with a large caseload to operate
from one emergency to another, never stopping to see what
direction a particular case is taking. Or, if he has a number of
difficult case situations to be handled, a worker may let the
quieter ones slip out of mind so that he fails to notice a slow
but steady deterioration. No case actually stands still. There
is always some movement in one direction or the other,
forward toward the goal or backward into old difficulties,
or possibly off at a tangent. There must be movement, if for
no other reason than that clients grow older as time goes by.

It is pretty evident that if we are to measure case movement
we should have a clear grasp of where the situation stood at
the starting point. What, for example, was the extent of the
problem when it first came to the attention of the agency?
People come for help, or are referred, for a wide variety of
reasons, some of which might be:

1. Financial need, caused by unemployment, insufficient
   income, or an inability to live on the available budget
2. Health problems, physical or mental, of the client himself or of some member of his family
3. Marital discord
4. Behavior problems of the client himself or of some
   member of his family
5. Delinquency and antisocial behavior
6. Abuse or neglect of children

The first two reasons for seeking help may or may not be
accompanied by emotional problems. The last four certainly
involve either mental or emotional imbalance. Sometimes
the client is aware of his own inner involvements. More often

he will deny vigorously that his behavior or attitude has anything to do with his unhappy situation and will project everything onto someone else: "It's not my fault that we quarrel
so much. If my husband (or my wife) would only be different . . . "; "It wasn't my idea to steal the car. Bill told me it
belonged to his brother and it would be all right to take it."

It is the caseworker's responsibility to learn the extent of
any external problem — poor housing, unemployment, or
whatever — how the client feels about it, to what extent he
has been able to deal with it, and what he hopes the agency
can do to help now. Even more important, and much more
difficult, the caseworker must discover the extent of the
emotional problem and the degree of insight which the client
has, if any.

So a number of judgments must be made concerning every
case that comes under the care of the agency. Some of these
judgments must be reached quickly, within a week or so of
the opening of the case, sometimes within hours. Is this a
battered child so severely abused that he should be removed
promptly out of harm's reach, or did he really get all those
bruises by falling out of the grape arbor as his parents insist? Is this an unstable man, liable to a dangerous psychotic
episode and better off in an institution for his own safety and
that of others, as his wife believes, or is she projecting her own
unhappy paranoid fantasies?

A diagnosis of the extent of the problem must be made at
the time of intake, or certainly very soon after the case is
accepted. Early in the case planning there should be an evaluation of the strengths and weaknesses of the persons involved,
children and adults. There must be also in almost every case
a careful evaluation of the strengths of the family of which the
client is a member (see Chapter XVII and Chapter XVIII).
Then a practical objective must be formulated in the light
of these strengths. We will not aim for perfection of adjustment. Sometimes even slight improvement of performance

is all that can reasonably be expected. Once the objective is formulated, we decide what is required to reach that objective.

All of these—diagnosis, evaluation of strengths, objective, and case planning—must be flexible and open to change as additional material comes to light. We may find that we must lower our sights, or raise them. We may see strengths that we missed at first, or discover that we overestimated them. And always the case planning must shift as the observed needs and objectives shift. The important thing is to have a plan and not permit the case to drift without direction.

Agencies vary in their demands as to the extent to which diagnosis, evaluation, objective, or plan should be set down clearly in the record, but it is my conviction that in any case in which supportive casework service is to be rendered it all should be clearly stated as early as possible. Certainly, to have the diagnosis and objective set down facilitates any later measurement of a case movement. Only then can we say that the situation was thus and so when we first knew it and it has now arrived at such and such a point, indicating thus and thus degree of movement toward the original objective.

If the case involves a family of two or three or four or more individuals, are we going to measure the movement of one person only? Of all members, evaluating one at a time? Or will we think of the family as functioning as a unit? This depends on the nature of the case, but usually we must take all the individuals, one at a time, interlacing the one-to-one interviews with family interviews to give us a picture of the functioning of the family unit. There can be situations, however, in which one person shows considerable growth while all the others remain unimproved or even regress, so that the functioning of the family as a whole is not much improved. Yet there has been progress for one individual, and this should be recognized.

Are we going to measure the amount of effort the caseworker has expended and the degree of skill he has shown, or are we going to measure what happens within and to the client himself, whether or not the changes have occurred as a result of casework effort? I feel that our measurements should be client-centered. There is certainly a place for recognition of casework effort and casework skill, which in a difficult situation may produce a discouragingly small amount of movement in the case. But I believe that here we should keep our attention on the client and should measure what happens to or in him. After we have done that, it might well be instructive to analyze the extent to which the movement was the result of casework effort.

Nor do we measure the end result of case movement against the ideal. We do not ask, "Has this person become a perfectly happy, mature individual functioning with maximum effectiveness?" Instead we inquire, "Is this person functioning more effectively or more comfortably than he was?" Medicine does not judge its success by any absolute standard of health. In many conditions, a 25 percent restoration of function may be considered excellent. We are concerned with the extent of improvement, not the ratio between the end result and perfection. There would be more movement in a case situation that was very bad at the start and pretty good at the close than in one that was pretty good at the beginning and ended the same way.

Hunt and Kogan define movement in a case as the "change that appears in the adaptive efficiency, in the disabling habits and conditions, and in the verbalized attitudes and understanding of an individual client and/or in his environmental situation between the opening and the closing of the case."[1]

Since I believe so strongly in the desirability of evaluating movement in a case periodically while it is active, I should like to change the last phrase of this definition to read, "during

---

[1] J. McV. Hunt and Leonard S. Kogan, *Measuring Results in Social Casework*, p. 25.

the period of time between the last evaluation and the current evaluation."

Now to define some of the terms used in this definition:

Adaptive efficiency. — This means changes in the effectiveness of functioning in any area, such as getting along with other people, running a home, handling financial resources. It might refer to improved schoolwork, new skills in planning, better ability to concentrate, wiser use of community resources, new habits of social behavior which improve personal relationships or functioning in various roles. Improved adaptive efficiency may come about as a result of increased knowledge, as might occur when a formerly inefficient home-maker is taught how to prepare meals, make a bed, or keep clothing in good condition. Or it might come about as a result of a changed outlook or an improved self-image, either of which may bring an improved relationship with people or a better performance of duties.

Change in disabling habits or conditions. — This might happen if an adolescent gave up delinquent behavior, or an over-anxious woman relaxed and grew less tense. It may also refer to improved health or the correction of any crippling physical disability.

Verbalized attitudes and understanding. — This refers to whatever a client may say about himself, other people, or his situation which shows better understanding, an improved attitude, or deeper insight. It is not to be expected of children, who rarely formalize motivation or any new grasp of relationships, and it is not to be accepted as a trustworthy indication of improvement unless accompanied by a change in behavior.

Environmental situation. — This refers to a change in the physical environment, such as improved housing, better clothing, better diet, or improved economic circumstances that might come with a better job or better salary. Or it may be an improved social environment, as when the attitudes of other people toward the client improve. The change in the attitude of parents toward a child probably indicate an improved adaptive efficiency on the part of the parents and an improved environment for the child.

Following is a suggested outline to use in evaluating case progress, either at the time the case is terminated by the agency or, better, at intervals throughout the period that the case is carried for service. This, like any other suggested outline, can and should be adapted to the individual case situation and to the special types of service provided by the agency.

OUTLINE FOR ANALYSIS OF CASE PROGRESS

I. Opening Picture
   This should briefly outline the concrete evidence concerning:
   A. How effectively the client was functioning in the various areas of his life, e.g., job, home, school, interpersonal relations
   B. What disabling habits and conditions interfered with his effectiveness, his interpersonal relations, his satisfactions with life
   C. What his attitudes were toward his situation and his understanding of it as gleaned from his own verbalization (not necessarily applicable if the client is a child)
   D. What his environmental situation was from the standpoint of clothing, living quarters, job, school placement, and from the standpoint of the behavior of other people toward him

II. History
   This should give only enough family history to explain statements made in Section I.

III. Casework Plan
   This should present very briefly the plan or objective as seen at the time the case was opened. If the plan changed, or was divided into phases, these different plans and phases may be described in Section IV.

IV. Casework Process
   This should outline briefly any action taken by the caseworker

during the period that the case was open: correction of poor health conditions; change of home environment; help through supportive relationship; interpretation to other individuals which might improve interpersonal relationships, etc.

V. Current Picture

This should contain concrete evidence concerning:

A. How effectively the client is functioning in the various phases of his life at the time the closing summary or transfer summary is being written

B. What disabling habits or conditions still interfere with his effectiveness, his interpersonal relationship, and his satisfaction with life

C. What new attitudes or understanding he has of himself, of others, of his situation. (In the case of adults or adolescents this may emerge through verbalization, backed by attitude and behavior. In the case of younger children it may be shown only through behavior.)

D. What his environmental situation is, especially from the standpoint of the behavior of other people toward him.

IX

MEASURING MOVEMENT IN THE WILCOX CASE

The Wilcox family came to the attention of the agency when the parents were charged with neglect and their children, aged four, three, two, and nine months, were placed in foster care. Mr. and Mrs. Wilcox, evicted from their two-room basement apartment for nonpayment of rent, separated, each going to the home of his own parents.

The case record showed that both Mr. and Mrs. Wilcox were alcoholic and had been given numerous warnings about neglecting the children. Mr. Wilcox had had several brushes with the law for minor delinquencies and for drunkenness. His parents' family had been known to a number of agencies, and had received public assistance help in the frequent intervals between the elder Wilcox's irregular employment.

The first half dozen interviews with Mr. Wilcox brought out some background information. He was the oldest of eight children. He had left school at sixteen when he was in the fifth grade and failing. He disliked school and was glad to be out of it. His work record was poor. He had never held a job for more than a few months, and was currently unemployed. He blamed his present predicament on his wife, who spent too much time walking the streets, never cooked a decent meal, never lifted a finger to make the apartment livable. He expressed affection for his children and a wish to reestablish a home for them, but his only suggestion was to take them into his mother's home. He knew his wife would never live with him there, but he was confident that his mother would take care of the four little ones. There were nine persons already living in this four-room apartment. His father was in the workhouse for nonsupport, but the mother was receiving AFDC help for herself and the five younger siblings who were eligible. The three oldest, including Mr. Wilcox himself, were living there too, but had no income and were constantly embroiled with the welfare agency, which was threatening to withdraw the AFDC grant if they did not contribute toward their own support. Obviously, a welfare grant intended to meet the need of six persons was being stretched to cover the demands of nine, three of them adults. According to Mr. Wilcox, however, his mother felt they could all manage somehow and had said that she would be happy to take in his four children also. She did not get along with her son's wife and would not welcome her in the home. Mr. Wilcox seemed to feel that it would be a fine plan to add his children to this ménage and to forget all about his wife.

The agency found that there was also a court record of the younger Mrs. Wilcox. She had been picked up several times by the police, wandering the streets aimlessly late at night. This had happened only within the last two years. They had no earlier record of her and none of her family. When she was warned about neglecting her children she had insisted that she always left them with a baby sitter, but the police woman who escorted her home felt that the sitters were too immature and too uninterested to be reliable.

Mrs. Wilcox talked less freely than her husband had, and it was necessary to see her in her parents' home many times before the whole picture emerged. Mrs. Wilcox, mother of four, was nineteen years old when the case was referred by the court. She had liked school, had reached the ninth grade by the time she was fifteen and was then obliged to leave because of her pregnancy. She was an only child, and her situation had distressed her parents very much. The mother thought that she should marry, but the court refused permission because of her age. The mother insisted, and arranged for the young couple to go to an adjoining state where they could marry without special court permission. The father was a quiet man, rather dominated by his wife. He had steady employment; in fact, he had held the same job for twelve years. He had asked for public assistance only once, when his wife has needed massive surgery for osteomyelitis. She was now a double amputee, but got around on prosthetic legs and managed all her housework without help.

The parents were quite willing for Mrs. Wilcox to remain in their home but felt there was not enough space for the four children. Mrs. Wilcox was sleeping on a couch in the living room while the parents occupied the only bedroom. Both parents were openly critical of Mr. Wilcox "who had got the innocent girl pregnant and now wouldn't support her." The mother especially was loud in asserting that he should be severely punished and was critical of the court for not putting him in jail.

It took several weeks of undemanding interviews before Mrs. Wilcox was able to talk with any freedom about her own feelings. When she did begin to talk she said over and over that she wanted to have her children with her. If they could not be with her all day and all night, she wanted to be able to visit them frequently. She said she did not want them to feel abandoned. She explained her drinking during the last two years, and her wandering the streets at night, as caused by her need to escape from the dingy apartment and also as an effort to show up her husband—if he got drunk, so could she, and that would show him how silly it was. She added that it wasn't much fun. It usually made her sick.

In one interview she suggested that she take the children with her, find an apartment, and apply for AFDC. Her mother, however, was against such a plan. Mr. Wilcox would not leave her alone. It wasn't right that a daughter of hers should be on relief. She would be ashamed to have it known that a member of her family needed public help.

Mrs. Wilcox's next suggestion was that she find a job and hire a housekeeper to take care of the children during the day. Her mother was against this plan also. Mrs. Wilcox had no training and no work experience. Her health was not too rugged. She had had four years of marriage which had been difficult—she needed a rest. In this the caseworker concurred although his reasoning was not quite the same. It seemed to him unrealistic to suppose that Mrs. Wilcox would be able to earn enough to pay an efficient housekeeper. She was very thin, with a bad complexion and very poor teeth. Her appearance would make it impossible for her to get work as a waitress or a salesgirl, the jobs for which her meager education might have fitted her. Mrs. Wilcox accepted the decisions of her mother and the caseworker, but again brought up her wish to see her children as often as could be arranged. The caseworker agreed to bring all the children to the office twice a month where Mrs. Wilcox could stay with them for an afternoon. Mr. Wilcox was told of the arrangement, and sometimes he also appeared for the visit. The worker observed that the young parents had little to say to one another. The children went naturally and easily to Mrs. Wilcox but were less interested in Mr. Wilcox.

Through his observations and through the content emerging from many interviews, the caseworker was evaluating the situation. Although neither Mr. nor Mrs. Wilcox had been adequate in assuming parental responsibilities, both had verbalized affection and interest in the children. There was no evidence of abuse of the children and no record of Mr. Wilcox striking the children or his wife, even when he was drunk. There was no report of marital infidelity. It was felt that their concern and sense of responsibility as parents might be reactivated and the home reestablished.

Mr. Wilcox was seen as the weaker and less promising of the two. His motivation was weak. He had been given little stimulation at any time toward self-improvement, either in school or in employment. He used projection to explain away his shortcomings, and was unrealistic in his planning. Nevertheless, it was decided to work with him. He was referred to Alcoholics Anonymous (AA). An effort would be made to help him find suitable employment and to stir in him some ambition for consistent self-support.

It was felt that Mrs. Wilcox showed good potential. She might well be excused for her initial failure as wife and mother since she had married at the age of fifteen with little preparation and no training. Observation of the relationship between Mrs. Wilcox and her mother suggested that the older woman would perform household tasks herself rather than take the time to teach her daughter, who even now did little to help the crippled older woman around the home. The worker felt that classes in cooking or baby care might give Mrs. Wilcox confidence and stimulate her to more effort. It was also planned to do whatever was necessary to improve her health. It was recognized that Mrs. Wilcox was now and probably always had been too dependent on her mother, a forceful and dominating personality. The caseworker decided not to initiate any discussion of this aspect of their relationship with either woman but to give Mrs. Wilcox every opportunity to talk about her feelings toward her parents, her husband, her children, and to release any hostility she might be repressing. Arrangements were made for frequent contacts with her children, both for their sake and to keep alive in Mrs. Wilcox her motivation for reestablishing a home for them.

Both parents were told the objectives toward which it was

hoped that the situation could progress, and both were told that the case would be reviewed at the end of six months, by which time there should be clear indication of success — or of failure. By that time Mr. Wilcox should have steady employment and be proving himself able to support his family. Mrs. Wilcox should have the improved health and the acquired skills which would enable her to carry her responsibilities. Both parents agreed with every appearance of eagerness.

A review of the case at the end of six months showed that the casework plan had been carried through, with a variety of results.

Mr. Wilcox had been referred to AA, and had been amiable about expressing a wish to change his ways and conquer the habit. However, he was inconsistent in working with AA, and the drinking problem did not diminish (an example of a verbalized attitude not accompanied by any change in behavior). During the half year he had worked at three different jobs and had lost one after the other because of absenteeism or inefficiency. He was still living in the home of his parents, where the situation was much the same as it had been. Mr. Wilcox still expressed an interest in his children and saw them at the office with fair regularity but could not offer any acceptable plan for them. He seemed to feel that if they could not be with him in his mother's home they were well enough off in foster care. He still said that the break in his family came about because of his wife's inefficiency as a homemaker. It was not his fault that he had been unable to provide adequately — what could a man do if there were no jobs available? The caseworker felt that in six months of work with Mr. Wilcox he had shown no progress in self-awareness, motivation, or reality of planning, and that there had been some regression in that he was sliding comfortably back into dependence on his parents.

Things had gone better with Mrs. Wilcox. She was in better
health and her skin condition was greatly improved. Her bad
teeth had been extracted, including all the front teeth, but
had not been replaced by any plate, and so her appearance
was still impaired. She now had a much easier relationship
with the caseworker, and was able to talk freely with him.
She admitted that she had not managed her life very well.
(Note that Mrs. Wilcox says that *she* had not managed her life
well. She was accepting responsibility.) She said she had
wanted to get away from her mother's domination and so
had been stubborn about continuing to see the boy of whom
both her parents disapproved, and had permitted herself to
become pregnant. She now considered that it had been a
mistake to marry him, but it had seemed the only thing to do
at the time. She said that she had blamed him at first for
everything that happened, for her pregnancy, for her having
to leave school, for his failure to take care of her and the
children. But now she saw that she had expected too much of
him. He had never learned to take any responsibility, and you
couldn't really think he would start now. She had got herself
into a situation in which the boy's behavior was inevitable.
Her pregnancy was as much her fault as his. Then she had
let things drift, and the rapid arrival of four babies in four
years put more responsibility on her husband than he could
ever be expected to carry. For a while she had blamed him
and her mother for the mess she was in but now she knew
that she could have pulled out if she had made a little effort.
She realized now that her drinking, which she pretended she
was doing to force her husband to act differently, was really
just a way of getting out of the housework she hated. She
should not have let herself get pregnant in the first place, she
should not have let her mother talk her into marrying the
boy, she should not have stayed with him after she realized
how things were going. She loved her children, but probably

they should not have been born. She would never go back to her husband; she would not have any more children. She did not know what she could do now that would be best for the children. She wished her parents would move to a larger apartment so that she could have them with her.

The caseworker recognized that Mrs. Wilcox's ability to assume responsibility for her situation indicated really remarkable growth. Her self-awareness and her freedom from projection were most promising, but she still showed dependency on her parents in spite of her admission that she had once longed to escape from them. There was no grasp of reality in her tentative planning since her father's income could not have met any higher rent than he was now paying.

The casework planning shifted slightly, to put less effort into work with Mr. Wilcox and more into trying to help Mrs. Wilcox move toward independence. The plan now did not include reestablishing this young family completely, but was concentrated on getting the four children back with the mother in some practical arrangement.

At the end of the second half-year period the case situation was evaluated again.

Contacts with Mr. Wilcox had been allowed to decrease. He had left his mother's home and moved to another city. At first this had been thought to be an indication of progress, but soon he was writing long, involved letters to the caseworker in which he claimed that he had learned that he was connected with the royal family of England. He signed his letters Lord Wilcox and demanded that all replies be addressed to him with that title. He never inquired about his wife or children. His letters dealt entirely with his royal connections, his right to be supported without effort on his part because of this connection. Correspondence with the public agency in the city to which he had gone indicated that Mr.

Wilcox was not employed and was making no effort to find work. The agency recognized his complete break with reality. He was receiving help from aid to the disabled. There appeared no need to hospitalize him, but his condition could only be regarded as serious deterioration.

Shortly after the first evaluation Mrs. Wilcox's youngest child was placed with her in her mother's home. With help from the caseworker and from a visiting nurse she developed ability to give consistent care to the baby. About four months after the baby was with her Mrs. Wilcox, without consulting the caseworker, abruptly removed herself from her mother's home, applied to the welfare agency for AFDC help and established a home in an apartment for herself and the baby. She showed considerable initiative in finding ways to get furniture through the Salvation Army.

She explained to the caseworker later that she could not stand having her mother take over the care of the baby. Mrs. Wilcox felt that this was her responsibility and she did not want to surrender it even if her mother was more proficient. She talked to the caseworker about having the other children with her, and by the end of the year they had been returned to her care. She was doing a creditable job of keeping her new home, herself, and the children clean and healthy. Her oldest child was now attending school and adjusting well. Mrs. Wilcox maintained contact with her parents, but refused to visit their home more often than once a week. By mutual agreement she took the children there for Sunday dinner and for holidays. She now helped her mother in the preparation of these family meals.

Mrs. Wilcox continued to receive assistance from AFDC for herself and the four children, but the case was closed with the child-care agency. At the time of the closing, when worker and supervisor together reviewed the case movement, it was recognized that the most significant event in the whole case progress was Mrs. Wilcox's leaving the home of her parents without consulting the worker. Mrs. Wilcox, remember, had been brought up in a mother-dominated home, and during her adolescent revolt she had fought against the domination. But the only thing she could think of to do then was to insist on continued contacts with a boy of whom her parents disapproved. When this relationship brought disaster, she was flung back into the old dependency, and the mother's habit of domination swept all before it, including the court's decision against marriage of this fifteen-year-old girl to an unsuitable man. Mrs. Wilcox's struggle against this trap in which she found herself was feeble and ineffective until the court action broke up the home. Then she went back to her mother. It would have been easy for her to slip once more into complete dependence. What prevented it?

1. When Mrs. Wilcox began to think about her own part in the various distressing situations in which she had been, the caseworker listened with understanding for her unhappiness but with no effort at any time to gloss over the part her own dependence had played in permitting the situations to develop. Too much sympathy at this point would have encouraged self-pity and continued dependence.

2. The caseworker's regular contacts with her had given her self-confidence. Mrs. Wilcox could believe that since he accepted her as an intelligent individual she must amount to something after all. Ignoring her or scolding her might have left her depressed and helpless.

3. The caseworker's confidence in Mrs. Wilcox was confirmed when he arranged for the return of the baby. Help from the visiting nurse gave her assurance that she could herself do the right thing for her child. Without advice from the nurse she might have depended too much on the experience of her mother.

4. Anywhere along the line of this case activity Mrs. Wilcox

might have been in danger of transferring her pattern of dependence from her mother to the caseworker, turning to him for approval and advice. In fact, she did just that for a short time as she talked to him about her immediate past. It would not have needed much encouragement from the worker for this young woman to lean on him completely. She was saved by her own basic strength, plus the worker's freedom from any need within himself to build his own self-image through a client's dependence. Her ability to make an important move toward complete self-reliance without consulting the worker was proof that the danger was past.

X

METHODS OF COPING

No one in the civilized world is able to give free rein to all his impulses. Nobody can allow open expression to every urge he feels. All of us meet in our daily lives a variety of restrictions and frustrations, and we all cope with them as best we can. We may feel like talking back to a critical employer, but we control ourselves because we do not want to lose the job. Since we know that love and loyalty are expected of us in certain family relationships, we may not be able to admit our resentment at the emotional demands made by a parent, a husband or wife, or our child, so we repress the real feelings, hiding them even from ourselves. Or perhaps we react by going to the other extreme and show excessive affection and concern. We are loath to admit a failure, and so we tell ourselves until we believe it that nothing was our fault—our supervisor never explained that to us; the teacher never told us about that problem. We do something impulsive, recognize too late what we have done, and produce high-sounding motives to rationalize away the inner selfishness that prompted the act.

We all do it. But a thoughtful person with self-awareness can be conscious at least some of the time of what he is doing, and of the contortions he goes through within himself to avoid facing the less agreeable aspects of his own personality.

All of us, caseworker and client, child and adult, meet challenges, any one of which carries the possibility of failure.

A new job, promotion to new responsibilities, a trip alone into unfamiliar territory, a new relationship in marriage or parenthood—any of these will involve effort, skills, knowledge, or sensitivity which we may or may not be able to provide. The methods which different individuals select for coping with a challenge, for handling frustrations, mirror his unique personality.

Techniques for avoiding discomfort, or for getting what we want from our environment, are generally learned in childhood in response to our childhood situation. These early techniques may be modified later by adult experience, but some vestiges of the first methods almost always remain. Neither the original learning nor the subsequent modification is an intellectual process. Rather both are the result of blundering trial and error. What is successful for us once we try again, and if it is effective often enough, that technique becomes a firmly entrenched way of life which we thenceforth follow blindly, sometimes in circumstances which could far better be handled in another way. A child who has found that a tantrum will get what he wants from his parents may well grow into a man who is aggressively demanding even where courtesy and a quiet request would win more cooperation from others. Yet we habitually rationalize, or "rush our fences," or always move so cautiously into a new situation that we may lose our chance through delay. I have known caseworkers who, confronted by a disagreeable chore (monthly reports, for example), shrug resignedly, say in effect, "Well, it's got to be done" and proceed to do it. This gets things done fast—but not always accurately. Other caseworkers characteristically procrastinate until the pressure is unendurable and the chore has become much more difficult than it would have been at first. Of course, we hope for a happy medium, and sometimes we achieve it.

Often it is the very fact that our clients are unable to find the middle path that has put them into the trouble that makes help necessary. Then they cannot live with themselves if they really face up to their own inadequacies, and so they must rationalize, or project, or withdraw from the struggle. Perhaps their coping method is to rush into a strange situation without thought or sensible consideration, or perhaps they procrastinate so long that nothing ever gets accomplished. Only by observing our client's habitual manner of coping with disappointment, with frustration, with pressure, can we ever know what to expect of his behavior in the future. What he promises verbally is a far less reliable guide than a study of what he has done in the past. Only through a realistic consideration of his personality can we plan how to help him.

Observation of a child's manner of coping is especially illuminating, partly because ways of coping are usually learned in childhood and forecast how this individual will react as an adult, and partly because a child's method of handling a challenge is frequently more open than the adult's, even though the adult is using the same technique. Children have not yet learned the devious ways in which motivations can be disguised, and often we can see what a youngster is trying to achieve more easily than we can determine the objectives of the more sophisticated adult.

During the first five or six years of life every child is confronted with demands to accept and come to terms with many varied situations that are new and strange to him:

1. The challenge of a new activity which may involve a possibility of personal failure — games, kindergarten, school

2. Orientation to new places that look, smell, and sound different from anything previously encountered, such as clinics, doctors' offices, hospitals, or sometimes a new neighborhood

3. Strange adults who may or may not constitute a threat—
   teachers, nurses, doctors, caseworkers
4. Children in large groups, in nursery school or kindergarten
5. New sensations—illness, pain
6. New emotions—new friendships, loss of old relationships; even separation from home and mother.

Try to imagine the feelings of even the best adjusted, most
secure child the first time he is faced with a large group of
strange children in nursery school, the first time he is lured
into playing an organized game with rules he does not understand, the first time he takes a lengthy trip with a stranger and
without his mother, the first time he walks into a foster home
that is nothing like his own home.

I remember taking a pugnacious, aggressive, little six-year-
old to an institution where he was to live for the next year or
so. He had been prepared for the move. It had all been
explained to him and he had agreed to go. But when we
drove into the grounds the first thing he saw was a group of
about thirty boys playing some sort of lively, noisy game
under the leadership of the athletic coach. My boy flattened
himself against the back of the car seat and said in a very
small voice, "I guess it's all right, but just let's sit here a little
while." So we parked and watched, while one small boy
looked the ground over and gathered strength to make the
plunge; this was his technique for coping with a strange and
frightening situation.

Any child who must meet any of these situations will
experience some degree of anxiety, and probably the more
sensitive and intelligent he is the deeper will be his anxiety
since he will sense the strangeness and will be alert to the
varied dark possibilities. His anxieties may be summed up in
seven questions which are not too different from those which
a grownup might ask in a comparable circumstance:

Who will take care of me while this is going on?
Who will help me?
Will I be able to do what is expected?
Will I be able to control my feelings and my actions, or will
 I get myself into trouble?
Whom can I love?
Who will there be to love me?
What is going to happen next?

If we have information about the social history of the child we might make an educated guess, even before meeting him, of what to expect of his behavior and his personality. Severe deprivation during early infancy, inconsistent or rough discipline during the toddler years, unresolved problems of identification or of establishing his own self-image, all show up later, each with its special type of characteristic behavior. But sometimes youngsters fool us. They may develop more ego strength than we would have thought possible. Or perhaps they have been hurt more deeply than a superficial review of their early experiences suggests, and will therefore have less strength than we had hoped. Moreover, two children from what seem to be identical backgrounds will develop quite different defenses and techniques for coping with their problems. There are probably forces at work which are not visible from the outside.

The differences in the way two individuals approach a situation should not mislead us into thinking that one is necessarily better than another. They may be equally good. If they are both socially acceptable, and both are effective for the individual, then they are equally good. But many adults, including caseworkers, are prone to have their own notions of how a child should behave. If the child's method of solving his particular problem as he struggles for mastery is the one which is convenient for us, or is the conventional type of good child behavior, we are glad enough to give it the stamp of our approval. But if the child is more deliberate, and therefore keeps us waiting, or if he fails to show himself as the affectionate youngster we fancy he should be, then we condemn him as uncooperative or antisocial.

So, as we observe the child, we must ask ourselves:

What does the child want? What is he striving for?

What techniques is he using?

Are the techniques really effective in helping him reach his immediate goal?

Are they techniques which will continue to be effective as he moves into adolescence, into young adulthood, and into heterosexual relationships, self-support, family responsibilities?

We must judge a child's method of coping, not in relation to our convenience, not against any stereotype of the model child, but in relation only to the child's own goals in his life situation, always remembering that what the child wants from life need not be at all what we think we would want if we were in his small shoes. When we are with a group of our peers we may want to participate, to be in the middle of activities. But perhaps this particular child wants to be let alone to play all by himself with plasticine in a corner.

Although the specific goals will vary from one individual to another, we may be pretty certain in general that what everyone wants, child or adult, when he is thrust into a new potentially threatening situation is to free himself as much as he can from anxiety, to master the situation, to feel confident that he can cope. He may tackle it by plunging in wholeheartedly. He may go in swinging, ready to fight everyone in sight. He may draw back and look the ground over cautiously. He may ask for reassurance by demanding answers to dozens of questions. Or, of course, the questioning itself may be an effective delaying technique. He may "put his head in the sand" and try to deny that the threatening situation exists. He may retreat, physically or emotionally.

A child may try to rig the situation so that his mother will be along. If that is impossible, he may turn to any available adult and ask for help, either verbally ("I can't tie my shoes. You do it for me.") or with body English by standing close to an adult, patting an arm, pressing against him, clinging to a skirt or coat.

Not all children, however, are able to put their trust in an adult, and some children value autonomy so much that they prefer to risk failure and tackle their problems alone. Some situations are tougher than others, so that the same child may be independent and self-sufficient at one time and ready to sacrifice autonomy to gain adult help on another occasion. The same situation will be more difficult for one child than it is for another, depending on his past experience, temperament, physical development and dexterity, ego strength, and general personality make-up.

Let us pretend that we are trying to get acquainted with an individual about whom we have no information. We want to assess his personality. What do we mean by "personality"? What is included in the concept?

How does he relate to people?

Is he trusting?

Is he skeptical?

Is he aloof and indifferent?

Is he dependent?

Does he seem to like people spontaneously, extending himself toward them, expecting confidently that they will like him in return? Or does he behave as though he expected to be rebuffed, hurt, or insulted? Does he make the first move, or does he wait passively for the other person to make all the advances? Once in a relationship with another, does he seem to need constant reassurance and approval?

Among his peers, is he a leader or a follower?

If he is a leader, does he behave with overweening aggression as though he could not endure not to be the chief? Or does he move to the front simply because he is bigger or quicker or brighter than the others? Can he still show a willingness to accept leadership from others if anyone appears to be more capable?

If he is a follower, is he that at all times? Or does he follow only when he feels less sure of himself but can take the lead in other instances? If the latter, in what kinds of situations is he insecure? In what kinds is he confident?

How does he handle frustration?

Does he show rage?

Is there a complete collapse of effort?

Does he accept temporary defeat while still maintaining assurance of success in another area?

What are his characteristic defense mechanisms?

Does he use substitution; accepting with good grace a satisfaction to replace one that is impossible for him?

Does he use denial; refusing to admit the existence of a realistic problem or the fact that a disappointment affects him?

Does he use displacement; attaching to some individual the emotions that have actually been stirred into existence by another person?

Does he use projection; refusing to admit responsibility for his behavior and putting the blame on somebody else?

Does he use escape; employing daydreams and fantasies to avoid facing a disagreeable reality?

Those defense mechanisms which involve a distortion of reality—denial, projection, displacement—are the ones less likely to be successful, and even if they are temporarily useful in childhood, they lead to trouble in later life. Fantasy, as a child uses it, may be a diversion employed with full awareness that it is not reality. Sometimes it is used half-consciously as a device to get past an emotional block.[1] It can then be

---

[1] "Laughing Tiger," as described in Selma Fraiberg, *The Magic Years,* pp. 16 ff.

abandoned when the need is over. Only when fantasy is used too persistently over too long a period does it become unhealthy. If a three-year-old squeals because you are about to shut the door on an imaginary Dodo's tail or sit in the chair already occupied by a purely imaginary child companion, do not lose patience. Play along. Neither Dodo nor the useful but imaginary companion has long to live. They will vanish from the scene in a few months. The time to worry is when a high-school student seems not to know the difference between the real and the fancied.

Dr. Moriarity reports on the behavior of preschool children who came to her clinic for intelligence testing. Some took the time to explore the situation, to try out possibilities, before really committing themselves to effort. The trying out might include manipulating and handling materials, or asking questions of the adult, or simply standing quietly to look things over.[2]

Some children used their own past experience to determine what they could or could not do: "I can do those buttons. I know how to button my coat"; or, "I can't do that. I never could do that kind of thing."

Many children made more or less open efforts to keep control of the situation, some by stalling for time without actually rejecting the intention of eventual cooperation with the tester: "I'm not ready yet"; "I couldn't do that just now"; "I'm tired; I think I ought to rest"; or, "I need a drink first."

Others insisted on maintaining control by refusing outright to do the required task, or refusing to do it as the tester requested: "I don't want to play with these. What else do you have?"; or, "I want to do it thisaway."

Some used substitutions when faced with imminent failure: "I can't do this, but I did the other okay, didn't I?"; "I can't

[2] Lois Barclay Murphy and collaborators, *The Widening World of Childhood*, pp. 86 ff.

just manage the scissors, but I can dance"; "I don't like this game; I'd rather string beads like I was doing."

Others reached for gratification through identification: "I can't do that but my mother can." Or they looked toward future achievement: "I can't do it now but some day I will."

Projection took the form of putting the blame on someone: "My mother never told me about that"; or, "You didn't give me time"; or, "Your scissors don't cut."

Difficulties were avoided in various ways: "I don't think I want to" (the implication being, of course, that he could if he wished); by shoving or scattering equipment; by concealing the answer sheet if the child suspected it would not be satisfactory; or by hiding essential equipment.

Children found various ways to release tension during a testing period, such as squealing excitedly, making animal noises, using body movements that ranged from squirming on the chair to dashing around the room, banging things, choosing noisy toys.

A child afraid that he might not be able to control his own aggressions might whisper, or speak in a hoarse tone, or he might sit or stand stiffly, barely moving.

Dr. Moriarity was testing and observing small children, but every one of these responses and defenses can be observed in adults, with the "language" changed only slightly to suit the age difference.

Here are some items to look for in observing an individual:

1. *Physical appearance.* — What does he look like? Is he big or small? (This might make a difference to his ego image and his self-confidence.) Is he good looking or very plain? (This can affect the response of other people to him.) What does his appearance indicate about his physical health? (Poor health adversely affects energy.)

2. *Body movement and use of body.* — Are his body movements usually quick or slow? (The body may reflect mental speed,

or health, or the person's characteristic emotional response. We must evaluate this in the light of the other observations.)

Does he seem "at home" with his body, or stiff, clumsy, unsure? (This may reflect, and will certainly affect, an individual's image of his own efficiency.)

Are his large muscles and small muscles equally developed for coordination, or is one more developed than the other? (This would influence the type of occupation at which a person could succeed.)

How much of what he is feeling is expressed through his body? (Whether much or little may be a matter of culture and training.)

3. *Facial expressions.* — How much of what he is feeling is expressed in his face? Do his reactions minute by minute show in his face? Do they show only when he feels intensely about something? Or does he characteristically maintain a "dead-pan" expression. (This may be a cultural matter, or it may be an indication of the openness of his approach to others, or of his "closed-in" attitude toward other people.)

4. *Speech.* — How much of what he is feeling is expressed through his tone of voice? Is his voice generally controlled, or does it express changing moods? If he is upset does he talk more, or less, than usual?

Is this a person to whom speech is an important means of communication, or does he speak rarely, communicating in other ways? Does he like to "play" with speech, making up chants, puns, stories? Does he answer questions briefly and to the point or with long, rambling *non sequiturs*? Does he use simple terms of everyday language, or does he attempt to find words a foot and a half long?

Is his speech fluent, average, choppy, inarticulate? (These characteristics are all indicative of his self-image and the ease with which he can reach out toward another person.)

5. *Emotional reactions.* — How and when does he exhibit happiness, anger, sadness, doubt, enthusiasm?

Does he seem to have too little control over his feelings? Too much? A good balance?

Do his responses seem appropriate to the situation? (There are occasions when the failure of a client to appear upset or worried is evidence of an inadequate grasp of reality, perhaps even an indication of a psychosis.)

6. *Relationships with other people.* — Does he seek out other people? His own sex, or the opposite sex? How and when? Does he seek only specific persons? Does he avoid others, or specific persons? Does he usually wait to be approached by another person before showing response? How does he respond to an invitation to social contact?

Is he generally a leader? Generally a follower? Sometimes one and sometimes the other? (This may be observed most easily within the family setting: is the husband the boss, or the wife, or do they share?)

Is he generally comfortable with other people, able to give and take and share ideas and equipment?

Is he unhappy unless he gets his own way?

Is he unduly inhibited about expressing his own ideas? (A good place to observe this is on the job. If it is not practicable for a caseworker to watch a man at work, his foreman could give valuable information which would deepen our awareness of the man's habitual method of coping.)

XI

THE INFANT

There are reasons why every caseworker should be well acquainted with the developmental phases through which a child moves in his progress from birth through infancy, childhood, and adolescence to maturity.

If the caseworker is involved with child care it is obviously advantageous to know what a child is feeling at each phase in his growth, what physical and emotional problems he is attempting to solve. At each step the child has need for a different kind of help from the world around him, and a child-care worker must know what those needs are and be able to determine whether or not they are being met. The child learns first whether he can trust someone to come in a minute to take care of him; then he must be encouraged to learn skills — precarious balance as he starts to walk; the meaning of language; control as toilet training starts. As he grows older, he learns to step out into the world of school and comradeship with those of his own age; learns to handle himself with the opposite sex. Finally, as an adult, he learns a little judgment in managing his own affairs, acquires a profession or other occupation and begins to support himself.

A caseworker involved with the parents of children needs equally to be aware of the children's requirements. Do the parents understand their child? When a two-year-old screams "NO NO" to everything his mother says, when a four-year-old boy is suddenly violently jealous of a father whom he had seemed to adore just last year, when an adolescent daughter shows no respect for her mother and has a strong tendency to imitate that sophisticated divorcee down the street, can parents really understand and continue to love their temporarily aggravating offspring without feeling offended or being punitive? The caseworker must be able to interpret, support, and guide.

A caseworker who is helping adults needs to have a grasp of the effects on adult personality of events that happened early in life. A child whose parents never approved of his small efforts but always held up an impossibly high standard of performance, always demanding that he be the perfect little gentlemen, that he win top grades at school, that he never get dirty, never answer back or quarrel with the boy next door, may well grow up to be a man miserably convinced that he can never meet expectations. Self-depreciation was a habit he learned in childhood and never could break. A child whose parents meted out extreme punishments may develop into an adult who resents and hates all authority, and even long after his parents are gone may still find it impossible to accept his boss's orders gracefully because of the habit of resentment he acquired from his parents' unjust demands. What happens to a child before he is six is likely to shape the pattern of his adult personality. Events of his early years settle into his subconscious, but even without the force of conscious memory they can go a long way toward establishing his habitual responses of self-confidence, of fearfulness, overdependency, aggressiveness.

Even things that happened to the infant while he was still in his mother's womb have subsequent consequences. We no longer believe that the baby will be born with a furry gray birthmark if his mother was frightened by a mouse but we do know that her health and, to a certain extent, her feelings about her pregnancy affect the baby's body. If the mother has certain diseases or takes certain drugs during the gestation period the baby may be born with malformation of body or mind. The position of the fetus in the womb may affect the amount of prenatal nourishment it can get from the mother's bloodstream. Extreme unhappiness or worry on the part of the mother will affect her health and with it the health of the unborn child.

Our understanding of the present depends on our understanding of the past. It is not necessary that we have specific details about Mr. M.'s mother, who was dissatisfied in her marriage, downgraded her husband, and clung to her son, overprotecting him for too many years. When we see that Mr. M. is fearful of stepping out into unfamiliar situations, clinging to the caseworker as his mother let him cling to her, it is enough that we recognize the sort of thing which must have happened twenty or thirty years ago and can because of our understanding be more patient now with this grown-up little boy's dependency. When we see a self-centered woman who gives nothing of love or security to her children, it is enough if we can realize that she has nothing within herself to give because no one gave to her when she was small. The awareness will make us better able to respond to these people as we would respond to any handicapped individual. We may not be able to like them much. We surely cannot approve of their immature behavior. But we can understand why they are as they are and perhaps we can do some little things to fill in the gaps even at this late date.

First, however, we must be able to recognize where the gaps are.

It is during the first few months of life that an individual learns to trust—or not to trust. What happens to him through the first twelve or eighteen months after birth, even to some extent what happens to him during the birth process itself, will go a long way toward setting the stage for a lifelong optimism and faith that people on the whole are pretty good, or it will set the stage for pessimism, apprehension, and a suspicion that what people do to him will be far more likely to hurt than to help.

It is easy enough to recognize that the helpless infant is wholly dependent on an adult to feed him and keep him warm and comfortable. What may not be quite so clear is that the way this is done is certain to affect his personality development. For physical survival he needs nourishing food, adequate shelter, possibly medical attention. To grow to emotional maturity he needs warm affection and cuddling — in short, the tender loving care which good mothering supplies.

It sometimes happens that adequate physical care is provided in a cold, sterile atmosphere without warmth or real personal concern. In the not-far-distant past, this happened in overcrowded and understaffed nurseries where babies were given ample nourishment but where there was no time for affectionate handling and cuddling. But doctors found that babies deprived of mothering became listless, apathetic, without a will to live. Such babies often ate voraciously but failed to thrive. They developed the ailment known as marasma. Medical men learned that such cases could be corrected by assigning one warmhearted nurse to do all the feeding of the marasmic child, to carry him about, cuddle him, talk to him, give him the feeling that it would really be worth his while to make an effort to live.

A baby must have mothering. But mothering of a minimal kind, barely enough to assure survival, may not be enough to assure adequate emotional or even intellectual growth. Everything that happens to an infant from the birth process itself on through the handling he gets after his arrival brings from the baby a response either of satisfaction or of discomfort, pain, protest, fear, anger. This becomes quite reasonable when we stop to think that the impulse toward survival is basic in all living things. The human infant must be instinctively aware of his helplessness. So any failure of help to appear when it is needed is a threat to survival itself. To be fed when he is hungry, made comfortable when he is wet or cold, to be cuddled and talked to and loved when he is lonesome, brings reassurance and a feeling of safety and satisfaction.

But any threat to survival will create anxiety. There is a certain amount of threat in the birth process itself. The infant loses the comfort and security of the womb where the temperature remained constant, where all sustenance required for growth, including oxygen, was supplied from the mother's body without his making the slightest effort. Abruptly he finds himself catapulted into quite a different environment. Cold air hits his skin. He feels a variety of pressures on his body. If he is to get any oxygen into his lungs he must do his own breathing. A baby born prematurely finds himself forced to breathe, to suck, to endure the shock of temperature change before his nervous system is fully developed, and all this is harder on him than a similar experience is for a full-term baby. Or perhaps the infant endures prolonged and painful pressure on his soft body during a difficult delivery. Such a baby will certainly be nervous and fussy for weeks as though he expected that every touch would be a repetition of the pain he experienced during the birth process. A baby born by a quick, easy delivery, and a full-term baby taken by Caesarean section with very little pressure on his tender body, will start life with quite a different temperament.

Given time and sufficient tender loving care, the premature baby, the baby who is fretful because of a difficult delivery, can be reassured. But without good mothering the baby who starts out with a poor feeling about life may never change his attitude. Even the full-term, happy, bouncy baby can be and will be disillusioned and embittered if he does not have adequate mothering.

The adequate mothering not only supplies nourishment for his body, but, as the mother handles the child, it helps to develop the intercostal muscles, thus making adequate breathing possible. As his mother carries him about, his sense of body position and equilibrium is strengthened. Body contact as the mother feeds, bathes, or changes him establishes a sense of personal relationship which increases as the infant grows older and more able to respond to his environment. If the care-taking person talks to the baby, or sings to him, that helps provide an awareness of sound as connected with human relationship and to connect for the child this sound with external stimuli. It also prepares the way for the baby later to imitate those sounds and thus to learn to talk.[1]

All of this fondling, handling, carrying, talking to, provides the baby with a feeling of physical well-being and a confidence that all is well in this best of all possible worlds. But if the baby is left for long periods alone and cold and hungry, uncomfortable, frightened, or in pain, he will surely learn apprehension, terror, anger. He does not learn these things intellectually, of course; for the infant has no intellect as an adult conceives it, but he learns through his nervous system, his glands, his organs. If nothing happens to break this habit of expecting the worst to happen, the baby will surely grow up to be misanthropic, pessimistic, resentful, and likely to hit back in any way he can at a life which has provided such scant satisfactions.

Of course, it is not serious for a baby to be unattended for a few minutes because his mother is on the telephone or in the tub when he cries, but to experience neglect over and over, day in and day out, will convince him that nobody cares, nobody is ever going to be on hand to help him, and the world

[1]Margaret A. Ribble, *The Rights of Infants.*

is an inhospitable place. He will grow up expecting the worst, and the good things that come his way after he is an adult will not do too much to change this basic deep pessimism.

If the handling he gets from his mother is rigid because of her own nervous tensions, or absent-minded because she is in a hurry to get on to occupations she prefers, or rough because she resents having a baby at all and finds no pleasure in taking care of him, then the baby will not know what it means to be warmly loved and sincerely wanted. Unless things change for him, he will never expect to be loved, he will never be able to trust people who try to love him, whether they are caseworkers or foster parents, teachers or friends. And in his deep anger at life he will probably behave in a fashion that makes it next to impossible to love him. Love is what he needs and most desperately wants, but his habit of doubt and suspicion makes him fend it off. Is this reasonable and sensible of him? Certainly not. But human beings are far more likely to act in response to emotions they do not really understand than they ever do to reason.

The tragic thing is that a child who has not had love and acceptance during infancy never ceases to want and need it, but the older he grows the more impossible it is for him to accept it even if it becomes available. The child-welfare worker can cuddle a baby. She can haul a long-legged, gawky, eight-year-old onto her lap, and if the early deprivation has not been too severe and suspicion and hostility have not gone too deep inside him, she may in time be able to make up, at least in part, for what he should have had eight years before.

By eight he may not yet be too distrustful to believe in good intentions. But by the time he is an adolescent and drawing away from dependence on adults anyway, he may be completely unable to think of himself as needing adult affection and quite unwilling to permit it. If he has never had much affection or acceptance he will have a poor self-image (which he tries to cover by bravado). He will by this time have convinced himself that nobody is going to love him anyway (and hides his insecurity behind a screen of scorn). He will be full of anger against life, and specifically against adults, and probably most especially against authority figures. He has doubtless tangled with authority several times, in school or in court, and he is convinced that they are forever "picking on him." He expresses this attitude by sullen withdrawal from those who try to help him, or by hitting back through the sort of delinquent behavior most calculated to upset the grown-ups and rouse them to the kind of punishing response that will justify his own anger ("See how mean that teacher is? I knew he hated me"). It is by no means ever easy to break through this wall. It takes time and great patience on the part of the caseworker, and an ability to give and give and give for months with no return and very few gleams to indicate progress.

It stands to reason, then, that the best time for a caseworker to help the personality which is starting out in an environment that lacks tender loving care is when that personality is two weeks old — not after he is eight years old, when helping him is awkward; not after he is fifteen, when it has become so difficult for him to accept any kind of help; not when he is an adult with a fixed and internalized pattern of self-doubt, resentment, hostility. The individual who grows to adulthood with no experience of love will, in his turn, be unable to give love wholeheartedly to anyone else, and so his children must, in their turn, grow up emotionally deprived, and the vicious circle starts again.

So, find the deprived child quickly and help him promptly.

This is easier said than done, of course. But if a caseworker is himself aware of the situations which provide the best emotional climate for the infant, he can be alert to those which are less than perfect, and be prepared to supplement where supplementation is needed.

Generally, a family environment is better for a baby than an institution since the family provides the opportunity for the baby to establish a close, confident relationship with one consistent mother person. Institutions, even those that are neither overcrowded or understaffed, are likely to have a changing personnel working in shifts, with no single individual who is always responsible for one infant, who always holds the baby in the same way, always speaks or sings with the same voice, to provide a sense of familiarity and the feeling of a strong one-to-one relationship. Group homes for five or six babies might be better than large institutions, but they too may leave responsibility with one person for so many babies that she cannot give any one what he needs. One nurse in charge of five babies cannot hold all of them as they take their bottle; cannot rock or carry all of them, and therefore some must be left in their cribs for too many hours without the personal contact with the mother person.

Perhaps we should mention that while in our culture the "mothering" is most often done by the biological mother, this need not be so. Fathers sometimes make first-rate mothers. So do grandmothers, aunts, big sisters, nannies, foster mothers, and nurses. Mothering can be done by anyone who is warm and giving, who loves babies, and has not too many to take care of at any one time.

While a middling-good private home usually provides better nourishment for a baby than an efficient but impersonal institution, it is nevertheless well known to all social workers that some homes have little or nothing to give an infant— homes, for example, in which the biological parents were themselves rejected and unloved as infants. If such parents cannot be helped, or cannot be helped soon enough to enable them to provide in time for the baby, then possibly it is wise to arrange for the unloved baby to be transferred to an adoptive home or a good foster home. But right here is where mistakes are easy to make. A shabby home with none of the amenities may have all the warmth that any baby needs—more warmth, perhaps, than one in which the parents have a good income, live on the right side of the tracks, but are too narcissistic to be able to love and reassure a child.

How can a caseworker know? Physical abuse, starvation, or battering comes to light readily with the baby's first medical examination. Emotional undernourishment may not be so obvious, especially if it is not so severe as to cause marasmic reactions. A small baby cannot express his frustrations by talking about them. A baby's only language is his body responses to the environment. Sleeplessness, for example, is a danger signal; or unduly prolonged spasms of colic; or abnormal amounts of vomiting; or persistent diarrhea for which the doctor can find no physical basis and which is not corrected by a change of formula. Any of these symptoms may have a purely physical basis, but if changing the physical situation does not correct the condition, then it must be borne in mind that early feeding problems may be directly related to the mother's feeling and attitude—and through her to the feelings of the infant. If this is the situation, then the caseworker's client is the mother, not the infant. Changing the psychological atmosphere rather than the feeding formula may be the only solution.

XII

THE TODDLER

If a small child has adequate physical and emotional nourishment during early infancy he is ready to move into the next phase of development sometime between his twelfth and eighteenth month. As growth reduces his dependency his aggressive self-reliance increases. This does not happen overnight, of course, and it does not come without many backslidings. One day he is still a baby; the next he insists on climbing the stairs all by himself, no matter how long it takes or how much it slows up a busy mother's progress. The next day he is a baby again, demanding to be carried. And the next he has clambered onto his mother's dressing table to spill perfume and scatter powder. And so it goes.

There is probably no period in any human life when an individual is called upon to learn so much, to absorb so many new ideas, to develop so many new skills, as between his first and second year. He must learn to balance himself on his own two feet—quite a stunt, considering the high center of gravity and the comparatively small base which the human foot provides. He must learn to coordinate his muscles until he can place one foot before the other in walking movements while continuing to maintain a precarious balance. He must imitate the sounds that adults make, arrange the sounds into words, and learn to associate the words with objects, activities, feelings. He must learn that hot stoves burn; sharp knives cut small fingers; insecure chairs can topple over and tumble small bodies to the hard floor; tablecloths, if pulled, can cata-pult dishes of hot soup onto unsuspecting babies. He has to start learning socially acceptable behavior. He now discovers that he is expected to eliminate, not when and where the impulse prompts, but only at the times and in the vessel regarded by adults as suitable. He must not grab other chil-dren's toys, nor pick the neighbor's flowers, nor bite people, nor smear his lovely squashy food all over his face. Eventually, he must learn not to bother adults who are busy, or interrupt when they are talking to each other. He is, he learns to his displeased astonishment, not the center of the universe after all, and some of his strongest impulses must be controlled if he is to be safe from hurt and if he is to get along with other people in this rapidly widening world of his.

This really takes quite a bit of doing, but fortunately he is helped by the fact that while the first instinct of any living thing is for survival, the second and equally strong instinct is for growth. So any healthy normal baby grows, physically, mentally, and emotionally. During the first eight or twelve or fourteen months of life his dependency needs must be satis-fied by the tender loving care of the mother person. During the next two or three years, while his aggressive urges are in the ascendant, he needs continued tender loving care but he also needs to be encouraged in his groping independence at the same time that he must be helped to develop firm con-trols. It is quite impossible to "spoil" a small infant by giving too much love and acceptance. But when his experimental investigations begin, consistent discipline must also begin.

A great deal of what a parent does and says during this investigative phase of a child's development must seem to the child like an unreasonable balking of his urge to learn, to experiment, to become his own boss. He wants to taste every-thing. His mouth, after all, has been up to this time the area of greatest sensitivity and the source of greatest pleasure, so of course he continues to use his mouth and his sense of taste and the feeling of his lips to learn more about this amazing world. Now that he can go places and clutch things, his scope has greatly widened. But he must be prevented from putting poisonous or unclean objects into his mouth. He longs to try out his new skill in walking and climbing, completely unaware of any danger to himself. But he must be stopped from walking into traffic or climbing where he could fall and be injured. He wants to touch and handle everything. But he must be stopped from touching the hot stove or a sharp knife. He has no sense of personal ownership—everything belongs to him as much as to anyone else. But if the family is to live on good terms with the neighbors he must be taught the difference between mine and thine. Also, since his mother by this time is getting pretty tired of washing diapers, he is asked to learn how to control his sphincter muscle.

All of this involves a truly impressive degree of self-restraint, of giving up what a small child wants at that moment, of stopping what he feels like doing just then, of accepting the present frustration involved in foregoing what looks to be immediately desirable for the sake of some future reward. The reward cannot be too long postponed, for toddlers have a short memory span. In a happy home, the chief reward consists of his mother's prompt approval, and the gradually growing awareness of being able to do what pleases his mother.

If earlier experiences during the dependency period have been satisfying, the toddler now has reason to believe that it is possible to win generous approval from his mother, and that the approval is worth making some small sacrifices. If, however, the toddler has never been given any reason to believe that he will ever get approval or acceptance no matter what he does, there will appear to be no reason for him to make an effort. On the contrary, earlier frustrations will already have nourished angry feelings which he expresses now by baby defiance — quite possibly by mulishness in the area of toilet training.

As every mother knows, no child is sweetness and light every hour of the day, but a child who has had a satisfactory relationship with the mother person will now have, on the whole, more good days than bad ones; and a child who has never had a happy relationship with an adult will have bad days in direct proportion to the extent of his earlier frustrations — days that are bad for the baby, for his mother, or for both. His feelings about his mother may be expressed through tantrums and defiance, or possibly he may be cowed by fear of punishment into a semblance of compliance, but discipline through fear will never develop inner controls.

Discipline there must be, for baby's immediate safety and also to help him develop the control of his impulses which will be required as he moves out into the world of school and, later, of adults. Successful discipline depends on the demands not exceeding the child's ability to accept and comply. Children differ in the age at which they develop this readiness. One child may accept toilet training easily at two years, while another in the same family may not be cooperative before he is three or older. No child is really able to control the sphincter muscle before he can walk. The wise mother adapts her demands to the individual child's capacity to conform.

At the same time, the wise mother keeps one short step ahead of her child in the encouragement and stimulation she provides for independence and self-control. A mother who enjoys her baby so much that she continues to dress and undress her small son after he is capable of learning to do it himself is performing no service for him. All of us, child or adult, find a sneaking pleasure at times in being taken care of, and a child whose mother does too much for him may never make the effort to accomplish the complicated maneuver required to tie his own shoes. Besides, he has probably learned that the way to win a pleasing response from his mother is to remain helpless and dependent. Very possibly his normal urge toward independence will be expressed by bossing her.

In a good home, the wise mother finds the right balance between making no demands on her child, and thus permitting him to remain overlong in the dependency phase, and making demands so stringent that he cannot meet them and develops a permanent conviction of his own inadequacy, and quite possibly a resentment against the demands of all authority figures which will be expressed later by disobedience in school and defiance of law-enforcement officers.

If a child has had an unsatisfying infancy with no adequate tender loving care from any parent figure, he will almost certainly move into an unsatisfying period of discipline unless the external situation changes. Parents who are too immature, too narcissistic, too concerned with their own unhappiness and their own unsatisfied needs to have the emotional energy for giving love to an infant will almost certainly be incapable of patience and consistency in stimulating and disciplining the toddler. That is why children who come to the attention of a child-caring agency when they are seven or eight or nine so often exhibit the undisciplined behavior of a badly trained child, and also the deep insecurity and distrust of a child whose dependency needs have never been adequately met. Then it is necessary for the caseworker somehow to give the child the tender loving care he should have had as an infant. Only by doing this can we hope to help him develop to the point where he can accept and use discipline through love.

Every child, even in the best and most understanding home, has some submerged feelings of anger and resentment as he proceeds through this difficult period of discipline. His mother's demands, no matter how gently conveyed, must often conflict with his own desires and pleasures, and no

child is always ready to give up what he wants for the sake
of his mother's smile. So, during this time, irritation, exhaus-
tion, and periodic despair normally alternate with any
mother's moments of pride and delight in the accomplish-
ments of her child. But the toddler who is in constant and
serious revolt against the demands made on him will show it
by prolonged temper tantrums, abnormal stubbornness. A
certain degree of mulishness is healthy and normal as a
child develops independence, but there should also be some
moments of happy compliance.

Frequently, the difficulties center in the area of toilet
training. This may show itself somatically by diarrhea or by
constipation, or by plain refusal to cooperate. A child may for
months refuse to have any movement while he is on the toilet
but habitually soil himself shortly after he is removed. And
who can blame him? If mother never did anything he wanted
her to, why should he do what she wants now, and here on
the potty he is in complete command. Mother is so much
bigger than he that she can pick him up and drag him forcibly
away from the mud he wants to play in. But nobody can make
him have a movement if he thinks he won't, and certainly
nobody can stop him from doing it in his pants. It is his perfect
revenge. The best advice to mothers in situations like this is
neither to scold him for his failures to cooperate nor praise
him for success.

It is during the toddler years that a child begins to learn the
difference between what is acceptable behavior and what is
not. But it is not to be expected that a child of this age should
have any notion of abstract right or wrong. To him there is
no important difference between messing his pants and staying clean; between eating his cereal with a spoon and pushing
his whole fist into the nice, warm, squashy stuff; between telling the truth and relating a fanciful tall story; between taking
things that do not belong to him and keeping his fingers off

the possessions of others. Probably the "wrong" thing is easier and often it is more fun, while the "right" thing is preferred only because it wins approval from Mommie. It takes weeks of consistent repetition before he grasps the general idea of right and wrong. Even then it is not conscience that makes him do the right thing, but the memory of parental approval reinforced by habit entrenched with increasing strength by repetition. It will be a few years yet before our toddler develops what could really be called a conscience. In these early years it is affectionate, firm consistence that counts. The affection provides the reward. The firmness stops the small boss of the family from being too bossy. And consistency forms the basis of habit which will stand him in good stead later.

XIII

THE PRESCHOOLER

At the age of three, or thereabouts, a child begins to recognize that his brother is made differently from his sister; that his mother is different from his father; that, in short, there are two sexes. This awareness may come a bit sooner to a child who has had the opportunity to observe the anatomical structure of a sibling being bathed or diapered, but it will come in time even without this. The child's growing curiosity about himself and about life will cause it to happen. As he matures, he is reaching out, intellectually and emotionally, to find his place in life, to discover what he is, to identify with some adult figure.

With any child living in a normally healthy family climate the first indication of the start of this phase of development is likely to be an increase in the warmth of his affection for the parent of the opposite sex and a corresponding jealousy of the parent of the same sex who so obviously enjoys a relationship with the beloved which the child does not share. This is a normal part of growing up, and nothing to worry about, but it can develop into a bit of a nuisance for the parents. The new jealousy may show itself in frank verbalization: from the little boy, "I wish Daddy would never come home and then I could sleep in Mommy's bed every night"; from the little girl, "Daddy, I want to marry you. You love me more than you do Mommy, don't you?" Sometimes the jealousy shows itself simply as a new reluctance to obey the parent of the same sex, along with increased sweetness and compliance toward the parent of the opposite sex. Little boys will not go to bed if Daddy tells them to. They quarrel with Daddy over which television program to watch and show a new tendency to be disagreeable at mealtimes if he is present. Little girls behave in the same way toward their mother. (The masculine gender is used more frequently in these chapters only because of the limitations of the language. During this phase small boys and small girls go through the same emotional experiences.)

Of course, all this does not happen overnight. The new mood may appear one day, may be gone the next, return a couple days later, go again, come back, and so on. If the child has had normal gratification of his dependency needs during infancy so that now he feels that he has a secure place in the family constellation, and if he has been given consistent discipline tempered by love during the toddler stage so that he has acquired confidence in his ability to manage himself without incurring social disaster, then he can weather this third stage. The first symptoms of jealousy wane, and the child moves comfortably into an acceptance of his own place in the affections of the parent of the opposite sex, and on to a normal identification with his own sex. There should be no need for anybody to do anything about it beyond bearing with him while he works through his conflicts and confusions. This is a portion of life's journey which a healthy child can and should walk alone.

The period, however, can be a trying one for a family which does not understand what is going on. The parent of the same sex who is bearing the brunt of the child's disobedience and resentment feels puzzled and hurt. He may be tempted to use increased sternness to nip in the bud what looks like incipient revolt. But any apparent withdrawal of affection will only delay the child's identification with that parent. The beleaguered parent would be better advised to take an attitude of patient waiting, enduring the sulks, preventing tantrums from getting out of hand, and never letting himself feel offended. His turn will come.

There are several areas in which mistakes on the part of a parent either during previous phases of the child's development or during this one, may result in permanent damage to the youngster's ability to identify with his own sex. If, during infancy or during the period of discipline, the child has had no opportunity to feel secure with the parent of the same sex, or has known only rigidity, sternness, and rejection from that parent, then he may never feel any impulse to move into an identification with that parent. How can a small boy get close to an absentee father, or to one who has always been presented as the punishing figure when there has been any naughtiness during the day? How can a little girl ever want to think of herself as feminine if the chief female figure of her life has been indifferent, unkind, or rejecting?

A child in a family where siblings of the other sex are openly favored may also have considerable difficulty in moving toward identification with his own sex. If the parents are more lenient with their daughters, or give them more attention and more favors, the little boy will quite naturally feel that it is safer and more desirable to be a girl. How can he enjoy his inescapable masculinity? He may even try to deny it by acting like a girl. Or if the parents wanted a son and talk about it in front of their daughter, or express openly their great pleasure when a son is born, then the small girl will recognize that her sex is belittled and unimportant. She may cringe in humiliation, or she may try to behave like a boy, but she will not easily find any pleasure in her feminine role.

Either of these circumstances might delay or even permanently block a child's progress toward acceptance of his own sex and of himself as a member of it. Another situation which makes for difficulties of identification may occur if either parent is hungering for more emotional gratification than he is able to find in the marital relationship. Then the mother, enjoying the increasing evidences of her small son's pleasant devotion, may be tempted to encourage its continuance in subtle, unconscious ways, perhaps fondling him more than usual, or responding to his requests to get into bed with her. Then it becomes all too easy for the little boy to stay on in this gratifying early stage instead of moving toward identification with his father as he normally would do. It is as though he felt that grown men were finding nothing as satisfying as what he is getting right where he is. So he remains a mama's boy, dependent on her affection, staying close to her, perhaps never leaving to marry or, if he does marry, expecting his wife to be a second mother to him. The same sort of thing can happen to a little girl if the father is too demonstrative, too seductive, while she is going through this particular phase of her development.

There is fortunately in all living creatures, including, of course, human children, a strong push toward growth and maturation. This push may be strong enough to carry a child through each stage of development in spite of errors and obstacles. But emotional development may be delayed, or it may be twisted and distorted, if the satisfactions of any one stage are made sufficiently gratifying to outweigh the urge toward growth. We have already seen that a small child may remain in the first stage of development far beyond the time when he should be moving out of his infant dependency. This may happen if a fond mama waits on him too slavishly and provides no stimulation for him to learn how to do things for himself. Or he can stay in the early phase of identification if a forward move seems frightening or unrewarding. A boy may not have any wish to become a man, nor a girl to become a woman, if there is no adult of the right sex to

provide an appealing model, or if the adult of the opposite
sex offers too much emotional allure for staying back.

Here is where the importance of the caseworker's knowledge comes in. If the caseworker is aware of what is happening
to the child as he moves through one stage of development
toward the next, if the worker is alert to the circumstances
which might block maturation, he may be able to help a
great deal. Perhaps all that is needed is an interpretation to
the parents of why the child who was so appealing yesterday
has become so thorny today, or of what may happen to a
child's development if he is given too much seductive fondling when he should be helped to move away from the parent
of the opposite sex into a comfortable, normal identification
with his own sex. It may be that what is needed is support
from an understanding caseworker as the wife tries to work
through her jealousy of her own daughter or a father attempts to conquer his feeling that his own small son is a
threat. The inadequacies and insecurities of the parents
themselves stem from things that happened to them during
their early years, and a caseworker who is aware of this can
be more understanding and tolerant.

It is toward the end of the preschool years, when the
child is four or five, that he really begins to consolidate his
gains. If he had what he needed of tender loving care during
the period of dependency, he now feels reasonably confident
that grownups like him, that he is an all-right person whom
people will accept and with whom they will be friendly. If he
has had consistent discipline, with enough affectionate approval for good behavior, he will have a fairly well-entrenched
habit of doing the acceptable thing, and if he has progressed
through this last period of identification with no emotional
blockades he will by this time be identified with an adult of
the same sex and have a realistic image of himself. With the
internalization of this identification comes also the internalization of conscience, the deep, by now largely subconscious

awareness of what in his family setting is considered right and what is wrong. Whether his conscience prompts him to do what is socially acceptable in the broader field of life depends on what he has incorporated from the adult with whom he has identified. Whether he is capable of performing in accord with his conscience depends on what happened to him during the first two stages of his maturation.

XIV

THE GRADESTER

If a child has had a reasonable amount of emotional satisfaction during the first three stages of his development—if he has learned security while he was a dependent infant, and has discovered during the period of discipline that he could control his own behavior sufficiently to keep out of trouble, and has moved into a comfortable awareness of himself as a boy (or of herself as a girl), identifying with an acceptable adult on whom to model himself—then he should be quite ready by the time he is five or six to take the next step toward growing up. When he has arrived at this stage the child is ready for school, and if all has gone well with him thus far, school should be a happy experience.

His natural curiosity has been increasing ever since his toddler age, and the chance to learn which school provides will help to satisfy this curiosity. In the period of identification he has learned to think of himself as a boy, or the girl has thought of herself as a girl, and so now getting out with a group of children, mixing with his own sex, increases his self-confidence and strengthens his self-image. Boys are ready to play with boys, girls with girls, and both are beginning to be ready for organized games and team play.

But children develop at different rates, mentally, physically, and emotionally. One child may stride off boldly to school when he is four. Another may not be ready before he is seven or eight. If a child is pushed too fast before he is emotionally ready, school can be a traumatic experience. Any child may whimper a bit with homesickness on his first day in school, and adjust comfortably before the week is out. But if he does not adjust, if he is really not yet mature enough for the experience, both he and his teachers may have trouble for years to come.

These gradester years, between approximately five and the approach of puberty at eleven or twelve, should be some of the most comfortable, both for the child and for his parents. The child has lived through the physical and emotional hazards of babyhood and has not yet arrived at the storm and stresses of adolescence. The fact that these in-between years are not always comfortable for anybody is due largely to whatever may have been lacking earlier for normal, healthy development.

If the trouble shows up first as a failure to learn or as obstreperous behavior in school, the caseworker must try to find out why things are going wrong. Probably a thorough physical examination would be the first move. Impairment of sight or hearing will certainly block a child from normal learning, and may affect his behavior adversely as he tries to work out his frustrations when he sees other children doing things he cannot understand. A low-grade fever from bad teeth, an ear infection, digestive upsets may be barely noticeable to the lay eye and yet be draining all the youngster's energy. Even more serious conditions may have escaped notice in a large, boisterous family but cause bizarre behavior in school where demands are more than the child can meet. It might even be desirable to arrange for an electroencephalogram. This test, familiarly known as the EEG, would reveal abnormal brain waves which might indicate brain damage or the possibility of epilepsy. However, there is a need for a double check here. Abnormal brain waves have been found in individuals whose behavior and learning ability have remained beyond reproach all their lives. They may also be found in persons whose behavior is not normal but whose personality problems come from quite a different cause. So if the EEG results are reported as "consistent with a possible epilepsy," do not assume that the villain has necessarily been tracked down. The EEG has only located something that *may* be the villain. Table it and look farther.

If the physical and neurological examinations bring to light nothing that explains poor school adjustment or inadequate performance, think next of mental tests. A child who lacks the intellectual capacity to keep up with others in his grade may give up, make no further effort, and sit doing nothing, escaping from his conviction of inferiority through day-dreams. Or he may attempt to compensate by "smart alecky" behavior, amusing the other children, or making them angry, but assuring himself of some kind of attention. Such a child may be in the wrong grade and should be permitted to drop back to one in which the work will be within his capacity. Or perhaps he is sufficiently retarded to need placement in a special grade.

It is also possible that the mental tests will show a superior IQ. Then perhaps the difficulty is that the child is simply bored by the repetition of material he grasped long ago and requires extra activities to use up excess energy.

In many areas the schools rather than the social agency arrange for these mental tests, but in any event there should be cooperation and frequent conferences between teacher and caseworker. For the most part, teachers are deeply interested in the children they teach, and are sensitive to their emotional or intellectual problems, but now and then a teacher may express impatience and exasperation about one troublesome youngster who is distracting the whole class-room. Surely she can be forgiven. She is probably trying to teach thirty squirming pupils simultaneously. The unseemly "shenanigans" of one hyperactive child can upset everyone, and the teacher would be more than human if she were not tempted to send him out of the room, or demand that he be excluded from the class, so that she can accomplish something with the rest of the group. In such situations a conference between teacher and caseworker helps. Even if the conference ends with the teacher still in despair about the possibility of any improvement, something will surely have been accomplished. It has happened that following a conference that closed on a note of utter discouragement, the small bad actor who had been the subject suddenly and inexplicably took a turn for the better. Although the teacher was unaware of doing anything in any way different, nevertheless there was a subtle change in the teacher–pupil relationship which the child sensed. Children are uncanny in their sensitivity to unspoken attitudes. What happens in this situation is that the child is subconsciously responding to the teacher's equally subconscious awareness of him as an individual, an awareness which the child has been needing and which was augmented by the previous day's conference.

If a child's school problems are not corrected by an improved physical condition or by a more appropriate grade placement, then probably the causes are more subtle and the solution more difficult. A child who is catapulted into school before he is sufficiently mature to accept its challenge may well develop a negative attitude that he never overcomes. His hearty dislike of school will be increased by the fact that he does not keep up with his companions at the beginning, so that he feels inferior. As a consequence, he falls more and more behind, which makes him hate school even more — a vicious circle that can be broken only by a taste of success which, of course, becomes increasingly difficult to achieve. Sometimes an especially sensitive and tactful teacher can help him, but it should be done before the child is asked to tackle third grade.

The third grade in our public schools is a critical period

in a pupil's career. At that time he is expected to drop the picture drawing, the game playing, the easy tasks of the earlier grades, and really buckle down to multiplication tables, what happened in 1492, and the location of Venezuela. A child who is slow but not too seriously retarded may reach the third grade without his handicap being identified. A child whose emotional problems interfere with concentration or with learning may encounter his first serious snags in the third grade.

The indication of some of the emotional problems that become manifest during the gradester years and which may well be the basis for school problems as well as for problems in the home and community are:

Temper tantrums. — Most children have tantrums during the period of discipline when they are first forced to recognize the rights of others, and the disappointing fact that they are not, after all, the center of the earth. This awareness comes hard, and harder for some children than others. If consistent limits are not set for them, or if they are not offered the award of approval for self-control, they may be very late in learning to tolerate the inevitable frustrations of life—if they ever do learn. A child who arrives at school age without having had any discipline or help to gain self-control is sure to have a difficult time accepting the limits that the schoolroom places on his behavior.

Fearfulness. — A child who has been severely punished for any independent experimentation, or one who has been over-protected by nervous parents who never dare let their child clamber about by himself or do anything without his mother to hold his hand, will surely be slower than other children to acquire self-confidence or to discover that strangers do not bite. Whether or not he is ever able to accept hazards as normal children do will depend on the extent of the early damage done by his parents and also on the degree to which they are still keeping him frightened and dependent. Sometimes interpretation to the parents helps, but this must be given with tact and understanding; for very nervous parents, uncertain of themselves and of their child, are what they are because of their own childhood and cannot be made courageous and fearless by a simple scolding. Help for them must be on a deeper level, perhaps deeper than a caseworker should attempt to reach without help from a trained therapist.

Rigidity.—Most children take their first steps away from their own home convinced that what their mother says is right, what their father does is the right and proper thing to do. But if the child has been given the normal amount of stimulation at home for experimentation, if he has a normal amount of self-confidence, he will soon be ready to try different ways. In an average home, parents remain the frame of reference up to a child's arrival at adolescence, but a healthy, reasonably confident child can still accept new ways, at least to a limited extent. He can try different foods, play different games, look at different television programs, read different books. But the child who can never bring himself to take a new risk, to try any fresh approach, always insisting on doing just what is done at home in just the way it is done at home, is going to have a difficult time in life unless he is given courage and self-confidence now.

Aggressiveness.—The child who is scrappy may be identifying with an aggressive parent, repeating a pattern seen at home, or he may be showing a reaction formation, a rushing to the opposite extreme from a real fear of admitting inadequacy. If it is the latter, the child is behaving like a bully to prove to himself that he is not afraid. Such a child will become less aggressive as he grows more secure within himself. A really secure child feels no need to prove anything; he can take his own courage for granted.

Sometimes a child's aggressiveness is directed against the

teacher rather than against his peers. In that case, the behavior is probably an expression of resentment against authority, transferred from the punishing parent onto all authority figures, with teacher (or social worker or police officer) used as stand-in.

Learning block. — This may show itself as an inability to learn anything in school, and if it is not due to intellectual immaturity or retardation, or to a defect of hearing or vision, it may well be due to a generalized anxiety that leaves no energy to be applied to learning. Children often show such a block if they come from homes where the friction between the parents worries the children, or where one of the parents is seriously ill, or where one or both parents have gone away, leaving the children to wonder why and to worry about what will happen next.

The child with a normal intelligence who learns other things but remains a nonreader has been the subject of a great deal of study, experimentation, and theory. One possible reason for an inability to read is a visual abnormality. Some children can do mirror reading with ease and learn later to read directly from the printed page. Another possible reason for the slow reader is lack in the home of any stimulation toward that particular type of learning. Either the child gets everything he feels he wants by watching television, or his parents read to him and he enjoys that too much to give it up. One father solved that problem by telling his child that he would continue to read stories aloud if the child would read one story for each one the father read. Another program which has been surprisingly successful is a summer reading camp for nonreaders with normal IQ's. The camp offers swimming, hikes, picnics, and such enjoyable occupations, plus one hour a day of individual tutoring in reading. The head of this camp[1] confesses that she does not know whether

[1]Summer reading camp on the shore of Otsego Lake near Cooperstown, N.Y., organized by Dr. Mary Goodwin, of the Mary Imogene Bassett Hospital, in Cooperstown.

the really outstanding success of the program is due to the individual attention the child receives, or to the pleasing association of reading and camping.

Truancy.—Truancy may be prompted by the fact that school—or home—is really unbearable because of the child's dread of failure, his expectation of punishment, his unpopularity with his peers, his memory of some recent humili ation. Any of these circumstances might be sufficient to prompt the child to seek escape from grim reality into a fantasy life, a make-believe that is more alluring. Sometimes children run away because of an urge to punish the parents or the teacher: "When I'm gone they'll be sorry." Or the running away may be a compulsive and unconscious search for a lost parent. The story *Runaway Alice* [2] points this up. When Alice found emotional security with her caseworker she no longer needed to run away.

Destructiveness.—This may be simply a result of inadequate home training. The child was never taught respect for the possessions of other people and was never trained to take care of his own. It is possible, however, that destructiveness is an expression of deep hostility, an urge to hurt because the child has been himself deeply hurt by the parents' failure to provide the affection and security he needed. This will be corrected only as the child is persuaded to trust in the real love of a concerned adult. This is not easy to accomplish; for with such a child the hurt has gone deep, and the suspicion is pretty thoroughly ingrained.

Enuresis.—The inability to retain urine is more likely to be a problem in the home than in school, although it may be troublesome in school too. There is always a possibility that the difficulty is a physical one, a real weakness of the sphincter muscle. If that cause has been ruled out, we can be certain that the problem is an emotional one. In that case, punishment of the offender will have no effect, and reduction of

[2]Frances Salomon Murphy, *Runaway Alice.*

liquid intake will have very little. Getting the child up once
or twice during the night helps some, but if the child's
unconscious wish to punish the parent is very strong he will
manage to wet the bed a minute or two before he is roused, or
five minutes after he has been put back in the bed. The
enuresis will be corrected when the child is sufficiently secure
so that he no longer needs to hit back at adults.

Withdrawal. — This is serious in a child, and doubly serious
because it may so easily be overlooked. A withdrawn child
gives no trouble to anyone. He may be able to learn fairly
well and therefore does not make himself conspicuous by
school failure. He does not misbehave at home or in the
classroom. He does exactly what he is told to do. In short,
he is the overly good child. But the healthy child is not all
that good. The normal child has a will of his own, and
feelings of his own, and sometimes he expresses them. The
withdrawn child shows no feelings, either of gaiety or grief,
of affection or dislike. This is an emotionally sick child, a
child who has been hurt and has crept into his shell to avoid
being hurt again. It is a child who has repressed his normal
resentments, his perfectly healthy anger over what has
happened to him, until he is no longer capable of admitting
any kind of feeling.

Caseworkers in child-placement agencies sometimes see
that kind of apparent indifference when a youngster is first
moved out of his own home into a foster home. This period
of peace has sometimes been termed the "honeymoon
period," but there could not be a more misleading phrase.
It is not the happy time that the words imply. The meek
behavior is the result of a temporary inhibiting of fear and
resentment which any child feels at the loss of all that has
been familiar to him in life. If the placed child is not too
seriously damaged, his inhibitions will dissolve within a week
or so, and his behavior thereupon will be more troublesome
to the foster parents — but far healthier for the child.

If the child's normal feelings do not find normal expression he may go through his whole life repressed and withdrawn, a small, pale ghost among the living. As an adult he may be able to function effectively, but he will never be able to admit any warm relationship with anyone. If he is faced with a stress which wears his control thin, he will develop neurotic symptoms—anything from a tic to a disabling claustrophobia. Or the withdrawn child may not reach adulthood without a break. If he does not get help while he is still young enough to accept it, he may go through the gradester years without calling attention to himself and then react violently in adolescence when the tumultuous emotions overwhelm his precariously balanced restraints. The too good daughter may become pregnant out of wedlock; the too good son may become delinquent.

These withdrawn children need help before they reach the breaking point. Warmth and undemanding affection from a concerned adult who can give without asking for response, who will not expect the child to pay for acceptance by good behavior, who can offer an implied permission for the child to show anger and resentment—this will in time melt the wall of reserve and allow the child to give up his deathly repressions.

There are several different attitudes which well-meaning adults may assume toward a child's undesirable behavior:

1. Rejection by the authority figure of the misbehaving child: examples of this would be the principal who expels the child from school, the harassed foster mother who insists that the child be removed from her home, and the social worker who avoids contact with an unappealing child.

2. Rejection of the existence of the undesirable behavior: the fond mother who refuses to believe that her child could possibly be guilty of the sin of which he is accused would be an example of this.

3. Forgiveness of the misbehavior because the adult is aware of the unfortunate circumstances of the child's life:

this is the temptation of the social worker who knows about the youngster's poor home background.

Not one of these attitudes is really constructive. It is not helpful to throw the child out; neither does it help to excuse or produce alibis. What the wise caseworker must do is determine the mood of which the bad behavior is an expression, to learn the basic human need which has gone unsatisfied and which the child was blindly trying to satisfy. Then, having looked through to the dynamics of the behavior, the caseworker must see whether the need cannot be satisfied in some more acceptable fashion. If it can, then the social worker must try to see that it is satisfied, either through a change in the child's situation and environment, or through his own relationship with the child.

A knowledge of the individual's home life and background helps but is not always essential. A worker who is aware of a child's unsatisfactory relationship with his parents will be able to make a very good guess of what early needs have been left unfilled. A worker who is trying to help an adult may have more difficulty learning about the early circumstances of the person's life, and must make his diagnosis from current behavior.

It may not be very easy to get the details of even a child's background. Parents may not be available for interviewing, and a child during the gradester years is not likely to verbalize. It does no good to ask him why he does this or that because his behavior is a response to unconscious urges of which his conscious mind is totally unaware. If he is pressed for explanations, he may give a fancy answer, an elaborate rationalization, or he may proffer only sullen silence. He may be able and willing to give facts about his background — or he may not. A withdrawn child will have repressed the vital information until it is beyond the reach of his conscious memory. The fearful or rigid child may be afraid to talk to the social workers, the aggressive child may not want to.

Helpful background information may be secured from medical reports, school records, social agencies, or police courts to which the parents have been known. But before the child can open up directly to the worker, a good relationship must be established, a climate of acceptance which gives the child permission to express resentment or anger without fear of retribution or loss of love.

Then, when the caseworker knows where the problem lies, he can figure out what is needed to solve it, perhaps through his own relationship with the child which gives reassurance and security, perhaps through affecting the child's environment at home or at school in some beneficial way.

XV

THE ADOLESCENT

Any caseworker who has adolescents on his caseload finds that he has problems and obligations not altogether like those he has with other age groups. For one thing, he must make some effort to steer the young ward with sensitivity and consummate tact through the characteristic adolescent revolt, at the same time probably offering support and interpretation to harassed adults who must live with their thorny teen-ager. Any young person from the age of twelve or fourteen on is in the process of finding himself, breaking away from family ties to start making his own decisions. Typically, he resents advice; hence the need for great tact. He may be more adequate than his anxious parents can believe, but almost certainly he is less capable, less sophisticated, less knowledgeable, than he himself would like to think.

Parenthetically, if a youngster in this age group is *not* thrashing around to some extent in an effort to be independent, that is a danger signal too, indicating low physical energy or a poor self-image such as may come from lack of emotional nourishment during the earlier years.

One of the important requirements for the healthy development of a teen-ager is an opportunity for plenty of stimulating, enjoyable activity in the company of other teen-agers. More than one adolescent has become involved in delinquencies because he had no chance to indulge in nondelinquent activities. This is especially a hazard for the children of financially and culturally underprivileged families. If a home is overcrowded, hot, noisy, if there is no neighborhood club or swimming pool or well-directed group activity available, what can a restless youngster do but hang around the street corner with his gang and think up a few exciting anti-social stunts with which to prove his cleverness to himself and his buddies?

Rural areas usually have 4-H clubs, Future Farmers of America, Boy Scouts and Girl Scouts, to provide a choice of healthy group occupations. In cities, unhappily, there are fewer resources in proportion to the temptations, but there are church groups, the Y's, neighborhood clubs, settlement houses, any of which may offer programs of sports, parties, dances, cultural and educational evenings. There are Big Brother and Big Sister movements to help in guidance, and various youth service agencies provide counseling for the adolescent and his parents. The caseworker must know his adolescent, and must try to direct him toward a group that will be to his taste—swimming, drama, sports, bird watching, hiking, whatever will catch the youngster's interest. But it must be done tactfully; for many teen-agers, especially those who have ever tangled with the law, are almost violently opposed to "do-gooders" or to any suggestion whatever that comes from their enemy, the adult. Teen-agers need to be with their own kind, but if they have located "their own kind" in the wrong setting before the caseworker has established a good working relationship, the task is triply difficult.

Then there is the matter of school. Among other life tasks that face every adolescent is the selection of, and preparation for, his lifework, the job by which he will support himself and his future family, by means of which he will make his individual, unique contribution to society. Every caseworker is very much aware that the more education a person has, the better his chances of finding a place in the career of his choice.

The caseworker also knows that good jobs are extremely difficult to find for a teen-ager who does not even have a high school diploma. So caseworkers try to prevent their wards from becoming those futile aimless creatures, school dropouts.

However, there are a few grim realities to consider. A college education is a desirable goal, and scholarships may make this a reachable goal even for young people who have no money. But the road is a rough one, and before the worker urges his client toward this goal he must be quite convinced that the adolescent has both the intellectual capacity and the emotional stamina to stick through four years of hard study (good grades must be maintained to hold a scholarship grant), of minimum social activity (there will be no surplus cash for fraternities, club dues, or entertainment), and probably of very little if any leisure (more often than not scholarships must be supplemented by odd jobs around the campus). However, if the adolescent is ambitious and capable, the caseworker should leave no stone unturned to help him apply for a scholarship, help him select the college and apply for admission. If possible, the worker should help him find the extra work he will need to keep going during the college years. But the caseworker must not push until he is pretty confident of the young person's interest and his ability. Flunking out at the end of the first semester may set him back a good many years in willingness to try anything ambitious again.

More caseworkers, however, will put all their energy into trying to keep their young client in high school long enough to earn a diploma, and here too there are a few not so pleasant realities to face. It is true that jobs are much easier for young people to find if they have graduated from high school, and so it would appear well worth while for them to stay the course. But the children of economically and cultur-ally underprivileged families are usually from two to four years behind their age group in grade placement. This is not to imply that "relief kids" have lower IQ's than children from the other side of the tracks. Not at all. But the "relief kids" may have had little or no stimulation at home. They may have been seriously hampered in their studies by lack of understanding or encouragement from their families, by noisy, crowded home conditions ill conducive to concentration on study assignments. Sometimes there are demands that they contribute to family support with part-time or weekend jobs that use up time and energy. Moreover, families with long histories of support from public assistance are prone to moving frequently, perhaps to avoid payment of rent or perhaps in the futile hope of finding better living quarters within their limited budgets. These moves may well mean many changes of schools for the children, and with each move a half year's setback. So while many more fortunate children finish high school by the time they are sixteen, the child of a welfare family may still be in the ninth or tenth grade at that age. Most states permit a child to leave school after his sixteenth birthday, and the temptation to do just that is strong in a restless, discouraged boy who feels that he is conspicuously bigger and older than his classmates.

It is difficult for a caseworker to find arguments to keep him in school, and it is almost impossible if the family is receiving assistance from an agency which drops children from the relief roll at sixteen.

The dropout does not always have a poorer mentality than class-mates who take hold and finish high school. He does always have poorer motivation. His chief characteristic is lack of interest, a true world weariness; he has lost the will to meet the exacting standards of society in his own times. Dr. Amos calls him "the young retired." Signs of a dropout's apathy may include a poor attendance record at school, no extracurricular activities, poor reading ability, a record of failure in one or more subjects so that it looks as though he will not be able to graduate with his class. He may dislike his teachers, choose friends who are much younger or much older. He may have a history of truancy or of absences based on headaches, upset stomachs, colds.[1]

What such a child needs is a strong incentive, a goal that is appealing and seems to be within his grasp. Certainly not for such as he is any glowing picture of college — that is far out of his reach. Nor does the mere acquisition of a high school diploma attract him — that is simply an uninteresting piece of paper. Probably the prospect of a better paid job if he graduates is no incentive either — that is too far in the future to seem very real, and there are too many obstacles in the way.

The incentive must be immediate and pleasurable in the teen-ager's terms. One sixteen-year-old girl, failing, discouraged, and bored, suddenly decided to stay in school when she discovered that she had a facility for baton twirling. She buckled down to study because she would not be permitted to participate in parades or sports activities unless she had passing grades. Eventually, she graduated with what was for her a creditable *C* average. A boy who found a summer job in a printing shop liked the work. His employer promised him weekend work during the winter and a job the next summer if he would stay in school, with the prospect of permanent employment if he graduated. He stayed in school and the promises were kept. Another boy was offered a place in the school band blowing a borrowed horn if he could keep his grades up, and for him this was sufficient incentive. The motivation need not be wholly academic.

Whether the adolescent finishes high school or drops out before graduation, the caseworker must provide practical help to the youngster in his search for work. The teen-ager should be encouraged to make his own application, either to a prospective employer or to an employment agency. Indeed,

[1]Dr. William E. Amos, Youth Specialist of the Department of Labor, quoted in Hilda Cole Espy, "The Tragic Problem of Dropouts in Our Schools," *Woman's Day*, August, 1964.

it is quite likely that an adolescent will resent too much close supervision at this time. Nevertheless, strong help from behind the scenes is definitely indicated. The adolescent may never have lived in a family in which any member was regularly employed. His parents are not going to be able to advise him how to present himself, how to sit or speak, even how to dress. This information must come from the caseworker, and it must be detailed and specific.

Appearance.—The adolescent must be persuaded to be personally clean, freshly bathed, free from body odor, with well-washed hands and clean fingernails. This, obviously, is more important to a girl who is applying for a job as a waitress or to a youth who wants to be a bus boy than it would be if the objective were to work as a mechanic. The caseworker can use discretion in the amount of emphasis he puts on cleanliness.

Hair styles should not be extreme, and the cut should be neat. Girls should avoid fashions which make their heads resemble last year's bird's nest.

Clothing should be suitable for the occasion. Girls are probably more prone than boys to err in this, but boys can be advised to avoid the black leather jacket, or whatever the local gang uniform may be, and to wear a clean shirt and tidy shoes. A girl may need more specific help. She should be dressed neatly and simply, with the minimum of jewelry and fussiness. No prospective employer is favorably impressed by a girl whose spike heels appear to be crippling her, whose stockings are sleazy or full of runs, or whose skirt is so tight or so short that she can scarcely sit down.

Inducing a girl to wear suitable clothes when she applies for work may take quite a bit of persuasion and a great deal of understanding on the part of the caseworker. An adolescent is in a period of strong peer identification, and sensible advice from some old fogy of twenty-five may not be too acceptable. The girl's image of herself as fascinating in tight skirt, jangling bracelets, and heavy make-up is not easy for her to relinquish. At the other extreme, we may be working with a girl who has never been too certain of her own charms and has defiantly dressed to prove that she does not care. But soiled slacks and her brother's sloppy shirt would not make a good impression either.

Manner. — An adolescent who is making his first application for a job should follow a few rules of behavior, and he will probably need to know from the worker what the rules are and why following them will help him get the job:

Do not chew gum.

Do not smoke unless the interviewer suggests it.

Sit up straight. Do not slouch.

For girls — do not cross your legs, especially if your skirt is very short.

Look directly at the interviewer, not vaguely out the window or up at the ceiling.

Do not talk too much, but answer all questions clearly, completely, and honestly.

Do not bluff about education or experience. The interviewer will certainly discover any untruth; if not during the interview, then later, when references are checked or as soon as the applicant starts on the job. Bluffing creates a bad impression and will be a large black mark against him in the future when he applies for other jobs.

The caseworker should feel free to ask a prospective employer about the work for which the application is being made. In fact, if possible, he should have given the adolescent information about the job, what the work will entail, the necessary qualifications in skills, appearance, and personality. This may well involve some advance research on the part of the caseworker, but it will be well worth the effort if it helps prepare the youngster for the interview, or even if it saves him from making futile and discouraging applications for work which he is completely unfitted to do.

The caseworker may find it helpful to arrange for a practice session, with the worker acting as the prospective employer and the adolescent dressing as he would for the interview, walking into the room, sitting, presenting his qualifications, and discussing the job opening. Doing this gives the worker an opportunity to correct solecisms and also will give the young applicant more confidence. Such a scheme will certainly be welcomed by an adolescent who really wants to find a job, and it might even stir a bit of enthusiasm in one who had not previously pictured himself as employed.

The caseworker's responsibility is by no means ended when the adolescent is earning a pay check. Perhaps even the most difficult task is yet to come, that of working with the adolescent in regard to the use of his money. It is to be expected that he will want to buy what he pleases and will not welcome control of his spending. He is likely at first to scatter his earnings defiantly, buying things which the agency, the caseworker, and his parents think are useless, but which he is convinced he must have to meet his conception of peer standards. The caseworker must maintain an uneasy balance between allowing too much freedom and applying too stringent control.

If the adolescent's family is receiving public assistance, it is to be hoped that the agency can have some flexibility in the budgeting of his earnings. Every adolescent has some tendency to cling to his earnings for his own individual use no matter what the financial circumstances of his family. If the adult world forces him to surrender most of his earnings, he will react with hostility. In public assistance agencies, the obligations of the adolescent as a contributor to the family are set by agency regulations; if those regulations fail to take into account the effect on the adolescent's personal development, a great deal of damage may be done.

Any adolescent who is a wage earner should be expected to meet his personal expenses and to pay to the extent feasible for his room and board. If the family has limited income he should contribute a specified amount to the other family expenses. He should be left free, however, to manage the rest of his money and to save or apply it toward education, career, or marriage. Much damage has been done from the insistence of parents and social agencies that an adolescent make relatively large contributions toward the support of the family... At the same time it is equally undesirable for employed adolescents not to participate in paying for their own living expenses. Learning to pay one's way provides a foundation for development toward mature independence and for later responsibility in marriage. In order to be able to assume responsibility for others, a person must first have experience in taking responsibility for himself.[2]

Certainly there should be a discussion about budgeting his earnings before the adolescent embarks on his first job. Unless he sees some advantage to himself in getting work he is not likely to try very hard. Not that having money to spend is the only advantage to employment, but it is unquestionably one of them, and may be the only one which a teen-ager sees at first.

The worker must be honest in discussing the budget and the amount to be contributed toward supporting himself in his parents' home or toward helping the parents. It would be most damaging to let him start out thinking that he will be free to spend all of his earnings on pleasures while he is supported from another source, whether welfare agency or parents. That is not realistic, and to spring a surprise budget on him after he has started work, demanding a large proportion of his earnings for his family's support, will result in anger, antagonism, and, very probably, a runaway adolescent.

[2]Frances Lomas Feldman, *The Family in a Money World*, p.54.

XVI

HELPING THE UNWED MOTHER

When a young and inexperienced worker starts out to help an unmarried mother or a girl pregnant out of wedlock he may find himself facing a few problems within himself. It is important that both he and his supervisor be alert to this possibility and together work through any conflicts he may feel.

If the unwed client is an adolescent and the caseworker not too far removed from adolescence himself, he may still have a good many residual feelings about emancipation. If the worker is married, and especially if the worker is female, married, and a mother, there may be strong feelings about the sanctity of the family, the importance of a father to a child's development. If the worker has no children and has had no sexual experience, his attitude may well be a mixture of envy, condemnation, embarrassment, and awareness of his ignorance of the physical aspects of the experience. A worker who has a tendency to overidentify with the client may be unable to think objectively about planning. His heartstrings may be pulled by the unwed mother who reveals her desperate need for at least one primary relationship in which she knows herself needed, as she will be needed by a dependent baby.

But planning must be done on the basis of what will be good for both the mother and the child, not only today, but a year from today, and ten years, and twenty from the present. The caseworker must free himself equally from any subconscious urge to punish the unwed mother and from an emotional, unthinking wish to use the baby to feed the young mother's needfulness.

Some unwed mothers can provide a better life for the child than could be secured in a foster home or even in an adoptive home. On the other hand, some, by reason of immaturity or emotional underdevelopment, could never give a child what he needs for growth. Each situation must be studied on its own merits, and each decision must be made on an individual basis. Planning must be guided by the mother's personality and also by the community's facilities for out-of-wedlock children. If the child is to be released to the agency, we should be sure that the agency has something better to offer than anything the mother can give. If the infant is to remain with the mother, we want to be confident that she can provide him with emotional nourishment, now while he is a helpless infant and later when he begins to move away from dependency and needs stimulation to attempt to think for himself. The worker's feeling about sexual acting-out must not be permitted to interfere with his objectivity in studying the strengths and the weaknesses of the unwed mother as a mother.

It is not only circumstances of the worker's personal life which may cloud his thinking. There is also a possibility that some vestige of cultural or racial prejudice may induce a worker to feel that out-of-wedlock pregnancies occur more frequently among the financially and socially deprived, the implication being that this indicates a weakness of moral fiber in these groups. It is a fact that statistics show more recorded out-of-wedlock births among the nonwhite and the financially underprivileged than in the higher incomes brackets. But this does not mean that out-of-wedlock coitus is necessarily confined to the "undeserving poor." A girl from well-to-do parents may use contraceptives. If pregnancy occurs and is carried to term, she can move temporarily into

a state where illegitimate births are not recorded as such—
New York or California, for example. She can thus keep her
condition a secret and arrange privately for adoptive placement of the infant without need to appeal to an agency for
help. There is little doubt that this happens, although in the
nature of things we can have no figures. Moreover, girls
from upper income families can, and sometimes do, arrange
for abortions if they find themselves pregnant. They and their
families are more strongly motivated to avoid revealing the
condition than are the low-income groups who have little to
lose whatever they do.

There is now and always has been a culture of poverty
brought about by the pressures that come from having too
little control over one's own destiny, the insecurity of never
knowing what tomorrow will bring, the grinding misery of
never having quite enough to eat and of having no resources
for legitimate social life. The culture of poverty offers special
temptations for out-of-wedlock intercourse, less inducement
to resist, and fewer ways to avoid its consequences.[1] Stimulation of the sexual urges is very much present in today's
society. Novels and stories emphasize boy-girl situations.
Movies, radio, and television stress sex. Popular music can
stir sexual impulses. Dancing is stimulating. Advertising
creates an image of success that involves popularity with
the opposite sex. Feminine dress emphasizes sex symbols—
exaggerated breasts and closely outlined buttocks.

The mores of our culture verbalize the ideal of limiting
sexual experience to the expression of unity and sharing
between a man and a woman who have joined their destinies
for the purpose of making a home and building a family.
Young people who have accepted the mores of our time, and

[1]Clark Vincent, *Unmarried Mother.* The author makes an interesting
contribution to information about age, social status, and income brackets as
related to out-of-wedlock pregnancies.

have through their own personal experiences in growing up developed adequate emotional strength and maturity, will be able to resist the multitudinous temptations to submit to sexual experience as a mere adventure or as a proof of personal popularity. Control may be more difficult in some socioeconomic levels that in others, but the dynamics which bring about out-of-wedlock coitus exist on all levels, and these dynamics are important for the caseworker to understand.

Leontine Young[2] discusses the various unhealthy emotional family climates which may induce a girl to turn to sexual acting-out. If the stimulation is strong, as it is in modern times, if resistance is difficult, as it so often is, especially for the underprivileged, if the inner emotional need is pressing, as it well may be in a girl whose early relationship with her parents has not been satisfying, then we may find ourselves working with an illegitimately pregnant girl. In order to help her we must understand something of the dynamics which have pushed her into this behavior.

A girl who reaches puberty without having known acceptance from parents who love and cherish her may in her desperate need yield readily to any opportunity that presents itself for sexual experience because it gives her a feeling of being close to another human being, accepted and cherished for however brief a time. If the experience has not resulted in any continuing relationship with the man, this girl is more than likely to attempt to meet her emotional hunger by the relationship with the baby whose helplessness makes him a safe object for her to love without fear of rejection. This girl will require a great deal of casework help if she is to make an adequate mother, able to stimulate the child to grow toward independence. It is possible that she will never be able to do

[2]Leontine Young. *Out of Wedlock: a Study of the Problems of the Unmarried Mother and Her Child.*

this. Then the caseworker must help her develop enough security to find a life for herself without the baby. If the worker can show her the concern and interest which her mother should have shown and did not, then possibly the girl will transfer her dependence from her own inadequate mother to the caseworker, who can build the girl's ego image until she is able to stand alone and, in time, assume a wife's role, giving as well as taking from her partner. If, however, the worker uses pressure to remove the infant, offering nothing to replace it in the girl's life, what will almost certainly happen is that the girl must turn to another illicit relationship and probably another pregnancy in her efforts to meet her emotional need.

It is disturbing to note how few of the unmarried girls with whom we work show concern for, or even much awareness of, the baby as an individual who will have developmental needs of his own as he grows. Sometimes they ignore the baby, leaving it in the hospital or handing it over to the agency without a second thought, as though the fact of having given birth was the important thing to them. Sometimes they are vigorous in their expressions of love for the baby—but it is the *baby* they talk about, not the child which the baby will become, not an individual with a separate personality and a life of its own. Often, too, they show very little interest in the father of the baby. Leontine Young says that in her experience they often do not even know his name, cannot describe him, know nothing of his background, his interests, his personality. "I think his first name was Bill," a girl may say. They met on a blind date, or as a "pick-up," and frequently the girl insists that they had intercourse only once. Even if they had a few weeks of relationship, the girl now shows no interest in continuing contact, again as though giving birth to a baby were the important thing, and once the man has served his biological purpose he is of no further concern. Very rare indeed is the unmarried pregnant girl who is promiscuous. Leontine Young points out:

The urge for a child is a fundamental biological force without which the race would not long survive but normally that urge is an inextricable part of love of a man and woman for each other. The success of the family as a basic unit of society is rooted in that fact. The serious problem of the unmarried mother is that her urge for a baby has been separated from its normal matrix, love for a mate.[3]

Girls who become pregnant out of wedlock, the ones who cannot think of the baby as an individual apart from themselves, may ignore the child's father utterly or want only to punish him, while they remain unable to admit that their own behavior or attitude had any part in making conception possible. These are sick girls. These are girls who have not had during their growing-up years sufficient emotional nourishment to make it possible for them to reach a psychological maturity.

If one factor can be considered fundamental in the family background of unmarried mothers it is the consistent pattern of domination of the home by one parent. With monotonous regularity one hears from girl after girl as she describes her early life of a family which has been shadowed by the possessiveness and unhealthy tyranny of one of the parents. Rare indeed is the girl who can remember parents who loved and respected each other and who shared family experiences and responsibilities with each other. In a great many cases an unmarried mother comes from a broken home and is brought up literally by one parent only, but in a large number of other cases the parents remain together and the effect is much the same. The domination of one parent deprives the girl of normal relationship with either.[4]

If the father has dominated through tyranny and abusiveness, the girl will want to strike back, and if she cannot strike effectively against her father, she will try to punish any man

[3]*Ibid.*, pp. 36–37.
[4]*Ibid.*, p. 70.

over whom she can achieve a position of power. Having an out-of-wedlock baby puts her in a position to punish the father of the infant, and frequently she insists on doing this very thing without admitting the man to any part of the planning for the baby or to any further part in her own life. She wants to keep the baby, not for the baby's sake, but because it can be used as a threat by means of which the man is forced to pay, financially and often socially and emotionally. If the girl's father has dominated her life through seductiveness during and after her period of identification, when she should have been learning to identify with her own mother and should have been starting to see herself as someday having a mate of her own, that girl will have a different problem. Her father's seductiveness will have blocked her from moving out of her childhood fantasy of being the lifelong mate of her male parent. She will as a young adult still harbor the unconscious fantasy of seeing herself in her own mother's place, and often she wants to take her out-of-wedlock baby home where she will assume, as it were, the role of wife to her own father. Not that the girl is ever aware of this motivation, but the strong probability of its existence should be very much present in the caseworker's awareness and should govern his handling of the situation.

If the girl's mother has been the dominating and possessive parent, the girl may want to use the existence of the baby to punish and embarrass the parent who deprived her of independence, or she may use her pregnancy in a sort of distorted rivalry with her mother: "Mother bore a child, and look, so did I." As in the case of the father-dominated girl, the motivation is always far beneath the surface of her conscious mind. No purpose whatever would be served by trying to discuss motivation with her. The worker must make his diagnosis by observing the girl and her parents together, or by listening to the way she talks about her relationship with her parents and the way she describes her childhood and her home life, and by the way she plans—or fails to plan—for the baby.

The mother-dominated girl, during her pregnancy and while arrangements are being made for her medical care and for the baby, probably will show either abject compliance with her mother's opinions and wishes or a defiance of everything her mother suggests. The latter will occur if the girl is able to resent openly the domination which has attempted to keep her a dependent child.

The extent to which the unmarried mother has achieved emotional maturity can be accurately measured by observing the extent to which she can think of the baby as a separate entity and can plan for his needs apart from her own. However, it does no good whatever for a caseworker to approach work with the unwed mother on the basis of logic or of what is best for the baby. Arguments will be accepted by her only if she has managed to work through her own unconscious dynamics. On rare occasions this comes with no special help from the caseworker. Much more often, if it is to happen at all, it will be through the caseworker's awareness of the dynamics that motivate this particular girl and his ability to meet the deep need through the client–worker relationship—not by reasoning or by logical discussion but wholly through acceptance and feeling.

It is not easy to work with a girl who is motivated by resentment of a dominating father. A male caseworker would fall into the general category of hated males. A female worker would very probably be regarded as nice but futile, since these girls have almost invariably known only weak and submissive mothers. (If the mother had been a stronger personality there would have been no opportunity for the father to be so dominating.) It takes long and patient work to help such a girl, and it may be that one's first efforts should be directed toward rescuing the baby and trying later to give the girl a better concept of mankind, or womankind, or both.

From the agency's point of view, planning for the mother-dominated girl is usually simpler. If the girl has reacted to the domination by submission, then planning for the baby will be done in the first instance through the mother while parallel and subsequent efforts are made to release the girl from this dependency. Usually, a female worker can be more successful here, and if she can establish a sufficiently strong rapport, the girl may transfer her dependency to the case-worker. This is good and should be encouraged. The case-worker herself, free from the neurotic urges which have directed the attitudes of the girl's mother, can understand that the dependency is a temporary crutch and can gently help the girl move away from her toward independence. If the girl can arrive at emotional maturity, she will not need an out-of-wedlock child either to "have something of her own to love," or to prove that she is as good as her mother. The girl will be able to fashion her own life along normal lines, looking forward to a mate whom she loves and a home and a family that she and her mate will share.

Whatever plans are made, whatever work is done, the caseworker must always keep in mind that his obligation is twofold—to plan for the best possible future for the child and to help the unwed mother move toward emotional maturity and a good life for herself. Sometimes this involves helping mother and child to stay together. Sometimes it means separating them, placing the baby for adoption and working with the mother individually. In either case, neither the unwed mother nor the out-of-wedlock infant should be sacrificed for the sake of the other. Both are clients of the agency. Both have a right to all the help the agency can give.

XVII

EVALUATION OF FAMILY
STRENGTHS

For years, caseworkers have been encouraged to think in terms of person-to-person relationships, husband-to-wife, mother-to-child, client-to-caseworker. They have been taught to study intrapsychic conflicts within the client, and to offer help in resolving those conflicts through the casework relationship, individually, one client at a time.

That is indeed a large part of casework, but increasingly the profession is becoming aware that it must work, not only with the individuals as they relate to the caseworker, but with the entire family constellation, as the family unit relates to society outside itself. Workers must diagnose, not only the intrapsychic, but the intersocial conflicts that may hamper the functioning of their clients, and conflicts in both areas can be aggravated by an unhealthy climate within the family group.

After all, individual clients do not exist in a vacuum between a caseworker's visits. A woman who is receiving AFDC help may be upset daily by telephone calls from her critical and authoritative mother who lives down the block. A temporarily unemployed man has to live with the remarks his wife makes about his lack of a job. Foster mothers may also have children of their own about whom they are concerned, or parents, brothers, sisters, who impinge on their daily lives and affect their feelings and their capacity to create a happy, wholesome home.

So we must think of the *families*, their strengths, their

weaknesses as families, what as families they can offer their own members, the foster children beneath their roof, adoptive children whom they may be seeking. Although it is true that the pathology of one individual in a family group can poison the atmosphere for all the others, it is also true that a group of individuals, no one of whom shows serious pathology, may fail to create a wholesome climate if the inter play of their personalities is grinding one on the other. Moreover, two less than perfect personalities may make a happy marriage and a peaceful home if their separate neuroses mesh comfortably, as sometimes happens — a dependent man, for example, and a motherly, rather domineering woman may be very well mated.

However, before we start talking about the specifics of family strengths, there are some terms an understanding of which will facilitate discussion, some concepts behind the terms a grasp of which will help to clarify our thinking of family relationships.

The term *social norm* refers to the rule of conduct which is accepted in any given culture. Such a rule of conduct may be established by law, by the folkways of a community, by accepted etiquette, or by current fashion.

Examples of a social norm established by law in American society are easy to identify and, usually, to understand. There are, for example, laws against murder, against appropriation of property that belongs to someone else, against destruction of property. The law determines between what ages a child must attend school, at what speed a motor car may be driven, and who is eligible to obtain a driver's license. Some laws apply to the entire Western culture. Other laws differ from place to place. Speed limits, for example, vary from one state to another. So do divorce laws.

In the middle-class American culture the mores, or folkways, demand, among other things, that husband and wife be domiciled together, that children be sheltered, supported, and trained by their parents, that our dead shall be interred with ceremony and in a specified place. The mores can slip over into law by almost imperceptible degrees. Health laws have something to say about the disposal of a dead body, but the social or religious mores determine the ceremony. There are laws to prevent the neglect of children. Custom suggests that the care be provided by the parents within the family; but if the child is adequately cared for elsewhere, by a relative, perhaps, the court does not step in. However, if the care is inadequate, the court pressures the parents, not the relatives.

Etiquette has established a social norm regarding stereotyped forms of greeting, ranging from the formal, "Good evening, Sir" to a casual, "Hi, there." Etiquette has also made clear what tools are to be used in eating, the manner of responding to invitations, and dozens of other gestures and words related to good manners.

Fashion sets the norm for dress (in so far as this has not been determined by local laws), hair styling, popular type of residence—ranch-type split levels today; three-story, ornate, Victorian mansions seventy years ago.

It is obvious that there can be and will be a much wider variation in social norms established by mores, etiquette, or fashion than in those established by law. Law is usually rigid within one geographical area, but the accepted norms dependent on fashion or etiquette vary from one social class to another within the same city, even on the same street. Style of dress, manner of greeting, choice of language, will have one standard in the country club set, another in the white-collar working group, still another in the laboring class.

It is imperative that a caseworker recognize the social norms of his client and on what those norms are based. It is sometimes possible, if it seems important to do so, for a caseworker to give a client sufficient motivation to shift his attitude and behavior in accordance with a social norm different from the one to which he was accustomed. At least, it is possible to effect a change in those norms based on fashion or etiquette. Quieter manners, more suitable dress, correct speech, may make better paid employment or wider social acceptance possible for the client. (Remember Eliza, in *My Fair Lady*, who managed with help to make a radical change in her manner of speech and thereby improved her situation.)

There are norms which should not be changed. The behavior of client and caseworker alike must conform to that aspect of the social norm established by law. This can be and should be presented to the client as a reality, not as a threat which the caseworker uses to pressure the client into a desired activity, but as a fact of life true for both client and caseworker. "A man who does not provide for his children as far as he is able will be brought before the court for nonsupport." This the caseworker must say in terms that the client will understand.

Still other social norms are almost impossible to change no matter how desirable a change might appear. Behavior which is a response to the mores of a group is often so firmly entrenched that any effort to change it can only create inner conflict. The cultural background may provide just as strong and just as unconscious an influence on behavior and attitude as any Freudian motivation. There are, in fact, a number of attitudes into which a caseworker may run head on that may seem to him old-fashioned but which he might nevertheless be well advised to accept since they are deeply embedded in the mores of some sociocultural groups. For example: a woman's place is in the home; the husband is the head of the household, and his word is law; it is an insult to masculinity to expect a male to do a woman's work, such as dishwashing or bedmaking.

One of the cultural areas in which a caseworker must walk softly, making no effort to change but needing always to understand, concerns the attitude toward revealing emotion. A self-contained and reserved caseworker may find an emotional client somewhat embarrassing, even repulsive, and he may consider such a client exaggerated and insincere. On the other hand, a more volatile worker may regard a repressed client as cold and unfeeling. In both cases the caseworker may be mistaken. A willingness on the part of a client to reveal himself probably denotes an ability and a readiness to relate to the worker, but the opposite is not necessarily true. Reserve may be wholly cultural.

The term *status* refers to the expectations which govern activities, behavior, or attitudes of a particular position within a social norm — that of doctor, for example, or pastor, or farmer, or longshoreman, or social worker; or husband, or mother, pupil, or employer. In a social norm with which we are familiar we recognize without difficulty the attitudes and behavior expected of any status. Unless we are cautious, however, we might easily be mistaken in our expectations within less familiar norms. What is expected of a husband or a father differs from one norm to another, and we cannot in justice criticize a father who comes from a norm other than ours for not performing as our father would. First we must find out the expectations that exist within his norm for the father status. Financial provider and nothing more? Stern disciplinarian? Planner and decision-maker? Pal to his son? He may, of course, be failing to live up to the expectations of his own norm. But he may be behaving in the fashion that he has always been led to believe is the correct behavior for the father of a family. Since that is one of the areas in which the norm is established pretty much by cultural mores, a social worker would do well to pause before attempting to make any change.

Incidentally, one of the centers of possible family stress arises from the conflict between the status expectations of an Old World father and a second-generation adolescent who has been absorbed into the norm of his new world. It is difficult for a caseworker to change the expectations or the behavior of either. Sometimes the best that can be accomplished is tolerance of each for the other through the worker's interpretation.

Another concept which we must understand if we are to have effective tools for diagnosing a family situation is that of *role*. This term refers to the norms that govern the activities in a relationship between two persons. It can be applied to the behavior of two individuals of the same status — doctor to doctor, for example, or one clubwoman to another clubwoman. Or it may refer to the behavior toward each other of two individuals of different status — doctor to nurse, doctor to patient, clubwoman to her gardener. During the course of a day one individual may enact several different roles according to the status of the person with whom he is in communication, or according to the social system he is in at the moment. A Shriner will enact one role in relation to other Shriners during a club meeting, and quite another role in the company of those same fellow Shriners when they are attending a convention. A man assumes one role at home with his family, a different one at a business luncheon, and still another if he seeks a loan at the bank. He may carry all his roles in a way acceptable to society, or he may manage one in a creditable manner and behave in a fashion highly objectionable in another. A kindly, indulgent father may be a tyrant in the office. A woman may be a braggart before her neighbors, self-deprecatory to her caseworker. A person will play the role in the manner that he thinks is expected of him or in the way which he feels will give him the most satisfaction, with either a practical or an emotional reward.

Here once again a social worker in assessing a family must be alert to the influence of the norm on the role expectations. Man's work versus woman's work, the place of a daughter in the home, who in the family carries responsibilities in what areas — all these strongly influence the roles assumed by various members of the family. Only by understanding the social norm of that family and the role expectations in that norm can a caseworker know whether or not that family and each individual in the family is living up to the expectations of that social system. A failure to understand role expectations may lead a worker into blunders which prevent the establishing of any helpful relationship. The father of the family may have been brought up to see the father role as one in which he exerts authority in money matters. In such a case it would be futile for a social worker to discuss the budget with the wife without including the man of the house. Any plan which excluded the man could and probably would be sabotaged in short order.

A role may be *instrumental*. It may involve action of some sort, doing something, accomplishing something. A doctor's role is to diagnose an ailment, recommend treatment, prescribe medication or surgery as required. The role of the wage earner is to bring home sufficient money to support his dependents. (This same wage earner may, of course, be simultaneously playing one or two other roles in the family setting.) A mother's role, in so far as it is instrumental, is understood in most Western cultures to be one of maintaining the home in good running order, seeing that meals are properly prepared, doing whatever is necessary to keep the family comfortable.

A role may be *expressive*. It may involve the expression of feeling, or the showing of some emotion, usually in response to the emotional need of somone else. A mother's instrumental role may be to make the beds and prepare the meals, but her expressive role, which is even more important, is to show love and warmth and concern for her husband and children.

A role may be *assumed.* It may be taken over and acted through by an individual without any special encouragement from any other person. An aggressive child may assume the role of leader in his gang, perhaps even over the protests of other children in the group.

A role may be *assigned* to one individual by another. A person in trouble may assign the role of confidante to an acquaintance whether or not the latter has any wish to listen to confidences. If the chosen confidante accepts the role assigned to him he will listen and show sympathy and concern, perhaps even take some action to help, thus making his assigned role both expressive and instrumental.

Sometimes a role assigned by one person to another is declined by the latter, thus leaving the former with a feeling of frustration, often of humiliation. If he tells his troubles to a friend to whom he has assigned the role of confidante, and the friend is not interested, offers no sympathy or help, he is likely to be embarrassed, even angry. A doctor who assumes the role of medical adviser in his office may decline the role if a self-centered hypochondriac tries to describe his symptoms at a social function.

Assumption of a role may be, and often is, an unconscious and unconsidered response to the role expectations in one particular social norm. In that sense, the social norm in which one lives goes a long way in fashioning an individual's personality patterns. The assigning of a role by one person to another may be equally unconscious and equally the result of the social norm's role expectations. Or the assigning of a role may be a blind reaching out for a way of filling an emotional need through the hoped-for relationship with the individual to whom the role is assigned.

Caseworkers who work with foster parents have seen that sort of thing happen. A foster mother, out of her own need, may assign to the foster child a responsive role. She hopes that the foster child will show affection, gratitude, compliance. As child-care workers very well know, this role often is declined by the foster child for reasons which many a foster parent has difficulty in understanding. The foster mother will feel hurt and frustrated, sometimes to the point of withdrawing abruptly from the mothering role which she had assumed.

Either the role assumed or the role assigned may be badly misunderstood by other people involved. The classic example is the mistaken assigning by a woman of the role of serious suitor to a man who does not have marriage in mind but sees himself only as a casual escort. If the date includes sexual intercourse, the results can be more tragic for the woman than a brief humiliation. A caseworker who assumes the role of helping person may have considerable difficulty in making this concept clear to the client who has assigned to him the role of threatening authority or punishing parent. Until there is reciprocity of role understanding, moreover, relationships can never be productive.

A grasp of this concept of role is vital in assessing family relationships and family strengths. As we study the interplay within a family, we must observe the role assumed by each member, the roles assigned by each to others in the family, whether the assumed role is carried successfully, whether the assigned role is accepted or declined.

As we look at families with this concept in mind all manner of tangles, conflicts, and contradictions come to light. There may be strong role conflict. When husband and wife both attempt to assume the role of authority, the inevitable result is arguments. There may be role overlap when both father and mother assume some part of the training and discipline of the children but are not clear as to the outline and limits of the responsibilities of each. If both mother and grandmother assume the mothering role, we may find jealousy either openly expressed or painfully repressed.

In families where the mother is either physically frail or emotionally immature, we sometimes find a role reversal, with the child mothering the mother. Sometimes an entire family unites to assign the role of scapegoat to one member who gets blamed for everything that goes wrong. All too frequently, this individual accepts the assigned role and sees himself as without worth or value.

A caseworker in assessing a family must be alert to the need-response pattern in the family. To what extent is the husband meeting his wife's emotional needs, and how is the wife meeting her husband's needs? To what extent does each parent respond to the needs of the children? To what extent does the family constellation fill the basic emotional needs of each member for love, for a balance between support and independence, between freedom and control? If the parents are not responding adequately to the needs of the child, how is the child handling his frustrations? Has he assigned the expressive role to someone else— an older sibling, a grandparent, a friendly neighbor?

Nor should it ever be forgotten that all of this is to be viewed in the light of the sociocultural factors, the family's resources, intellectual, emotional, and financial, and also in the light of whatever crisis has brought the family to the attention of the agency.

XVIII

OUTLINE
FOR THE EVALUATION
OF THE FAMILY

Every department in a welfare agency must think of families as well as of individuals. The family climate creates the environment for each individual who is a member of that group. It may be a wholesome environment conducive to full development, or it may be so charged with the poison of dissent that any individual growth must be stunted. In general, welfare agencies are dedicated to holding families together, but sometimes relationships are already so bad that efforts to patch them up would mean a waste of the caseworker's time and prolonged damage to the vulnerable individuals in the home. So we must be able to assess every family as an environment in which the several individuals comprising the family can develop to their full potential. What are the values or the hurts accruing to each individual in the family?

A family is a group of individuals with destinies intertwined. Usually, but not necessarily always, they are domiciled under one roof. (A son or a daughter may be away at school; a father may be in the armed services; a mother may be enduring a lengthy hospitalization.) Usually, but not necessarily always, the individuals within the family constellation are related by blood or marriage. (An adopted child surely and, it is to be hoped, a foster child will be incorporated as an integral part of the family. Sometimes a long-time boarder or a "nanny" is accepted as a family member.) The basic family in our culture consists of father, mother, children, including biological, adopted, and foster children, and one, two, three, or perhaps more of the extended family, such as grandparents, uncles, or aunts.

There is one thing that all social workers should keep well in the forefront of their thinking as they work with families who are in need of public assistance or who are before the court charged with neglect of their children. These families may seem pretty inadequate by our middle-class standards, but remember that any family, our own included, would surely react with a lowered threshold of strength and stability to difficult situations, such as inadequate income, poor housing, irregular employment, racial conflicts, or any of the other social ills to which society may subject them. But even depressed personalities remain viable, and a social ill that attacks a family from the outside can often be corrected or at least minimized by environmental manipulation. Maybe the father is irritable and hard to live with because of his tension over money problems, or the mother may be a poor homemaker because she lacks adequate equipment.

Perhaps these misfortunes can be corrected through the services of a welfare agency. However, even adequate service to a family which has been long underprivileged will not correct undesirable attitudes and behavior instantly. There may be too much internalization of despair, hopelessness, resentment, not to mention suspicion of the good intentions of a social worker. Change will not come overnight. We cannot move a family from a shack into a modern apartment and say, "All right. Here you are. Now you can start being neat and efficient and happy." It simply does not work that way. Without long and patient help from a homemaker, the mother may never learn how to clean an apartment acceptably, or do the laundry without leaving tattletale gray. The children will have no training in hanging up their clothes, or brushing their teeth. The father may have had too many years of being rejected by one employer after another to have much hope now. Perhaps he cannot make any real effort to find work even though he starts out the day from a better address. These things change gradually. The family may not even like their new apartment. It may seem cold and inhospitable after the cozy, crowded, familiar mess of their shack. They may not really welcome the interference of a well-meaning social worker. It may take a long time before the apartment feels like home, or before the caseworker is accepted as a friend, this new way of life as really their way. During this long delay we must not jump to hasty evaluations or decide that the family climate is wholly bad.

Welfare agencies mirror middle-class standards. We believe that a father should assume financial responsibility, hold a steady job, support his family, and pay his bills. We believe the mother should cook nourishing food, keep a tidy, well-ordered home, see that the children behave properly, dress properly, wash behind the ears, and attend school regularly. We expect family members to tell the truth, obey the law, remain sober and industrious, affiliate with some religious organization, and see their dentist twice a year.

These are good, solid standards, and the observance of them has carried a large segment of Western civilization into comparative prosperity. But they are not the only standards, and it is possible for a family to observe only some of them, fail signally in others, and nevertheless remain an integrated unit able to give one another more warmth and security and stimulation than any single member of such a family could find apart from his own.

We would like to know that the family has some sort of orderly routine in their daily lives, within a home of adequate comfort and cleanliness. We hope that the family can meet their physical and emotional needs with the financial resources

available to them. We want to feel that the adults have respect
for one another and a certain amount of pleasure in one
another's companionship. We want the parents to be considerate of each other, to find satisfaction in their life together,
in their sexual relationship, in their social contacts, and we
would like to see a mutuality of standards and interests. We
want both parents to be equally concerned for the children
and we want all the children to be welcome in the family
and warmly loved.

That would be the ideal. How can we, outsiders, truly know
the degree to which any family approaches the ideal? How
far below the ideal may a family drop before we feel that it
should be broken up in order to save some of the individual
members?

Our assessment of, and our standards for, the family will
vary somewhat according to our purpose in making a study
of that family and any plan we might have in mind. We have
slightly different expectations for a foster family than we
have for an adoptive family. An adoptive family must be
able to accept a child as their own, permanently, assuming
responsibility for that child's nurture through all the stages
of his development and on to adulthood. A foster family
must be able to provide warmth and acceptance for a more
limited period, and at the same time be able to share the
planning with the agency which carries legal responsibility,
and they must be prepared also to share the child's love and
loyalty with his own parents. Although no agency would
knowingly place a baby for adoption with a mother who
would not be able to handle that baby when he became an
adolescent, we might very well place a baby with a foster
mother who was warm and loving with dependent infants
but admittedly could not work effectively with a teen-ager.
So our researches into the personalities and capacities of the
two homes would differ. We would demand more economic

security and social acceptance of the adoptive, or even the foster, family than we would of a family already established with their own biological offspring. We would not be likely to place an adoptive child with a family unable to maintain themselves financially, but we would surely not think of separating children from their parents for financial reasons alone.

With these variations clearly in mind, let us examine the following outline for the evaluation of a family's strengths and weaknesses for providing an environment conducive to the development of each of its members. Not all the items are of equal importance in any study. Some are important in assessing a family for one purpose but can be ignored for another purpose. Like any outline, it can be useful only if it is used with flexibility and judgment.

We can glance over the whole outline first, and then come back to study the items one by one:

OUTLINE FOR EVALUATING THE FAMILY

I. Environment
    A. Acceptability of the neighborhood
        1. Socially — from the point of view of the family
        2. For health — from the point of view of the Department of Health

    B. Living conditions within the house
        1. State of repair — roof, walls, etc.
        2. Type of heat
        3. Type of lighting
        4. Water supply — hot and cold water
        5. Absence of vermin

    C. Household appliances
        1. Housekeeping tools — vacuum cleaner, iron, etc.
        2. Cooking equipment — stove, utensils
        3. Laundering facilities — washing machine; space to air and dry
        4. Refrigeration

D. Household articles
   1. Living room furniture
   2. Television set
   3. Alarm clock
   4. Telephone
   5. Books, magazines, newspapers
E. Cleanliness and orderliness of rooms — especially kitchen and bedrooms
F. Condition and repair of furniture
G. Floor covering
H. Available bed space
I. Sleeping arrangements — how many and what sexes of children sleep together?

II. Health
   A. Physical health of head of family
   B. Permanency of ailments if any
   C. Medical attention received
   D. Nutrition of children
   E. Mental health of head of family
   F. Mental health of children

III. Sexual stability
   A. Marital status
   B. Degree to which parents fill one another's needs sexually and emotionally
   C. Role assignment and role acceptance
   D. Outsiders living in the home who have a detrimental effect
   E. Consistency of paternity — number of fathers involved

IV. Employment
   A. Employment status of head of family
   B. Consistency of employment
   C. Occupational abilities
   D. Occupational training — past or planned for future

V. Financial management
   A. Bills paid or unpaid — rent, utilities, time payments
   B. Food shopping habits
   C. Adequacy of clothing

VI. Child rearing
   A. Cooperation of parents in child rearing, training, and discipline

   B. Consistency of discipline
   C. Scholastic performance of children
   D. Regularity of school attendance
   E. Scholastic ambitions for children
   F. Dropouts

VII. Home integration
   A. Contact with law enforcement — children; adults
   B. Dining habits — separately or as a family unit
   C. Play facilities for children — playroom; yard
   D. Entertainment habits — as passive spectators or as participants
   E. Hobbies — individual, or as family enterprise
   F. Social life outside the home — individual or in common? Are friends seen in the home, or do children find social life on the street corners and father in the bar?
   G. Family loyalty — does it exist, or does each individual project blame on another family member?
   H. Family scapegoat, if any

   1. *Environment.* — The neighborhood may establish the social norm for the family, and for any family we would like a neighborhood which favors a norm established by the law of the land.

   Is the neighborhood acceptable from the point of view of the family? It matters little on which side of the tracks the home may be situated just so it is adequate from the point of view of health. But the feeling of the family toward their neighborhood matters a great deal. A family living in an environment of predominately different religion or different race or different financial standing from its own can easily run into tensions and discontent, especially as the younger members start school and begin to see themselves as part of an out-group — or, perhaps, just as unfortunate, begin to develop arrogant attitudes because they feel themselves above their comrades. It is even worse if one member of the family feels himself out of place. This discontent might be a strength

if the family is in a substandard neighborhood and one unhappy member can goad them into improving their situation.
But if the discontent means that one individual will break
away from the family, but will be unable or unwilling to pull
the others with him, then we have another matter to consider.
Will the loss of this one individual weaken the family structure irretrievably, or can the others close ranks and carry on
without him?

What are the living conditions within the home. The items
under this heading, like those under "household appliances"
indicate the degree of interest the family has in the home
setting, and also suggest the ease with which the housewife
can handle her job. However, judgments must be made with
caution. It is to be hoped that a young caseworker who has
grown up in an air-conditioned apartment or in a ranch-
style home with gas-fueled furnace will not think the less of
a family that lives in a remote rural home heated by wood-
burning stoves—one in the kitchen, one in the "setting
room," and probably none in the bedrooms. A housewife
has a more laborious job cooking on a wood-burning stove,
doing a family washing with water carried from a well and
heated by the pailful, than she would if her home had
electricity or gas. Yet for generations meals were prepared
without refrigerators, floors were cleaned without a vacuum,
clothes were laundered without a washing machine. Families
were healthy, happy, and affectionate even in those dark ages.

Lack of labor-saving equipment may be wholly a matter
of unavoidable circumstance. A rural family may be beyond
the reach of electric lines. Lack of equipment may be a matter
of finances. When food and clothing have been supplied,
perhaps there is nothing left over to put toward the pur-
chase of a refrigerator or a steam iron. It may be necessary
to choose how the available funds are to be spent, but a man
who spends his pay check on alcohol instead of a washing

machine for his wife is probably not a considerate husband, nor is he concerned for the welfare of his family. Living conditions in the house, appliances, furniture, books, and so on may indicate nothing more than the economic situation, or they may indicate the degree of interest the family feels in its home. In using the presence or absence of appliances and comforts as a measure of assessment the caseworker must consider the family circumstances and the motivation that prompted the spending of cash in one way or in another. If a whole family, hard-working housewife included, is giving up comforts in order to pay off the mortgage, there is a positive. If the husband hoards his money for a bigger barn or more blooded stock while his wife whimpers and complains, there is a schism in the family, a poor emotional climate, and a negative. If the absence of luxuries shows only a standard of living different from that of the caseworker, it may mean nothing more than that — a variation of standards — and before a caseworker can turn thumbs down on a family that is concerned about their home but does not share his feeling about central heating, he must know a great deal about the emotional climate in the home.

Household articles. Again, the absence of certain articles may be wholly a matter of finances. A family that is receiving public assistance probably would not be able to pay a telephone bill or buy magazines and newspapers. But if a family can afford such articles and is not interested in having them, we can come to certain conclusions about the extent and type of their concerns.

Living room furniture that is comfortable and looks used, whether it is shabby or new, usually implies a family that likes being together and enjoying home life. Furniture which is too spic and span may mean a family that cannot relax for fear of soiling the upholstery and children who are not allowed to play or enjoy themselves in the family room. But here again the caseworker must take into account the family's habits. The old-fashioned, chilly, uncomfortable front parlor, open only for funerals and state occasions, has not entirely vanished. Some families still do their communal living in the dining room or the kitchen.

A telephone provides contact with people outside the immediate family. A family that can afford a phone and does not have one may be a seclusive family, but the caseworker must consider this in conjunction with other observations. Books, magazines, newspapers, indicate an interest in events and thoughts outside the four walls of the home, and their presence can almost always be counted an asset. The meaning of a television set can be determined only if we observe the use to which it is put. Does the family use it for occasional diversion and for keeping up with news events, or do they sit before it, phlegmatic and mesmerized, letting the flickering lights and blaring sound be poured into their senses without any effort on their part to make judgments, or even to choose programs?

An alarm clock is an article whose importance as a clue goes far beyond what the size and cost of the item might suggest. A family who owns one and uses it has a sense of time and of organization. They are able to get the man of the house off to work on time, the children ready for school on time. Perhaps some few families have an inner metronome and can accomplish this without a clock, but more often the lack of a timepiece suggests an indifference to schedules, a carelessness about appointments, and a general lack of organization. It seems to me that a clock, by its presence or absence, is the most indicative of any of the household articles.

The next few items are self-explanatory: cleanliness and orderliness, yes, we want them, especially in the kitchen, where food is prepared, and in the bedroom, where the family spends eight or more hours out of the twenty-four sleeping. Tidiness in the family room, the playroom, is less important, and disorder may mean only that the rooms are much used and enjoyed. For that matter, we would prefer a little gray fluff under the beds to rooms maintained by a "lick-and-polish" compulsive housekeeper who cannot let anyone in the family relax and enjoy the home.

We want sufficient bed space so that children do not sleep with adults or with children of the opposite sex, and so that each individual, child or adult, has room to stretch out comfortably at night. One child to a bed is best. Two children of the same sex to a bed is possible. Three children to a bed — no. The middle youngster gets pushed.

II. *Health.* — Poor health of the head of the family is a negative, but how heavily this negative weighs depends on the extent of the disability. Can he carry the role of wage earner expected of him? If the mother is the head of the family, can she in spite of poor health give the necessary care to the children? Even more important for family integration, to what extent does poor health affect the mood and tempera-ment of the individual and how heavy are the demands he makes on other family members for services or for smypathy?

If either adults or children are not receiving the medical care they should have the caseworker must be sure that the family is made aware of the fact and knows how to get what is needed. Failure to provide proper nutrition or to obtain medical attention may simply mean that the others in the family do not realize the seriousness of the situation. If, how-ever, they are paying no attention or do not care, that is indeed a black mark against them as a family.

Failure to recognize a child's poor mental health may be wholly an inability to interpret symptoms, and here the obser-vation, the understanding, and tactful interpretation of the social worker are required. A great deal of emotional support will be needed to accept a child's mental illness. Parents sometimes react with deep guilt. They did something wrong in raising him, it is all their fault, they feel, and this guilt may be so disabling that they cannot give adequately to their normal, healthy children, let alone to the mentally ill child. Or the inconvenience and embarrassment caused by the behavior of the mentally ill child may rouse so much anger and resentment that the parents either shower fruitless punishment on the child, or hide their anger behind reaction formation and overprotect the child, punishing themselves by insisting on keeping him at home instead of arranging for psychiatric help in an institution. The damage which a mentally ill or a retarded child can cause in a family depends on the extent of the illness or the retardation, but even more it depends on the attitude of the others, especially the parents, toward the condition. A caseworker should work first toward freeing the parents from guilt and from reaction formation sufficiently so that they can look at the facts realistically and plan whatever is best for the afflicted child and for the rest of the family.

III. *Sexual stability.* — In all families with which we work we must pay some attention to the marital relationship if both parents are in the home. How many fathers have been involved? How many marriages has each parent had? What were the reasons for their termination? Does the current marriage seem stable, or is there a history of repeated separations and desertions? We want to know the degree of helpful concern which each parent shows for the other, whether they attack family problems together as a team, and the degree of reciprocity there is in the gratification of both the emotional and biological needs of each. What is the affectional relationship between husband and wife, and in what manner and with what success does each sustain the other? Does one, for example, build up his own self-image by downgrading the other? Or do they help one another in ego building? Does one, or do both, turn to sources outside the family for satisfactions? To do so may mean marital infidelity, but it may mean something less dramatic but just as debilitating to family unity. For example, in many middle-class homes the man's feeling of self-worth comes from his job; the woman's, perhaps, from her activities as a clubwoman or from her social successes. This may not be a bad system if each has a reasonable degree of interest in, and respect for, the basis of the other's self-esteem so that they can talk to one another, sharing their respective triumphs or disappointments. But if the woman persistently downgrades the man's earning capacity or the importance of his work, and if the man has only sneers for the wife's activities, then the family is not healthy.

We would be interested in the extent to which the parents share responsibilities for, and interest in, homemaking. We do not necessarily expect the man to wash the supper dishes, but we are interested in knowing whether both husband and wife are equally concerned about the appearance of the home, the efficiency with which it is run. Do both share in making the home life pleasant and smooth, or does one carry all the responsibility while the other remains an indifferent or a carping, complaining onlooker?

We would like to know, too, how the family social life is maintained. Are there shared values in religion, culture, leisure activities, and in their relationships with the extended family outside the home? Or are there constant arguments about which church to attend, or whether to attend church at all; about whether to go to a movie or a picnic; whether to spend the summer holiday at a swank hotel or camping in the deep woods; whether to visit his family or hers or neither.

Concerning the sexual life of the parents we should learn the shared values with respect to the form and the frequency of the sex act. A child in a family where either parent finds no satisfactions and no gratification in the sexual act may well be faced with serious problems of identification as he approaches school age. If either parent is tempted to use the child's response as a substitute for the satisfactions he fails to get with the marital partner, then the child is surely headed for trouble. This might also be the case in a one-parent family, though not necessarily so. If the remaining parent is sufficiently strong not to use the child for his own emotional sustenance, then the child may find a good object of identification in a grandparent, uncle, aunt, or the friendly adult down the street who likes children.

An inexperienced caseworker may feel considerable diffidence if he is faced with the need to delve into intimate matters. But if he can conquer his own embarrassment, regard himself as a professional person, just as a physician is professional, he may be able by his very attitude to open the way for communication. Questions about a couple's sex life should come fairly naturally in the course of an adoptive study, since the reasons for childlessness would be an important part of the study. Similarly, such discussions would be a normal part of work with parents who ask for marital counseling. Direct inquiry is less necessary in a study of prospective foster parents or an investigation of eligibility for public assistance, but an alert caseworker will be able to observe details which indicate whether or not both parents are finding emotional satisfactions in each other.

Caseworkers in general, by habit and by training, are given to greater awareness of pathology than of strengths. We must, of course, be sensitive to the limits which any pathology imposes on the diagnosis, social planning, and prognosis, but we must also keep in mind that pathology is not necessarily all encompassing, and a family may operate in a modified way if there are some encouraging strengths to offset the negatives.

IV. *Employment.* — The questions we must ask concern the

success with which the adult wage earner can hold steady
employment and earn enough to meet the needs of the
family, and how he feels about his job. Is he proud of the
work he does? Bored? Embarrassed by the kind of work he
is forced to do? Angry with his boss? All of this will be
reflected for better or for worse in the climate in the home.

V. *Financial management.* — We need also know how capably
the family handles its budget. If there is no family member
able to assume the role of wage earner, so that the family is relying on public assistance, the vital question is how skill-
fully can they keep within their limited resources and still
meet the family's needs. Here, of course, the criteria will
differ according to the reasons the agency has for working
with the family. We hope for a higher financial standing in
an adoptive family than in one applying for public assistance,
but in both we hope to find an ability to live within the
available resources.

VI. *Child rearing.* — Here we want to know to what extent
both parents assume responsibility, in what areas each carries
responsibility, and what reciprocity there is between them.
Does the mother do it all, while the father remains a critical
observer, taking no action? Who gets up at night to give the
two o'clock bottle? Who feeds the toddler in the high chair?
Who reads the bedtime stories? Who takes action when reproof is called for? Does the mother provide physical care
while the father is the disciplinarian? Or do both parents
share in both areas? If they do, how complete is their agreement? Have they fallen into the trap of permitting the child
to play one parent against the other? What agreement is
there between the parents in their ambitions for the children.
Does the mother want advanced education for her son while
the father insists that he leave school and start contributing
toward the family support? And how does the son feel about
it?

VII. *Home integration.*—This is of the utmost importance. Most of the items listed are self-explanatory, with the possible exception of "family dining habits." I feel that this is indicative of family attitudes far beyond what might appear on the surface. A family in which each member grabs a bite from refrigerator or kitchen shelf whenever he happens to be hungry, eating on the run, is surely a family with the minimum of organization, planning, or unity of interest. A family that has its meals at the family table, all together, is a family that enjoys doing things together. This enjoyment of being together is an important barometer of the family climate. A family that likes doing things together, whether it is eating dinner, cleaning up the yard, going on picnics, or working on mutual hobbies, is surely a family with a feeling of unity. A family all of whose members respect one another's daily occupations—the children's schoolwork, the mother's home duties, the father's job—is a family that can provide security, a feeling of belonging, to one another and to any child they accept and take unto themselves.

XIX

EVALUATION OF TWO FAMILIES

THE DENTON FAMILY

On the second of October, the Fourteenth Street School referred the Denton family to a social agency because of the failure of the parents to provide adequate medical care for Tommy Darrow, a twelve-year-old boy living with his mother (Mrs. Denton), his stepfather, and siblings. The school reported that Tommy wet and soiled during the day, probably because of a physical defect which might be corrected if he had proper medical attention. He had a history of *spina bifida*,[1] which in his case resulted in weak control of the sphincter muscle. The situation in the school was intolerable, and becoming increasingly so as Tommy matured. His behavior was good, but he was understandably isolated from other children. He seemed unhappy, and he had deteriorated intellectually, dropping from a reported IQ of 87 to 77 during the last four years. He was doing poor work scholastically, and was one and a half grades behind his age group.

The boy's family had been consistently uncooperative throughout the six years that the school had had contact with them. The mother had ignored repeated demands that she come to the school to talk to the school doctor. She had also

[1]*Spina bifida* is a congenital defect in the closure of the spinal canal, with hernial protrusion of the meninges of the cord. The hernial sac contains cerebrospinal fluid and sometimes nervous tissue. The effect of the condition is poor coordination of the lower extremities, sometimes a complete paralysis. The degree of the disabling depends on the place in the spinal canal where the defect occurs. The symptoms can often be decreased by proper medical care.

ignored requests to send clean underclothes to school with Tommy so that in case of accident he would have a change. The school authorities found it impossible to work with these parents. At one time, resentful of a teacher's reproof of another Denton child, the parents removed the little girl from school and attempted to place her in a private Catholic school. They were refused and, to quote the school letter, they "had to eat crow and bring her back to Fourteenth Street." It was the opinion of the school that this family would refuse to cooperate with any authority and should be brought to Juvenile Court on a charge of neglect since they had failed to provide the necessary medical care for Tommy. The school hoped that the judge would order that the medical care be provided by the family, or that Tommy would be removed to a foster home under supervision of an agency.

In response to a letter from the agency, Mrs. Denton phoned the office. Although the letter suggested only that the agency might be able to help her, Mrs. Denton instantly assumed that a complaint had been made, and wanted to know who had complained, what was it about, was it about one of the children, nobody had any real reason to complain about her family, and so on. She was told that these things could not be discussed over the telephone: could she and her husband come to the office? She produced a number of excuses: her husband couldn't take time off from work; she was pregnant and afraid she might lose the baby if she made the trip; she didn't like leaving the children home alone; her husband had the car and she was afraid to travel by bus. However, one by one, these were disposed of. She admitted that she went downtown by bus several times a week to do her marketing, and the agency was no farther away from her home. The children were all in school during the day. Tomorrow was her husband's day off, and she could have the use of the car. She agreed to come next day.

Without having seen any member of the Denton family the agency already had a few valuable hints about them and about Mrs. Denton's method of coping. It seemed probable that the family had considerable unity since Mrs. Denton's instant response to the slightest hint of a threat was that "Nobody has any real reason to complain about the family." We did not know anything yet about Mr. Denton but we did see that his wife had no fear of him. She was clearly assuming that if he were not using the car she would be free to do so. Remember the children mentioned in Chapter X who "make more or less an open effort to control the situation by stalling without actually rejecting the intention of eventually cooperating"? That was exactly what Mrs. Denton was doing by making one excuse after another for not coming to the office. We also knew from the school's referral letter that her response to criticism was to withdraw from the field. (In the child's language, she would take her dolls and go home.) We could also guess without too much difficulty that the school may not have been too tactful in dealing with her, for the referral letter showed an almost triumphant vindictiveness.

We did not yet know the medical diagnosis of Tommy's condition. We did not know the family's financial situation. We knew next to nothing about Mr. Denton or about the other children. But Tommy's symptoms, his unhappiness, isolation, and intellectual deterioration surely spelled trouble. However, the agency was inclined to approach the problem in a manner different from that used by the school. If six years of work had brought no cooperation it was clearly time for a new technique.

When the appointment time arrived, Mr. and Mrs. Denton both appeared, accompanied by Mrs. Denton's married sister, Tommy, and five-year-old Becky Denton. The two youngsters were asked to remain in the waiting room while the parents were interviewed, and Becky immediately climbed into the chair beside Tommy with a magazine so that he could show her the pictures. The worker attempted to indicate by his manner that he was assuming that Mrs. Denton's sister would remain in the waiting room with the children, but Mrs. Denton said to her sister, "You come too." When the worker offered a mild protest, Mrs. Denton insisted. So we knew that she was apprehensive, and just as a child will rig a situation to keep his mother near, so this grown woman was arranging to have reinforcements at hand.

Mrs. Denton was a short, stocky woman with high color. She wore a clean cotton dress that stretched tight across her abdomen. Her hair was combed smoothly back in a tight bun. Mr. Denton wore a dark-colored work shirt, mended at the cuffs, and clean denim pants. (So Mrs. Denton's failure to send extra underclothing to the school for Tommy was not due to any careless lack of concern for cleanliness.)

Mr. Denton came into the interviewing room behind his wife, took a chair in the background, and assumed very little initiative during the conversation. Mrs. Denton took the chair closest to the caseworker's desk and was belligerent and defensive at once. She said angrily that the school was blaming her and Tommy's stepfather for Tommy's condition. (So she knew all the time the reason for the request to come to the office.) She said that the school seemed to feel that they had abused Tommy but this was not so. They never lifted a hand against any of the children. Mr. Denton was a good father to all the children, those of her first marriage as well as his own. Mr. Denton nodded at this and mumbled that he sure loved all the kids. Mrs. Denton went on to accuse the principal of being prejudiced against the whole family. She insisted that Tommy was scared of his teacher because she seemed to be watching him all the time, and this made him nervous and accounted for his loss of control. They couldn't afford to pay for any fancy medical care for Tommy. Mr. Denton nodded agreement from his corner. The school had told them to take Tommy to the city clinic, but they wouldn't do that. Mr. Denton was working, and clinics were for paupers. They wouldn't want people to think he wasn't supporting his family.

The faces of the other two members of the family reflected complete agreement with what Mrs. Denton was saying. It occurred to the caseworker that the family cohesiveness, the rebellion against the somewhat tactless pressure by the school, and their resistance to any suggestion of financial dependency might all be part of a cultural heritage. The address of the Dentons showed that they lived in a section of the city inhabited now by second-generation Americans, very few of whom were receiving public assistance or had any history of conflict with the courts.

The worker expressed sympathy with Mrs. Denton over the amount of laundry that must be involved in caring for an encopretic boy, and indicated appreciation of Mr. Denton's concern for his stepchildren. The worker said that the agency would move step by step to see what help it might provide. This recognition of the parents' problems and the implication of deliberate movement without pressure apparently reassured the Dentons, who visibly relaxed. Mrs. Denton then asked the worker to get Anna Denton's school reports. Anna, she said, had been getting real good grades. Translated, this meant, "Let me prove to you that I am the mother of a good and clever child. I may not have done so well producing Tommy, but Anna is all right." Mrs. Denton went on to say that Becky was enrolled in kindergarten but so far attended only in the mornings. She was a bright little trick; the teacher said so. Mr. Denton beamed and nodded vigorously.

As they were leaving, Mrs. Denton's sister hung back to say to the worker that he must not let Mrs. Denton's abrupt ways bother him. She was quick tempered but she loved her kids and did right by them. So the worker knew that loyalty included the extended as well as the immediate family.

Back in the waiting room Becky was still cuddled against Tommy, who was showing her pictures. Both children stood up, smiling, when the worker and the family entered. Both seemed to have an easy, normal attitude toward the parents, and both looked like happy children. The worker chalked this up to weigh against the school's report that Tommy was not a happy child. Apparently, the unfortunate school situation had not carried into the home.

During the series of visits to the home, enough information came out by easy stages to enable the worker to get a fairly clear picture of the background.

The present marriage was the second for Mrs. Denton. She had previously been married to Henry Darrow, by whom she had three children, Anthony, now seventeen, Tommy, twelve, and Susan, ten. Mr. Darrow had never supported her or the children adequately and eventually deserted them while she was pregnant with Susan. Things were rough for a while, but her mother had helped out. Anthony, then six years old, had gone to stay with his grandmother and later, after the divorce and his mother's marriage to Mr. Denton, he had remained with the grandmother, who found him good company and wanted to keep him. He came home to visit quite often and usually had Sunday dinner with his parents.

Mr. Denton had been quite willing to support the children of the first marriage and, in fact, was fully supporting Tommy and Susan. He also bought all of Anthony's clothes and sometimes gave him spending money. He was a real good man, Mrs. Denton said, and she was much happier with him than she had ever been with her first husband.

Mrs. Denton spoke of all her children except Tommy with pride, stressing their good school performance. She excused Tommy's failings on the ground of his "nervousness" and the way the school "picked on him." She did not mention the attempt to withdraw Susan from the school, and the worker did not bring it up. Mrs. Denton seemed much gratified when she found that the caseworker had, in fact, asked for and received Anna's school reports which were, as the mother had boasted, very good. "I told you my kids were smart," she bragged. "Susan's good, too, and you ought to hear that Tony play the horn. He's in the school band."

Mr. Denton was not so volatile nor so articulate as Mrs. Denton, but he was able to reveal his feelings in some areas. He expressed himself strongly about Tommy. The boy could control himself if he really tried. His wife was a good woman, but she babied that boy too much. It was humiliating to have a big boy like that messing his pants. What that boy needed was a good thrashing—then he'd remember to get to the bathroom in time. But Mrs. Denton wouldn't let the kid be punished, and he wouldn't go against his wife. He never laid a hand on Tommy. But it was tough. His wife was getting on—probably wouldn't have another baby after the one she was carrying now, and probably that would be another girl. Just his luck: only two boys in the family, one living with the grandmother and the other a kid like Tommy. Then three girls, Susan, Anna, and Becky. He loved the girls all right, but a man wanted a son to be proud of. And who could be proud of Tommy? One was always afraid to take him out anywhere for fear he'd mess himself in public.

A study of Tommy's medical history verified the school report of *spina bifida*, and proved that Mr. Denton was incorrect in thinking that the boy could control himself if he tried.

The medical records of Tommy's very early life showed that he was baptized by a Catholic priest immediately after birth since there was grave question of his survival. At seven days of age he had been operated on for the *spina bifida* condition, but his mother had failed to take him back for the aftercare. The hospital had had several subsequent contacts with the child, but always the mother had failed to follow through with the recommended care. The latest report, dated five years ago, stated that "the patient was noted to be an arrested hydrocephalic and has remote *spina bifida*."

Although we do not have all the information that we would like to have before making a complete diagnosis of the strengths and weaknesses of the Denton family, yet we know enough to justify some tentative conclusions.

The family is self-supporting and proud of it. (Mrs. Denton rejected the suggestion of taking Tommy to the city clinic, which was for "paupers." She wanted the neighbors to recognize that her husband could support his family.)

Although the children had been fathered by two different men, they all appeared to relate to the present husband as the father person. The current family was stable. (Tommy's easy attitude was observed by the worker as he greeted his stepfather in the waiting room, Anthony, whose separation from the family had been arranged before the second marriage, came home for visits, and the stepfather was assuming some of his financial support. The half brothers and sisters got along well together, as shown by the way they spoke of one another and especially by the five-year-old Susan's confiding way with Tommy.)

Mr. and Mrs. Denton showed mutual concern and respect for one another and, in fact, seemed eager to build one another up before the caseworker. (Mrs. Denton described her husband as a good man and said she was happy with him. She emphasized his willingness to support his stepchildren and his ability to do so. Mr. Denton disagreed with his wife's handling of Tommy but did not openly oppose her, and told the worker that she was a good mother.)

Both parents are proud of all the children except Tommy. (They made a special point of asking the worker to look at Anna's fine school reports and they bragged about Anthony and about Becky, the "smart little trick.")

Thus far the family showed strengths that promised well.

However, faced with the reality problems created by Tommy's physical disabilities, they refused to admit facts. Mr. Denton was convinced that Tommy could control himself if he tried. Mrs. Denton did not blame the boy, but projected the blame on the school authorities who were making him "nervous." Mr. Denton expressed bitterness over Tommy's inability to assume the role of honored son which the stepfather would like to assign to him. Mrs. Denton refused to admit that his condition could have been in any degree corrected by different behavior on her part. Both were avoiding personal responsibility. In their defense it might, however, be mentioned that they came from a culture which traditionally has had little contact with the medical profession. Their experience had not prepared them to accept readily what the caseworker saw at once as the physical basis for the boy's difficulties.

Mrs. Denton's unhappiness in her first marriage may well have kept her so self-centered that she had no energy left over for Tommy's early problems. Mr. Denton's disappointment in having no son probably accounted for some of his blindness now.

Both parents were independent and by temperament and tradition given to rebellion against pressure. The school authorities had tried to "drive" them, but the agency caseworker decided to try "leading." The school, faced with the problem of an encopretic twelve-year-old boy, asked the agency to evoke the authority of the court, but the worker felt that this step would do more harm than good. The court could order the parents to secure the medical help required for Tommy, but it could not successfully order the family to love him, or accept him, or change the role which they were assigning to him.

The worker's expression of appreciation of Mrs. Denton as the mother of clever, well-behaved children, his avoidance of any implication that she was to be blamed for Tommy's condition, his sympathetic listening to Mr. Denton's desire for a son to be proud of, all helped to give this family a better feeling about themselves and about Tommy, and a readiness to accept interpretation from the worker. His next move was a tactful explanation of the nature of Tommy's physical condition, and what the medical profession could do to help it. Once this was understood, he was in a position to offer practical suggestions for getting the help in a way which the Dentons would not feel was a threat to their autonomy.

With understanding of why these people thought and felt and behaved as they did it was possible to insure a happier life for Tommy and still hold the family intact.

THE SPARROW FAMILY

Mrs. Sparrow came to the agency without appointment. She was a thin, unhealthy-appearing woman in her late twenties. She fidgeted uneasily in the reception room while she waited to be interviewed, and when the caseworker called her, she came forward with swift, plunging steps. During the interview she sat twisting her fingers as she talked in a tight, jerky voice. Her right eyelid twitched, and she rubbed her eye several times.

Mrs. Sparrow asked first for help in finding suitable day care for her four children, aged eight, seven, four, and two, while she was at work. When she was told that, unfortunately, this service was not available through that agency, she did not wait to learn where it could be secured, but asked if the agency would place the children in a foster home. She said that she thought her husband had deserted her.

When the worker repeated, "You *think* he has deserted?" Mrs. Sparrow explained that he was a truck driver, often absent for two or three days at a time on long hauls, but this time he had been away for two weeks. She did not know where he had gone. He seldom told her about his trips. She had phoned the company where she thought he worked and learned that he had been fired a month ago. He hadn't mentioned this to her, and she hadn't noticed much difference in his behavior or his daily routine. Maybe he had picked up odd jobs as a driver's helper; she wouldn't know. Her money was getting low. She had about enough to last another week, but she didn't dare wait any longer. She hadn't anybody to help her but she could get a job. She was sure she could. She had worked before her marriage and off and on since but she would need to put the kids someplace. They were good kids, but they were getting on her nerves.

The worker asked whether she had been able to find someone to stay with the children while she came to the office. Mrs. Sparrow replied, "Nobody helps me. But the oldest girl is real reliable. She watches the younger ones."

The worker felt that Mrs. Sparrow's nervous tension was extreme. She seemed near the breaking point. In her present condition could she possibly find employment, or keep it if she found it? The whole situation needed further study. The worker suggested that Mrs. Sparrow might apply for AFDC help and remain with the children until she knew more about her husband's plans.

Mrs. Sparrow flared into quick anger: "I don't want relief. They treat you like dirt in that place." She jumped to her feet. "Never mind!" she exclaimed, and in spite of the worker's protests, ran out of the building.

The following day the worker attempted to reach Mrs. Sparrow at the address she had given and learned that early that morning Mrs. Sparrow and the four children had left, saying that they were joining Mr. Sparrow.

Two months after the first contact, the agency received a letter from a child-care agency in California. Mr. and Mrs. Sparrow and four children had arrived there. Mrs. Sparrow had left again two weeks before the date of the letter, and was thought to have returned to Cleveland. Mr. Sparrow had recently gone off on a cross-country trip with a truck, leaving the children alone in the care of the eight-year-old girl. Because they became frightened at night, the children had gone to a neighbor, who reported the situation to the court. The oldest girl had been able to give information about her parents, including the mother's present address in Cleveland (she had received a letter from her mother). The California agency agreed to place the children in foster homes while waiting for the Cleveland agency to establish the family's residence and accept custody.

Mrs. Sparrow was found at the address given. She said she had come back to Cleveland because she knew she could get employment here. She thought the children were being cared for by her husband, who was not working when she left California. She didn't know why he had walked out on them but she wasn't surprised; it was just like him. She had planned to send for the children when she had money enough but she couldn't pay their fares yet. She would like to have them back in Cleveland but she did not want to give up her job. She had made up her mind. She would never again try living with her husband.

She complained bitterly about his neglect, his frequent desertions. He would go off, leaving her with innumerable unpaid bills. They had once started to buy a house in Cleveland, but his extravagances and unreliability had caused them to lose it. When the agency hadn't wanted to help her, she had decided to go to California, where she had heard that her husband had work. But he had lost the job before she got there—he always lost every job he ever got. So she had come back to Cleveland where she knew she could find employment. She had not brought the children back because she hadn't money enough for more than her own bus fare, and she had thought they would be all right with her husband until she could send for them.

The caseworker made a mistake then. He said, "You did

not tell us that you thought your husband was in California, but you started out to go to him the morning after you were here. And it seems to me you were hardly justified in leaving four small children in his care if he is as unreliable as you say."

Mrs. Sparrow flared into temper and, according to the worker's subsequent recording, "accepted none of the blame for having deserted the children. She seemed more concerned with the troubles she herself had had than with anything that might be happening to the children."

However, the Sparrow family clearly had residence in Cleveland, and the children were the responsibility of Cuyahoga County. The California agency was notified that we would accept them and place them in foster care. We met the children for the first time when the worker from California brought them back. They were all attractive, well-mannered youngsters. The eight-year-old girl seemed older than her years, and it was evident that the others were accustomed to relying on her. The California worker said that the child had assumed most of their care during the trip, behaving like a "perfect little mother."

In the course of working out plans with Mrs. Sparrow we learned quite a bit about her background. She was the only child of an unmarried mother. She confessed that she had always had difficulties in her relationship with her mother. She refused flatly to give us her mother's address, other than to say it was in Albany, New York. She never wanted anything to do with her again and did not want her mother to know about her present situation. She had managed to go through business college, but had left Albany just as soon as she graduated. She went to New York City and got a job but found it difficult to manage alone. She met her husband in New York and married when she was nineteen.

Mrs. Sparrow talked about her marital difficulties in terms of the differences between what she wanted and what her husband wanted from life. She longed for a nice home but every time she tried to establish one, her husband's shiftlessness resulted in its loss. Moreover, he was not clean personally, and many of his habits were so disagreeable that she could not bear to have him around. He got worse as time went on. Each of her four pregnancies had occurred when he forced himself on her while he was drunk. She had not wanted children. She would have preferred to work and contribute to the family income.

She talked of the clean, well-ordered life she felt she had a right to expect. She was willing to work to earn the life she wanted, but the difficulties her husband had forced on her had so far made that impossible. But this was the end. She did not know where her husband had got to, and she didn't care. She never intended to return to him. She knew her children needed a father, but she thought they might better have no father than one who was drunk and dirty like her husband.

When the worker asked about her husband's family, she at first refused to give information but when she was assured that the children would not be sent to the paternal relatives against her wishes she gave the addresses in New York City where they might be found. But they were a no-good bunch, she insisted. She should have known better than to marry into that crowd, but her husband was good looking and a smooth talker, and she had thought he was different.

Correspondence with the New York City agency confirmed Mrs. Sparrow's estimate of her in-laws. No financial help could be expected from them. Mr. Sparrow himself was never located. If Mrs. Sparrow heard from him she did not tell us. The agency took the usual action to find the husband but did not put pressure on Mrs. Sparrow, choosing to accept her statement that she had no idea where he was. Her confidence that she could find work in Cleveland had been promptly justified. Her employment was steady and she was reported to be a good worker. She regularly made partial payments toward the cost of the children's care, and she visited them every Sunday. She did not suggest making any change in her way of life that might enable her to have the children with her.

As months went by Mrs. Sparrow appeared much less tense. Her health improved. The twitching of her eyelid disappeared. Her voice became softer, and her quick bursts of temper vanished. About ten months after we had taken the children in care, she reported that she had secured a divorce from Mr. Sparrow. She added that she had met another man who was interested in marrying her. He knew about her children but had never met them. If he and the children liked each other she thought she would marry him. He had a good job and was steady — quite different from Mr. Sparrow. She was older now, she said, and had more judgment. She would not marry him unless things were right between him and her children but she thought they would be. She discussed with the worker how best to introduce this man and her relationship with him to the children.

Perhaps we are not completely justified in presenting Mrs. Sparrow and the four children here for family evaluation. We never met Mr. Sparrow and knew him only through Mrs. Sparrow's descriptions, through the reports from his employers of his erratic work record, and through the New York City agency which told us about his relatives. Still, the family as represented by Mrs. Sparrow and the children illustrates some points worth our consideration.

Initially, Mrs. Sparrow made a poor impression. Observe the somewhat derogatory terms used by the intake worker in describing her, and the criticism expressed when she was located after her return from California. But was this poor impression justified? It must be kept in mind that she had come to the agency in a time of stress, and behavior during stress is not a reliable indication of what behavior will be at calmer moments. No accurate evaluation of this woman's capacity as a person or as a mother could have been made at the first contact, nor at the second. But as the weeks and months went by several things emerged, the importance of which could be recognized by hindsight—always so much easier than foresight.

1. Mrs. Sparrow was not emotionally ready to be a mother.

She seemed concerned for what was happening to herself rather than for what might be happening to the children.

She was willing to leave the children in the care of the oldest girl, assigning without a qualm the mother role to an eight-year-old child.

She was able to leave them with the father, whom she admitted she had had no reason to trust.

She would not apply for AFDC for herself because of the humiliation she thought she would feel, but did not hesitate to ask that her children receive agency care.

She had no identification with any mother figure—usually an indication that a woman will not see herself in a mother role. Her description of her relationship with her own mother showed her lack of identification.

2. The tension and the twitching eyelid evident on the first contact and for some time thereafter suggested some unresolved inner struggle beyond the financial stress of the moment. Such conflicts use up emotional energy and interfere with accomplishment. Did the stress come from the marital difficulties, or from guilt over her failure in the mother role? Hard to say, even by hindsight. But we see evidences that the conflict dwindled as her situation became happier.

3. There was no acceptable father figure.

Even if Mr. Sparrow had been located and had proved to be less undesirable than his wife pictured him, the probability is that her attitude toward him had already ruined him in the eyes of the children.

4. The parents were finding no satisfaction in one another. There was no mutuality of concern.

Mr. and Mrs. Sparrow had quite different values. She wanted a "comfortable, well-ordered home," but Mr. Sparrow did nothing to make that possible, and apparently on several occasions spoiled their chances of having such a home.

Mrs. Sparrow's criticisms of her husband as dirty and repugnant to her showed that she found no emotional gratification from their sexual life.

Since Mrs. Sparrow felt as she did, and seemed to have no reticence about expressing her feeling, it is most unlikely that Mr. Sparrow had any satisfaction in his relationship with her. This was confirmed by his frequent and prolonged absences from home.

These are strong liabilities. But as we became better acquainted with Mrs. Sparrow we found some definite strengths in her:

1. She was not dependent.

She got herself to California without help, and when that plan failed she got herself back again without help.

She found employment for herself.

She decided on a divorce and got it without asking for advice or help.

2. She knew quite clearly what she wanted from life and had strong motivation to go after it.

3. She was personally fastidious, which would suggest an ability to establish a home that was at least physically appropriate.

4. As she began to surmount her personal difficulties some of the liabilities decreased.

The indication of nervous tension disappeared. The tic of the eyelid vanished. Her voice softened.

She was able to show more concern for the children. She contributed regularly toward the cost of their care and she visited each week. When she was first seen in the agency perhaps she had been "too unhappy to be kind." When she grew interested in the possibility of marrying again, she was eager that the relationship between the children and their stepfather should be good.

5. She had both the ability and the motivation to work. She was very highly spoken of by her employer, and she kept the same job.

The situation shows almost as many weaknesses as potential strengths. What would be the prognosis? What would be the plan? An effort to get the children back with the mother? Or acceptance of permanent placement for them, with Mrs. Sparrow relating to them as a part-time mother?

Mrs. Sparrow married her second husband. He visited the children with her and was gentle and tactful with them. They accepted him happily. Within three months the mother came to the office to tell us she was very happy and had decided to give up her job to take care of her husband and her home, and to get ready to have the children with her.

For the first time Mrs. Sparrow showed real awareness and sensitivity concerning the children. She said she would like to have them come back to her one at a time so that she could "get acquainted with them all over." She asked to have the oldest girl come first: "She's much too grown up for her age. She needs to be the only one and be babied for a bit."

So the oldest girl went home, and reveled in the pampering. She was given dolls to play with and was introduced to neighbor children of her own age, and was given no responsibilities. When the worker called at the home a month later he found her sitting on her stepfather's lap while he read *Winnie the Pooh*.

The other children came home for weekend visits for a period of some months before another child was added to the permanent household. Then it was the second oldest who came, at the mother's request: "He's independent. He won't expect big sister to tie his shoes or take care of him, and I don't want her sliding back into her old habits of mothering the gang."

Two months later, the last two came home together. By this time the mother was pregnant and looking forward to having a baby by the second husband. Both parents were proving themselves adequate and affectionate to all the children—including, later, the small half brother.

Perhaps one of the most interesting aspects of this case is that the emotional problems and the environmental difficulties were both solved by means outside the function of the agency to which the distraught mother had first turned for help. The agency's acceptance of the children for foster care did relieve the immediate stress, providing an opportunity for the troubled woman to resolve her own confusions and to relax her tensions. But the important part of the "casework" was done by her second husband.

XX

FAMILY INTERVIEWS

In our culture, people more often than not live in some sort of family setting. There are, unhappily, children who spend years in large child-care institutions. There are handicapped persons in nursing homes and hospitals, and there are isolates living in rooming houses or one-room apartments or in remote shacks half way up a mountain. But normal life in America is family life—a group of individuals with destinies intertwined. Husband lives with wife, children with parents, or grandparents, or married older sister, or with foster parents. The elderly often live with adult married children. So social workers must think in terms of family health as well as in terms of the mental, physical, or emotional health of an individual. Our attention, both in diagnosis and in treatment, if it comes to treatment, should be turned to the interpersonal component within the family group in addition to the intrapsychic make-up of any individual member.

This applies if we are studying the family of a child in placement to determine whether or not we can work toward his return to his own parents. It applies if we are studying a prospective foster home or a potential adoptive family. It applies for workers in protective services who are observing a family to learn its strengths and its potential for remaining intact with agency help. It applies for workers in public assistance who are providing services for AFDC families where the relationship between the mother and children, or perhaps between the siblings can create a climate for making or for breaking the lives of the individual members. It applies in a welfare family where the friction in the home may be so wearing on the breadwinner that he is unable to keep his attention on securing or holding any paying job.

Any diagnosis of a family's potential must be based on its current behavior, not on an introspective study of the development of any individual member. However, the present grows out of the past and has continuity with the past. We must not lose sight of this, but our emphasis in diagnosis must be on today—and tomorrow. We use the past only as a help to our better understanding, and perhaps sometimes as a help in interpreting to a client why he acts and feels as he does. But we offer this interpretation only if some aspect of the past is really blocking a solution to the current problems.

In assessing family strengths, the worker must remain aware of the family's past opportunities—or lack of them. What have been the educational opportunities, the job training, the stimulation toward improvement, the recreational possibilities? Also, he must be aware of events in the past which may be blocking activity now. There is, for example, no true reintegration into society for a man who served a jail sentence or is known to have been in a mental hospital.

A caseworker must differentiate between problems inherent in the maturation process of the individual, those that are precipitated by external events, and those that are caused by internal or interpersonal difficulties. A family's essential functioning can be seriously affected by any or all of these types of problems.

The caseworker must remain alert to the part played in the family constellation by each member of the family group. Caseworkers, especially those in child-placement agencies and in home-finding departments of child-care agencies, have a tendency to emphasize the mother role in a family, to forget the father and the siblings, and to pay little or no attention to the way in which the family functions as a unit. It is easy to understand how this might happen in a child-care agency. Such an agency is child-oriented, and the mother of the family is usually the one who dresses the child, washes him, prepares his meals, gets him up in the morning and in bed at night, starts him off to school, and provides his afternoon snack when he comes home again. She is often the one who carries the role of disciplinarian and sets the standards of behavior. Also, of course, she is usually the member of the family easiest for the worker to locate since she is oftenest in the home and available during his working hours; whereas the father, if he is employed, must be seen at odd times—lunch hours, evenings, or Saturday afternoons.

But it is a serious error to ignore the father. He is a part of the family group if he is at home at all. His role is usually thought of as that of wage earner, and he has either accepted or has declined that role, he is either succeeding or failing to carry it. He is also the one who provides, or fails to provide, emotional satisfactions to his wife. He may well be the one whose attitudes and expectations assign the role to the mother which she accepts gladly, accepts under protest, or declines. He may be the real disciplinarian.

More often than not a foster father is by no means the retiring weakling which child-placement workers assume him to be. By their failure to see the father, to talk to him, to include him in the planning, the caseworkers assign him the role of nonentity, and the dominant role to the foster mother. Perhaps both parents accept the assigned roles in their relationship with the agency but not with one another or with the children in the home.

The best, perhaps the only way we can make an accurate family evaluation is to observe the family all together, watch the interplay between them, see their gestures, their facial expressions, listen to the tones they use and the words they employ with one another. As a technique for diagnosis and often for treatment, the family interview has an important place in social work. It must never, however, be thought of as replacing the tried-and-true personal interview in which the caseworker talks to an individual client alone. No, the family interview can never be the only technique employed, but it is a most important supplement. Caseworkers have added another dimension to basic interviewing practice by this relatively recent technique of combining planned, purposeful group activity with the traditional one-to-one approach.

Seeing a family all together has numerous purposes and numerous advantages. We can learn things in one multiple-client interview that would never be unearthed in any number of interviews with each individual separately. The multiple-client interview can clarify distortions which may be given consciously or unconsciously by individuals alone. It can improve communication between family members. It reveals, clarifies, and sometimes improves role functioning. It will bring into consciousness the goals and values of the family and it will strengthen family identity. It avoids the dangers attaching to single interviews with separate members of the family that one individual will play the worker against another, that any individual will feel left out or will feel undue responsibility for what has gone wrong or unduly bound to carry the full load for correcting the situation.

Inexperienced workers tend to avoid multiple-client interviews, to be afraid of them. Such family interviews do take rather more skill than the one-to-one interview, but they offer so many advantages that they are worth trying. There is a technique for conducting multiple-client interviewing which a worker can acquire and can improve with practice.

The caseworker should attempt to get the family members

to talk to one another. At the start, however, the worker may find himself asking questions and listening to responses directed to himself, but as tensions relax the family members will begin to talk to each other across him, and he can withdraw bit by bit from active participation in the discussion and become the observer, watching reactions and making his diagnosis. In the beginning, while he is still active in the discussion, his manner and his attitude can demonstrate how to be patient in the face of monotonous repetition or unjustified criticism, how to draw out a shy person, how to be tactful and courteous, how to talk to an aggressive person, perhaps how to handle an obstreperous child.

A caseworker was once interviewing a man and wife who had applied to adopt a child. A previous interview with the couple had brought little from the man, who barely opened his mouth, and an interview with the woman alone had shown her to be aggressive and prone to downgrade her husband who, according to her, never had any opinions, never had any sensible ideas, and "wouldn't have known enough to come in out of the rain" if she had not been around to call him in. In this second joint interview the worker made a special point of addressing most of his initial remarks to the husband, of asking the husband's opinions, and listening with obvious attention and interest to all his responses. The husband blossomed under this treatment, and made a number of worthwhile remarks. The wife, who had started to interrupt and override her husband, finally quieted down and listened. After he had left to bring up the family car, the wife said to the caseworker, "Well! That was a revelation. I never knew he had that much sense or thought like that about things."

However, during a family interview it is possible for communication between the worker and the family members to be obstructed by the defenses of individual members who may be uneasy about revealing themselves to others in the family.

Or sometimes there may be so much bottled-up hate in one or more members that the whole interview is swamped by recriminations. If this is beyond the worker's ability to handle, the interview might better be stopped and the individuals seen separately.

In one case a worker was interviewing the parents of a ten-year-old retarded boy while the boy was present. The parents had asked for help to arrange an institutional placement for their son. The worker's plan was for a discussion of such placement, with the parents helping to interpret to the boy the reasons for his leaving home. What the worker failed to recognize was the strength and bitterness of the parents' rejection of the unfortunate child or the degree to which the husband blamed his wife for the child's condition. Both the rejection and the blame came out in the open during the interview, with the boy listening. He was unable to take any verbal part in the discussion, but he could act out his feelings of frustration and resentment, which he did by savagely attacking his father with a knife. This family interview might be said to have been valuable diagnostically, but it was highly damaging to the intrafamily relationship, to the retarded child's self-image, and to the case planning. In this situation diagnosis was of far less importance than helpful planning would have been. The worker should have ended the interview the instant that the parents' rejection of the boy began to emerge; better, he should never have attempted such an interview with the child present. It is seldom wise to include in multiple-client interviewing any individual who is able to understand the feeling tone of the discussion but is unable to take a verbal part.

Sometimes a family interview is blocked by the caseworker's own lack of self-awareness so that he is blind to the effect that he is having on the group. Nobody will reveal himself more than he can help to a person whom he regards as punitive or critical. If the worker thinks of the parents in this family, not as troubled people, but as inefficient tools for the furthering of the child's welfare, he will get no self-revelation from them, but only defenses, projections, and rationalizations.

The multiple-client interview can provide the worker with his best opportunity for obtaining a cross-sectional view of the family. Such a view of responses and interchange between family members can serve to correct distortions in the individual client's reporting of attitudes and feelings. It can also reveal the behavior pattern of an individual which stems from unconscious attitudes and therefore has not come to light in any individual interview.

The caseworker must avoid becoming involved in charges and countercharges, in appeals to act as referee, in requests to make decisions for any one member of the group. For example, a mother and teen-age son were arguing about the type of gift the boy should give his current girl friend. The son wanted to give jewelry. The mother thought he should select a book, and the argument became quite heated. They demanded that the caseworker decide which was right. He managed to avoid the trap and instead kept the discussion on why such an issue provoked so much heat between them.

The worker should see to it that all members of the family participate in the interview, and he should never permit one member of the family to override any other.

The nonverbal communication—the behavior, attitudes, gestures, roles assigned, and roles enacted—ought to receive as much attention from the worker as the verbal interplay. Often a worker's comments about the nonverbal manifestations are as meaningful to the family as are his responses to the verbal.

If one member of the family is striving for a status different from that of the other, the worker must decide whether the striving will tend to separate that person from the family group, or whether his success will carry the whole group to a different status. If it is the former, the question must be asked whether the loss of that member will have a disintegrating effect on the remaining members, or whether they will close ranks and be more strongly united without him. One often sees a teen-age son or daughter going through, not only the normal adolescent revolt against parental domination, but a much more specific revolt against the status of the family. This may occur in any family but appears often in second-generation American children brought up by Old World parents. Such a striving on the part of an adolescent is not likely to carry a whole family along, nor, painful though it may be, does it often result in the complete disintegration of the family. The trickier situation comes when the father of a family aspires to a change of status. Then we ask ourselves whether he can pull the whole family along with him. If not, and he must leave the family, how disastrous will his desertion be to those who remain? The answers to those questions strongly affect our diagnosis of the family's strengths, and the answers can probably be most rapidly and most accurately determined through family interviewing.

To recapitulate quickly:

In diagnosing a family, ask whether the present crisis or breakdown has been precipitated by external circumstances. If so, can those circumstances be corrected by environmental manipulation?

Is the crisis caused by the weakness or personality failure of one individual in the family? If so, is that failure caused by some event or circumstance, or by the lack of opportunity in that individual's past, such as lack of educational opportunity, loss of employment because of automation, or inability to find employment because of a history of prison sentence or mental illness? If so, can the situation be corrected or ameliorated, or can it be interpreted to the other members of the family so that they can accept it?

Are all the roles assigned to any family member by any other family member accepted and assumed efficiently and gladly? If any individual is declining the role which another attempts to assign, how are the others taking the frustration?

What is the pattern of need response in the family? Is any member failing to find satisfaction of his emotional needs? If so, can the need be interpreted to the others with any hope that they will be able to provide what is required?

Is the social norm of the family such that it can be acceptable within the culture where the family is now living? If not, can any interpretation be given without risk of the total disintegration of family norm and status?

XXI

THE USE AND MISUSE
OF AUTHORITY

Authority is a two-edged sword. It is a useful and sometimes a necessary tool in casework, but if it is used inappropriately it is capable of doing great damage, both to the client in whose behalf it is supposed to be wielded and, equally, to the caseworker who may be handling it clumsily.

There are occasions, easily recognized, when authority should be invoked. If a man is bashing in the head of another, if a woman is caught shoplifting, if a parent is beating a child, then we do not hesitate to call in the authority of the law to protect person or property. It is when a client's activities appear to be injurious to himself alone that the caseworker must think twice before using authority to change that behavior. Even here there are few clear-cut situations. A mental defective who is unable to care for himself must be institutionalized. Most of us are inclined to agree that a person should be prevented, by force if necessary, from committing suicide. But what about the woman who remains with a sadistic or alcoholic husband, complaining all the time but remaining nevertheless? What about the man who persists in keeping a hunger strike, or holding to an unhealthful diet, to the point where he no longer has the energy to carry a job? What about the elderly client who prefers her familiar but inconvenient house without plumbing or central heat to the comfortable "rest home" recommended by her worker? What about the adolescent who prefers reading a book in a corner to taking any part in the organized games of his peers?

Here is where decisions become delicate, and "authority" melts imperceptibly into "influence." Perhaps we would not go so far as to threaten withdrawal of assistance if the wife of the alcoholic did not leave her husband, but we might be tempted to exert our influence as a person whom she trusts. We might make it abundantly clear to the woman that separation from her husband would meet with our approval, or let it be known that we feel highly critical of a man who eats so unwisely that his health suffers, or that we strongly disapprove of an old lady who lets her long-suffering neighbors cut her wood and carry her water and worry about her when there are trained personnel paid to take care of her if she would go to them.

But are we justified in showing so clearly our personal preference and bias?

Florence Hollis says: "In the days of innocence when workers were universally thought to be wiser. and better informed than clients, advice was one of the 'visitor's' stock in trade."[1]

Make no mistake, "advice" from a trusted caseworker who is in a position to give or withhold approval, or even practical assistance, amounts to a form of authority. The threat of loss of approval from such a one can be almost as effective as a court's threat of imprisonment.

Dr. Hollis goes on to say:

Now it is recognized that to use the client's trust in the worker as a vehicle for influencing his behavior is sometimes a very useful form of treatment, but three safeguards must be observed. First, the worker must be reasonably sure that he knows enough about what is best for the client. Especially in important decisions, the worker rarely knows enough to justify influencing him .... For instance, in a decision to break up a marriage, a third person cannot sufficiently appreciate the subjective feelings and needs involved to weigh them adequately along with the objective realities that seem, perhaps too obviously, to point toward the wisdom of separation.[2]

[1] Florence Hollis, *Casework: a Psychosocial Therapy*, p. 89.
[2] *Ibid.*

Any caseworker, especially one not yet sufficiently experienced to have been exposed to a wide variety of off-beat personalities, will be tempted to apply his own standard of what makes a good life. To the caseworker, perhaps any degree of loneliness would be preferable to a drunken marriage mate and an uncertain income. But different people feel differently about drunkenness—and about loneliness. It is the client who must be led to weigh the alternatives and to make a choice in the light of what is most important to her, not of what the caseworker would approve.

So first, before we try to influence a client's way of life, we should be sure that we really know what is best—and we almost never do. Objective factors we may see clearly, more clearly, perhaps, than the client sees them, but we seldom can truly and deeply know the subjective element. That the client alone can grasp. The subjective elements are often actually much stronger than the objective ones. Thus we may find a client appearing to accede to the plans the caseworker is imposing on him, accepting the arguments offered by the worker, only to sabotage the whole scheme in a matter of weeks. The woman returns to her drunken husband. The adolescent manages to fumble in all sports until the group is relieved to have him go back to his book and his corner.

Dr. Hollis continues:

A second safeguard is to be quite sure that the need for advice rests in the client and not in the worker. This is a matter of self-examination for the worker. It is so tempting to tell people what to do; one feels so good to be called on for professional advice! All the negative connotations of the word "authority" can be removed simply by putting "professional" in front of it and thereby transforming "authoritativeness" into "strength for the client to lean on." That there is such a thing as professional authority is not to be denied, and under certain circumstances it can be put to very good use. However, the need to see oneself as an authority is not sufficient reason for invoking that role.[3]

[3] *Ibid.*, p. 90.

Instead of expressing or implying his own opinion of what a client should do with his life, the caseworker would be advised to persuade the client to think things through for himself. This is the third safeguard against the overuse of authority. To accomplish this may take time, and it will certainly demand patience and self-restraint on the part of the worker who thinks he can see so clearly what ought to be done. Some clients (as well as some other persons) do not like to think, partly because to do so may force them into admitting impulses and attitudes that could be embarrassing, and partly because it is so much pleasanter to have somebody else to blame if things go wrong. But it is worth all the caseworker's skill and effort to persuade the client really to examine all alternatives and to make his own choice, based on the way he feels, not on the way he thinks the caseworker wants him to feel.

With these precautions in mind, we must still recognize that there are occasions when authoritative intervention is necessary. One such occasion, as we implied at the beginning of this chapter, exists when we see a client doing actual physical or emotional damage to a weaker individual. We would remove a child from a home where he is subjected to cruelty or severe neglect. Before doing so, however, we would probably attempt to interpret to the parents the needs of the child, the ways in which the parent is failing to meet those needs, and what will happen if he does not manage to meet them: "If you continue to tie the child in bed and then go off and leave him there alone for the evening, the Juvenile Court will certainly step in." This is not so much the use of a caseworker's authority as it is a factual presentation of the realities of our culture.

There are three important cautions to keep in mind in a situation such as this. The caseworker must be very certain of his facts, that the parent *does* tie the child in bed and *does* repeatedly leave him there alone. Secondly, the caseworker must have evidence better than the hearsay evidence of a hostile neighbor who says somebody told her that this happens. Thirdly, the caseworker must have confidence in the attitude of the Juvenile Court. What the caseworker says to the client must be an accurate prediction of what really will happen if the client does not change his behavior. If the worker makes such a prediction and the client does not change, and the Juvenile Court fails to take any action after satisfactory evidence has been presented, the client will surely regard his words as an empty threat, and the worker will have forfeited any relationship he may ever have had with the client and will probably have made the home situation worse for the child than it was before. (If the worker takes the matter into court and then fails to present adequate evidence he has only himself to blame.)

Another situation in which use of authority might be indicated is one in which a person by reason of immaturity or inexperience cannot be made sufficiently aware of the consequences of his acts in time to save him from damage. Suppose that a child runs out on an icy road in front of a car without realizing that the driver can neither stop the car nor redirect its motion in time to avoid hitting him. We would shout in our most stentorian and authoritative tones, ordering the child out of the road, and explain later. A thirteen-year-old girl with a good potential for learning runs away from school, heading for Hollywood with the avowed intention of becoming a movie star. She knows nothing about the business of acting except its spurious glamour. She must be brought home, with the help of law-enforcement officers if necessary, and this must be done before she gets into a situation she cannot foresee and might have great trouble getting out of undamaged. The very young, the very aged, the emotionally immature, may be incapable of controlling impulses, of knowing with any accuracy their own limitations. Authority may be required to save these people from disaster.

But again, the caseworker must use his authority with caution. He must always follow the authority, or accompany it, with understanding and acceptance of the impulse which the client is expressing, with a reasonable interpretation of the dangerous consequences in terms the client can understand, and always with the opportunity for the client to talk about his feelings and to express his frustrations. He would say to the child, "You must not run into the road because the road is for cars and you could get hurt." Or to the adolescent adventuress, "You must stay in school at least until you are sixteen because that is the law in this state. That is the way things are, and you must go along with it. Besides, if you didn't find a job quickly, you could get very hungry." If the child and the adolescent are resentful and angry, the caseworker should let them talk. He should listen—and not be patronizing.

There are occasions, too, when clients ordinarily capable of self-direction may need and appreciate a short period of authoritative guidance from the caseworker. This may happen, for example, at times of crisis when a client feels temporarily overwhelmed and unable to think clearly. Sometimes this may be the situation when a client first comes to the agency since it is often a crisis which sends a person to an agency for help. But the worker must use judgment in applying authority even in severe crisis, since some individuals fear loss of autonomy even more than they dread the precipitating problem which has sent them there. In any event, if a caseworker loans his strength to help an anxious client in an emergency, he should be alert to the danger of encouraging continued dependence, and he must be ready to ease the client back into self-direction as soon as the person can use his own resources.

Another situation in which tactful use of authority may be a help is one in which the wisest action on the part of the client would create within him a crippling sense of guilt. For example, a mother overwhelmed by her own personal problems may be finding it impossible to give her child the undeviating love and feeling of security which any child needs. She may be unable to work through her own difficulties realistically while she is distracted by the demands of the child. It would be better for both if they could be separated for a time, but if the mother herself requests placement of the child she will be filled with guilt and even less able than before to solve her own personal problems. However, if the worker from a child-placement agency should make the decision for her and say, "For your child's sake, and for your sake as well, we are insisting that this child be placed for a time away from you," the mother would then be simultaneously freed from guilt and from the child's daily demands which had been draining her emotionally. A decision to take such an action must rest on the worker's sensitive diagnosis of the mother's real needs, and the authoritative act itself must be carried through with skill in handling the child's feelings over the separation as well as with tact in interpreting to the mother. Such a plan is undertaken to give the mother an opportunity to find herself. The separation may be brief, it may be lengthy, it may even be permanent — as it is likely to be if the mother is immature and unmarried — but it is *not* in any sense a punishment of the mother.

Misuse of authority, I said, may hurt the caseworker as well as the client. This is true, and perhaps the statement could be amplified.

Some caseworkers, especially before they have had much experience in diagnosis, are timid about assuming responsibility for planning the life of another human being. It is to be expected that at first a worker may avoid making decisions on his own initiative. He is likely to quote agency policy, presenting it as inflexible and undeviating. Probably this initial approach to casework problems is not too unhealthy. Certainly it is to be preferred to a brashness which might plunge a tyro into complicated situations before he had sufficient knowledge for handling them. The danger to the client, the agency, and the timid caseworker comes if the worker avoids the effort necessary to acquire the necessary knowledge of human dynamics and the necessary skill in diagnosis which he needs to make decisions without the crutch of "agency policy," or if he continues for too many months to use authority at one remove instead of assuming responsibility for thinking out his own decisions. Any caseworker must operate within the framework of his agency, but no agency is so rigid that it grants no leeway for approaching individual situations in different ways. If a worker persists for too many months in leaning on a generalized "agency policy" without understanding it himself, without being able to give the client adequate interpretation, and without seeing the client and his situation as unique and worthy of individual study and individual help, then he is doing his agency a disservice, and possibly deep harm to the client. Moreover, he is permitting himself to regress into unthinking dependence. The exercise of a quoted authority, while at the same time avoiding understanding and dodging responsibility, cannot be other than debilitating to any caseworker's character.

Another equally harmful misuse of authority comes about if the worker, finding himself, perhaps for the first time, in a position of some power over the lives of others, leaps all too joyfully into the habit of swinging the "big stick" for the pleasure he feels in seeing himself as Authority rather than because he has taken the trouble to understand the need of the client. Remember the words we quoted earlier:

. . . be quite sure that the need for advice rests in the client and not in the worker.... It is so tempting to tell people what to do ... the need to see oneself as an authority is not sufficient reason for invoking the role.[4]

What it boils down to is this: do not be afraid to use authority when authoritative direction will save the client or help him. The caseworker should be quite certain that he really knows what will save or what will help the client. And never should he use authority simply because to do so is fun. He must try to understand the client, his capacity for making his own decisions, his special needs at the moment.

And the worker must try to understand himself.

[4] *Ibid.*

XXII

WHEN A CHILD MUST BE TAKEN
FROM HIS OWN HOME

The parents of children who are removed today for placement in institutions or foster homes are much more disturbed
than were the parents of placed children a generation ago.
This is partly because there are more resources today for
holding families together. There is no reason now for
separating children from their parents for financial causes
alone. We have public assistance, AFDC, social security and
survivors' benefits. More agencies are making efforts to use
day care to keep children with employed parents, or homemaker services to help a father care for motherless children
at home. So now if the parents have sufficient internal
strengths they can use such resources as these without giving
up their children.

Also, we are far less complacent than we used to be about
separating children from their parents. Time was when
there was a strong tendency to punish apparently inadequate
parents by taking their children away from them: "You don't
keep your children clean. You don't provide good meals
for them. You don't deserve to have any children." Today
we have begun to recognize what separation does to the
child, and so we make much more of an effort to work
through difficulties in the home without breaking up the
family.

Thus it comes about that when children must be removed
from the home it is because the parents are needful people

who cannot give what the child should have for emotional nourishment. So caseworkers in child-placement agencies find themselves working with parents who have few inner strengths and many physical, mental, or emotional problems of their own.

In most states neglect or abuse of their children is sufficient cause for bringing parents before a juvenile court. If the complaints are found to be justified, the court may place the children in the custody of a child-caring agency. Sometimes the court's decision makes it mandatory that the child be removed from his own home; in other situations, the decision is left to the agency, which may then either place the children or attempt to help the parents while the child remains with them.

Serious mental or physical illness or feeble-mindedness on the part of the parents sometimes makes it impossible for them to give good care. Or, because of their own emotional problems, parents may be so incapable of handling the child with understanding that their relationship with him is seriously damaging. If such an acute disturbance of the parent–child relationship exists, it will usually be apparent in the personality or the behavior of the child, as in his withdrawal into himself, or in learning difficulties, sex problems, destructiveness, or in delinquencies, stealing, truancy. If the parents are hospitalized or incarcerated, or if they have deserted, then someone must be found promptly to provide for the children. If no relative, no grandparents or kindly aunt, can be located, the children must go to a foster home or an institution. But if one or both of the parents are at home it may be possible to provide sufficient casework help to rehabilitate the family without subjecting the children to the shock of separation.

Sometimes the parents are facing what for them are overwhelming reality difficulties — poor housing, race prejudice, marital discord, a repetitive pattern of desertion and return. Adults who are emotionally immature may be able to maintain life in the community only if the stresses are not too severe. They may be able to cope with two children but not with eight. Or they may be able to handle their life situation with supportive help from a caseworker.

Before any decision is made to remove a child from his parents, there is one inescapable truth to be considered. However bad the home may be, we now recognize that it is *always* traumatic for the child to be separated from it. The parents may not have been able to give much, in material things, or acceptable training, or even perhaps in love, but when a child is taken from the only home he has ever known, no matter how inadequate it has been, the last small shreds of security vanish, and he is left not knowing what he can expect from life. Even when parents are found guilty of gross neglect or abuse, even in situations so severely damaging that we are convinced we must take the child away from the parents for his own safety, even then it is traumatic. The best that can be said is that we may be choosing the lesser of two evils. Even if the parents have abused and terrorized the child, removal, necessary though it may be, is still a serious blow if for no other reason than that he is made aware that his parents, his family, from whom he sprung, of whom he was a part, have been regarded by society as inadequate and undesirable. If we must take a child away from his own home we do so, but always with an awareness of what this break means to the child.

Legally, the two terms "abuse" and "neglect" are thrown together. Psychologically, they are very different, and they put families worlds apart in the prognosis for rehabilitation. Neglect may come from ignorance of what the child needs, physically or emotionally, or from ignorance of how to go about securing what he needs—adequate medical care, for instance. Or the neglect may come from a lack of inner resources out of which the parent can give to the child.

Abuse is a different matter. Abuse is not a failure to give because of ignorance or inadequacy. Abuse does not come from lack of knowledge. It comes from the parents' sick desire to inflict pain. Abuse may be physical or emotional or mental or all three. Nor is sadistic behavior confined to the low-income groups, although the upper-income groups are better able to conceal what they are doing and have a stronger motivation for concealment. But on whichever side of the tracks the abusive parents may live, they are sick people. In situations of real abuse, the caseworker should not be sweet, passive, and understanding. He should act fast and with firmness. If a parent beats a child black and blue, or shuts him in a dark closet for hours at a time, then community pressure or the law must be brought to bear to get the child out of the reach of the abusive parent.

However, it is not always immediately apparent whether the behavior of the parent stems from ignorance or from a pathological pleasure in giving pain. If the child is being damaged it may be necessary to remove him from the home, but before we act impetuously we should pause and consider whether the damage is going to be more serious if there is a week or a fortnight's delay. If the neglect is a matter of unwise diet or lack of cleanliness he will not suffer much more if he remains where he is a little longer while we make our diagnosis. It may be possible to help the family without subjecting the child to the trauma of separation. If the child is being physically abused, probably we better get him to a safe place, and then make our study of the dynamics behind the abuse. Apparent abuse, like neglect, may be a matter of ignorance, a sincere belief in "spare the rod and spoil the child." Then, possibly, interpretation, environmental changes, or supportive casework may be sufficient. If the abuse is pathological, probably the parents need psychiatric help which the caseworker is not equipped to give. Perhaps their sickness goes so deep that they cannot be helped, and permanent separation of the child from the parents is the only way to save him. But caseworkers should take time to make as clear a diagnosis as they can.

If a complete break from the parents is necessary, the earlier in the child's life the separation occurs, the easier it will be to find a way to compensate for the damage. That is one reason we remove infants from immature, inadequate, unmarried mothers as soon as possible. However, even to a small baby a substitution of one mother person for another is frightening. It involves a change in the manner of holding, in the tone of voice, in the rapidity and type of the response to his cry, and all of that makes life for a time seem unpredictable and a bit threatening. But if the baby finds a warm substitute mother quickly he can soon adjust to new ways of finding satisfactions.

After a child is old enough to know and recognize his parents any abrupt separation is more threatening, and this will be true even when the parents have had all too little to give him. After all, they gave him *something*. As an infant he could not have survived a week of complete and absolute neglect. Perhaps the little they gave him was not adequate, but it was all he had, and to lose that small scrap is frightening.

If a child is torn from his moorings and dumped in a strange foster home with no interpretation, with no opportunity to work through his feelings about his relationship with his parents, he surely is headed for trouble. The placement may be successful for a while, only to fail during his adolescence because of his lack of parental identification. He may never have any clear idea of who he is or where he belongs, no sense of his own identity. Or he may be stopped short in personality development at the stage he had reached at the time of separation from his parents, and cease to grow emotionally beyond that point. Or he may have so deep a feeling of being unloved and unwanted, since his parents seemed not to love him enough to keep him, that he can never bear to permit any other close relationship with anyone, expecting from it only another hurt, another rejection. Or he may harbor a deep guilt because he suspects that he was the cause of the family breakdown: if he had been a better boy his parents would have wanted him to stay with them; they would not have permitted him to be taken away; they would not have found it necessary to go off and leave him behind. As a result, he may never be able to think of himself as worth while, and will never really try to do anything with his life.

So, unless we have determined that permanent separation of the child from his parents is the lesser of the two evils for him, we will try to arrange a continuing relationship between the child and his family. If it is at all feasible, we work with the parents while he remains with them. If that is realistically impossible, or if helping them is going to take so long that the child will suffer more by remaining with them than he would by leaving them temporarily, then we attempt to involve the parents in the placement process. It is good if they can be persuaded to help interpret to the child the reasons for the placement. What his parents say always means more and seems truer to a child than anything a strange caseworker can say.

There may be some advantage in having the parents included in a preplacement visit to the foster home. It would then seem to the child that they had some part in the selection of the place. Also, they can describe it ahead of time to the youngster, and this will go far in helping him accept the placement. If such a visit is not possible, the worker should describe the place to the parents so that they can pass on the details which will interest the child — the color of the buildings; where he will sleep; how many other children there will be and their ages; what sorts of things they will have to eat; where they will play; whether there is a television set.

It also helps if the parents can include the child in preparations, letting him select the clothing or the toys that are to go with him, accompany the parents and caseworker on shopping expeditions, pick out pictures or mementos that he would like to take along.

When parents have been asked to interpret the reasons for the placement they frequently say they cannot do it, they would not know what to say. The worker can tell them not to fib, but to avoid saying things that will make the youngster pity the parents, or that will make him worry about them while they are apart, and to say nothing which will imply that placement is a punishment for either child or parents. This is not always easy and is sometimes impossible for parents who are feeling upset, guilty, or resentful, but the worker can assist by making concrete suggestions suitable to the specific situation. The child is going away to school—or to a place where it will be easier for him not to get into trouble with other kids—or where he can be comfortable and well taken care of while his mother has a rest until she can do more for him than she has been able to do recently.

It always helps if one or both of the parents can come along when the child is placed. If they do, they should be advised to say good-by when the time comes, not to sneak away when the child is out of sight, a temptation they often feel because of their own dread of the moment of separation.

The parents' continued participation after placement helps to ease the child's feelings of rejection or worthlessness. It prevents the growth of fantasy in his mind of an unreal, idealized parent—a fantasy doomed to be shattered when the child does eventually return to his own home and is faced with his parents' human frailties. A vision of the unrealistic ideal during the placement will block a child from accepting the merely human foster parents, thus making it difficult if not impossible for them to provide the emotional nourishment he needs for development.

To accomplish any of these ends will take patient, skillful casework help; for parents whose children must be placed even temporarily are not often the kind of parents who have the strength within themselves to do any of these things alone. We must never forget for one minute that we are working with immature and desperately needful people. It will accomplish nothing whatever to ignore their need and preach at them about what the child needs and what they, the parents, ought to have done and failed to do.

Often a mother is shy with her own child after he has been placed, especially if her visits are made in the presence of the foster parents or the caseworker. A woman not too glib in verbalization is self-conscious if she must sit quietly and just talk to her child instead of throwing out side remarks as she goes about casual housekeeping chores in her own home. Often a mother's love shows itself in doing things, dressing her child in the morning, feeding him, cuffing him when she thinks he needs a spot of discipline. If these activities have been deemed inadequate, the mother is at a loss. Somebody else, the foster mother, is performing all those services now. So what can the child's own mother do or say? Sometimes all she can think of is to talk about her own troubles, either ignoring the child or appealing to his sympathy.

However, the caseworker can help immensely in re-establishing the mother–child relationship. Perhaps he can himself start a conversation with the child about things that will interest the youngster until the mother can take part. Or he can suggest that the child tell his mother about the pony ride he had at the fair, or the nice things his teacher said about his spelling paper. Or the worker can get down on the floor and play with the child, gradually pulling the parent into the game. In any event, both worker and foster mother should try to avoid a situation in which the parents talk over the child's head to other adults, and the worker especially should try to prevent any conversation that emphasizes the parents' guilt, or grief, or current difficulties. Children are prone to worry about absent parents too much as it is; they need no encouragement in that direction.

If visits between parent and child are not practicable, then by all means encourage the sending of letters, or the making of telephone calls, or the exchange of pictures or small gifts. Anything is helpful that will keep the child aware of the existence and continued concern of the parent.

Remember, the parent of a dependent or neglected child does not want to be a bad parent. In his need to see himself as a good parent in spite of what the Juvenile Court may have said about him, he is very likely to make promises to the child and in his weakness fail to keep them. He will agree to the caseworker's suggested plans, and then cannot carry them through. But any caseworker who thinks of neglectful parents as neglectful on purpose and by deliberate intention will never be able to help the home situation. It accomplishes nothing to tell such a parent that if he really wanted the child to come home, as he says, he would pull himself together and clean up the apartment, or try harder to locate steady work, or cut out the drinking, or do any of the things that would bring about the child's return. Scolding such a needful individual does not help. It can only make him more defensive and less able than ever to do any of the sensible things that should be done if the family is to be rehabilitated. Only if the caseworker sees the inner need of the parent himself and responds to it will the parent ever be able to give to the child.

When a child must be removed from his own home, unless the parents are suffering from a pathology beyond the help of casework or psychiatric treatment, we should start from the moment of removal to plan toward his eventual return. We can set out with two assumptions:

1. The foster home placement should be regarded as temporary, to be used only until the home is repaired. If the foster home placement must be prolonged because of the inability of the parents ever to be full-time parents, then the placement should be thought of as a kind of adjunct to their own home, with parental contact maintained.

2. Whatever wrong or inadequate home condition prompted removal of the child will not change spontaneously but will need casework services. On very rare occasions some chance influence outside the sphere of casework activity may correct the poor environment, but this cannot be relied on.

If the placement of the child is made without clear planning, either for rehabilitation of the home or for his permanent separation from it, then the child may be left dangling with no contact with his parents, neither close to them nor emotionally released from them, living in a never-never land without roots. Or the child may come to the end of the placement period only to be returned to an unimproved home, and all the corrective work accomplished for him during placement will be promptly undone. Moreover, parents for whom no casework help is provided have a distressing ability to sabotage the placement itself.

Neglectful parents are often badly disorganized. They cannot get any effective routine into their lives. Meals are haphazard, efforts toward cleanliness erratic. They cannot assume continued responsibility in any area. These people cannot respond to any appeal made to them on the basis of what is best for the children because they themselves are so needful. An immature, inadequate parent must necessarily be helped to find some satisfactions for his own personal needs before he can be expected to have any surplus out of which he can feed a child's emotional hunger.

The job of the caseworker who is trying to repair a situation which has resulted in the placement of a child away from his own home is twofold. First, he must minimize as much as possible the trauma to the child of the separation; and secondly, he must help the parents prepare themselves and their home for the child's return.

There are a few guides for accomplishing the minimizing of the trauma:

1. The caseworker should give the child as much interpretation as he can understand of why the separation occurred. Give it as soon as possible, preferably before he leaves home so that he has some small opportunity to digest the interpretation.

2. The worker must remember that children see and understand a great deal more than most adults give them credit for. So open the way for the child to say why he thinks he must leave his home. He may have an amazingly clear and realistic picture, or he may harbor the notion that he is the cause of it all. If his thinking about his own part is distorted he must be set right, and the sooner the better. But find out first what the child himself thinks.

3. The caseworker should give the interpretation to the child with the least possible implication of criticism of the parents. Tell the truth, but perhaps not the whole truth. Avoid loaded terms, such as "neglect," or "dirty," or "drunk," which would give the child a feeling that parents are to blame or are being downgraded. Say that the parents are sick, or they had a lot of problems they wanted to work through so that they could take better care of him, or that difficulties sometimes get too much for grownups just as they sometimes do for children, and even grownups need a rest before they can do what they would like to do for their child. All this will not be easy for the youngster to accept. To a child, parents, good or bad, loving or rejecting, are sure to appear all-powerful, and it is difficult for a child to grasp the concept of a parent who needs help, who needs rest, who is a

vulnerable human being. One does not often see his parents as people until one has himself reached adulthood. Thus to a child the separation seems to have been at the deliberate wish of the parent, and he will feel accordingly rejected. That is the misery which we must attempt to minimize.

4. If possible, the worker should persuade the parent to do his own interpreting to the child and to involve himself in the placement process.

5. If possible, unless permanent separation is definitely indicated, the caseworker should encourage the parents to maintain contact with the child by visiting, writing, and sending gifts or, at least, messages.

6. The worker should give the child every possible opening to talk about his parents, to ask questions about them, to express without fear of blame or retribution any anger or resentment he may feel toward parents who, from his point of view, deserted him. Foster parents frequently remark that a placed child shows no curiosity and no concern about his own parents. But the caseworker must be aware that this reticence by no means indicates any lack of concern or feeling or curiosity. It is far more likely to be the child's response to what he thinks the foster parents wish. This will be especially true if the foster parents let the child sense that they have a poor opinion of their own parents, or are a bit jealous of the child's loyalty to his own parents.

7. Everything possible should be done to avoid letting the child feel that he is worthless or unlovable. He is vulnerable in that area either because of the parents' outspoken rejection of him before he left home, or because of the separation itself, or because of any criticism of his parents that he may have heard during the court action or from neighbors or school pals or (unhappily) from his foster parents. To a child, downgrading of his parents is a downgrading of himself. Good foster parents who can love a child and still share his loyalty

with his own parents, who can accept a child for what he is and refrain from negative comments about his own home, can do a great deal for a child's morale. The caseworker's repeatedly expressed interest and concern can also help.

8. The caseworker must remember that a child's unacceptable behavior — resistance to kindly foster parents, destructiveness, school difficulties — may well be his reaction to the original poor parent-child relationship. Interpret this to the foster parents so that they will not think that they are failing or that the child is incorrigible. Give the foster parents all possible support. Also, give the child implicit permission to verbalize his feelings about parents who have failed him. Talking about it will provide an outlet and reduce his need to act out.

Our second assumption was that the conditions in the child's own home which brought about his removal will be corrected only with casework help. Here are a few suggestions:

1. The worker should keep clearly in mind that these parents are needful people whose objectionable behavior is the inevitable consequence of their own deprived childhood.

2. Contacts with the parent should be based always on a recognition of *his* needs, *his* difficulties, *his* problems, and not alone on the needs of his child.

3. The parent must be seen as an individual in his own right, not merely as an inefficient caretaker of the child. Talk to the parent as a person who has his own problems.

4. Since the present needfulness of the parent is a result of his not receiving what he needed most and should have had from his own parents, it may be that the only way to help him is for the caseworker to assume the role of the good parent who cares what happens to him, who wants things right for him, who will listen to his troubles, who will understand and forgive his failures.

XXIII

HELPING RESISTIVE PARENTS

Social agencies are required repeatedly to try to help families in which the parents strongly resist help. Why do these people resist? Obviously, they have problems. They are probably in trouble with their neighbors; they cannot live within their income; they have tangled with the law; they cannot get along with their spouses; their children are failing in school, or have been reported to the authorities as running wild, or disrupting the classroom, or as being underfed or inadequately clothed, or as stealing candy from Woolworth's or cars from the parking lot. Of course these people have problems—and probably the referral to a social agency and the caseworker's subsequent visit seem to be just additional troubles on top of those they already have.

Yet they resist help and they deny that they have any problems. Why? They deny because they could not endure living with themselves if they admitted their need and faced their situation without a cushioning of excuses.

Remember, there is really no difference between the client who denies that there is anything wrong and the client who has learned all the expected answers, admits that her children are in difficulties, says she knows she needs help—and then avoids help in a variety of subtle ways. She misses appointments, she is not home when the worker calls, or she insists that she herself has no responsibility in the matter and somebody ought to make her husband assume more authority; or she declares that the caseworker should punish Johnny and make him be a different kind of boy.

But whether they deny the existence of any problems or whether they say the right words but cannot involve themselves in any plan for changing the situation, the effect on the family life is much the same, and the same kind of skill is required of the caseworker to improve the home. Both types of parents are afraid to look squarely into the horrid abyss of their own inadequacy which their early experiences in life have given them every reason to believe will exist unchangeably and forever.

The parents who deny the existence of any problems are people whose own parents gave them when they were children no faith in themselves, no reason to see themselves as individuals who would ever be worth loving, no picture of themselves as ever succeeding in anything, or ever making anything good of their lives. But that outlook is too depressing. They cannot face it—nobody could. So they say it is somebody else's fault. "Everybody picks on me. If the police would leave me alone"—or the school—or the neighbors— "I'd get along just fine"; or they say in effect, "If I just don't look, it will go away and there won't be any trouble"; or, "Don't bother me. I don't want anybody snooping in my business. Go away."

By the time these deprived people are chronologically adult and have children of their own, their defenses have been pushed far down deep inside, out of their conscious awareness. They honestly believe that they behave as they do for logical reasons. Actually, of course, they are operating wholly out of their emotions, not at all out of any thinking process. They do what they do in a blind groping for some satisfying experience that they should have had when they were small children. They get drunk every night, or they run out to the garish racket and friendliness of a honky-tonk dance hall, or they accept sexual advances from anybody who will give them a momentary illusion of closeness and acceptance. They lie abed all day hoping that there will be somebody willing to take care of them as they should have been taken care of as small children. They scream at their children and cuff them when they interfere with this futile search for emotional satisfactions. The things they do, of course, do not come within miles of meeting their inner needs. But they keep on groping, and they think up nonsensical excuses for their unendurable failures.

Life has always criticized them and attacked them and pressured them. With every new attack they patch up their defenses a little more. They crouch behind their defensive wall, becoming every year more incapable of emerging to do anything practical for themselves, let alone for their children. They have never been given to—so now they have nothing to give. They are needful themselves—so how can they fill the needs of their children? A child cannot be a wise mother or father to another child, but that is what we are asking these immature, childish, resistive parents to be.

What can a caseworker do for these people?

First, she can refrain from attacking. This is not always easy. We see children suffering from a lack of physical or emotional nourishment. The parents *look* grown up, and it is difficult to remember that emotionally they are only two years old—or six—or ten—or whatever age they managed to reach before they had used up the meager nourishment they received from their own inadequate parents. They are stunted, even though it does not show from the outside.

We are always tempted to side with the children against these pseudo grownups, to blame inadequate parents for failing to do what they so obviously should do. Maybe we have been taught not to scold our clients, but unless we are very careful, very much aware of ourselves, we let the blame creep through in the tone of our voice, our facial expressions, our impatient gestures. Then up go the client's defenses, and we get exactly nowhere. For these immature, childish adults are uncannily sensitive to the way we feel toward them beneath our façade of courtesy.

So not only do we refrain from attacking, we must not even *feel* like attacking. We must feel all the way down to our heels that these clients are needful individuals who are doing the best they can with what they have, and it is not their fault that they have so little. Until we give them more they will not be able to do more. We must in all sincerity make them realize that we have faith in them, concern for them, confidence that they can manage their lives so that things will really be better.

It will take time. There will be months, years perhaps, of slow effort on the caseworker's part before these parents really trust, can really accept what the worker has to give of concern, friendliness, emotional support. But unless the caseworker does manage to get through to them, unless he does persuade them to accept what they cannot admit that they need, they will never be able to give to their children.

But we must be sincere. And how do we manage that? A caseworker cannot turn his feelings on and off like a faucet. Inexperienced caseworkers especially have difficulty in feeling any sincere empathy for a drunken father, a slovenly mother. Inexperienced workers have trouble standing up to the onslaughts of a hostile client, or keeping in mind that the ugly insults the client is flinging are not really aimed at the worker but at authority, which the client has had reason to fear; at society, which has offered so little and criticized much; or perhaps at a father long since dead who never gave the client what any small child should have from a father, but whom she never dared insult as she is now insulting the worker in his place. It is difficult to focus on what is behind this disagreeable front, but we must do exactly that. The clients are quick to catch any negative feelings the caseworker has, and if his attitude unfortunately remains one of disgust or dislike he must do something about it. What can he do?

The first rule is to think of the parent as a person who is probably about three years old emotionally, no matter what her exterior appearance may be. The worker must listen to the parent as though she herself were the really important part of the case situation. Stop thinking about the child and listen to the mother. Think of *her* troubles, troubles which are too much for her to handle, immature and childish as she is. Let her talk. Let her explain how it is all the school's fault, or the neighbor's, or the court's. Let her complain about the stingy welfare that never gives her enough to live on. The caseworker does not correct her, or reason with her, or explain how it really is. He *listens*. He nods his head and makes sounds to show that he is listening. He does not ask questions for if he does the client will answer from her head. If he keeps quiet and listens, she will talk from her emotions, and her emotions are what the worker needs to understand. What she says may be far from the mark factually, but it will certainly provide clues to her unexpressed, unadmitted needs. The worker will catch on to what it is she has always wanted from life and never had, and that gives him his starting place.

We are taught to start where the client is, but that is easier said than done. How do we know where the client is? Our client cannot verbalize. She has no adequate vocabulary. Or our client talks too volubly and never comes to the point. Or our client is more emotional than we find agreeable. And of course our client has no self-awareness.

But if we listen and keep on listening, if we accept what the client says without argument or contradiction, if we make

clear by our expression and our posture that we are interested, that we think the client is an important person and
worth listening to, little by little she will find the courage to
emerge from behind her defensive wall. She will give us
more and more clues even if she does not know herself that
she is telling us anything about her inner needs.

Probably she will never tell us directly. How can she? She
has pushed all awareness of these early unsatisfied needs
far down into her subconscious because she has been convinced that they will never be met, that she does not deserve
anything, that she should never have hoped. It is safer to
forget. But whether or not her conscious mind is aware of
them, the needs are still there, unsatisfied and festering. So
in spite of herself she will tell us indirectly, perhaps by symbols, and if we listen "with the third ear" we will know what
she means.

A woman who had been deserted by her husband was receiving
AFDC help for herself and her two little girls, aged 8 and 10. Reports
came to the agency that the girls were running wild, were completely without supervision. Reports also reached the agency that
the mother was entertaining men until late into the night, that they
staged noisy drinking parties. The landlord notified the agency that
he had asked the woman to move — too many tenants were complaining. With the change of address the case was transferred to another
worker. Following is the report of this second worker's first visit
to the woman in the new apartment.

The interview was conducted in the living room, but the little
girls were not present. Mrs. M. welcomed me cordially and invited
me in, explaining that the girls were out on the playground. I
suggested that she call them in so that I could get acquainted with
them, but she said she would do so later. She thought it would be
nice to talk to me first without them.

She was very pleasant with me. She was neat enough, but her
costume could have been more appropriate. She had on very tight
toreador pants, high-heeled sandals, a frilly blouse, and a wide
ribbon in her hair, which was dyed to an improbable shade of red.

The apartment needed painting, and I remarked on this. I asked

her why she had moved from the other apartment, which was in a
newer building. She said this was a better location to bring up children. There was a playground. She said the neighbors in the other
apartment house had not been friendly. They had circulated rumors
about her, and she was afraid to stay there.

I brought up the complaints which the agency had received about
her late drinking parties. She said she never drank anything but
beer, and she would give that up if the caseworker wanted her to.

I mentioned the complaints about the children running all over
the place, going into other people's apartments uninvited, and so
on. I said I thought it was particularly bad that she should make
threats of punishment and then let the girls do the same thing all
over again. She denied that this ever happened. She said she was
very strict with them. Sometimes she thought she was too strict.
If she scolded them any more they might not love her. I explained
that making threats that meant nothing and promises that were
not kept would encourage them not to believe anything she ever
said and to lose faith in everyone. She said she knew it and wouldn't
do it any more.

She then told several unsavory stories about the girls. She told
how the older one had poked a nail into the eye of another child
at school and injured him so severely that he had to be taken to the
hospital to have his eye treated.

I had heard nothing of this, and it seemed unlikely that the
school would not have reported so serious an incident to the agency.
I told Mrs. M. that I thought she must be exaggerating and I would
investigate.

When I got up to leave she made much of being frank with me.
She seemed overanxious to bare her soul and made it quite clear
that any personal questions I might feel like asking she would not
hesitate to answer.

That interview is well worth our attention. Everything this
woman said or did provided ample clues to her needfulness,
and the worker missed every one.

The caseworker started out by saying, in effect, "I am not
interested in you. I am interested in the little girls."

The woman responded by saying, "Please pay attention to
me. Please notice me."

The manner in which she was dressed may have indicated a cultural pattern, but the chances are that it indicated another reaching out for attention. The manner in which the worker described the costume shows clearly that he felt it was in bad taste, and quite possibly this was reflected in his expression.

Then the worker asked Mrs. M. why she moved, although he had been told that the landlord asked her to go because of complaints from the neighbors. His asking Mrs. M. to explain forced her into the defensive. Naturally, she paraded the best excuses she could think of to put herself in a favorable light.

When the worker scolded her for the way she was bringing up the children she first denied making any mistakes, then promised to improve ("See, I am trying to please you"), then presented incidents to prove how bad the girls were ("I can't do any better. I try, but this is all too much for me").

The worker, for the second time in the course of the interview, said he did not believe what she was saying. ("You are exaggerating. I'll check with the school.") Her meek acceptance of this suggested that she had not expected to be believed — people never did believe her.

But she was resilient. She made one more try. At the end of the interview as the worker was leaving she really said, "Pay a little attention to *me*. Listen to *me*. I need a friend. I need to be understood. Help *me*."

Throughout she had been saying, "I am no older than my two daughters. I need more than they do. I can't be a mother to them. I am the same age as they are."

Not once did the caseworker listen. Not once did he hear what the woman was crying out to him. His manner and his remarks throughout said clearly, "You are not important. Only your two girls are important. You are of concern to me only as somebody to take care of the girls and you are doing a lousy job of it. You ought to do better. I don't

believe a word you say. You are silly and foolish and a liar
and of no account whatever."

So what happened?

The woman kept on trying to find satisfaction and acceptance through parties and a crowd of men around her to
prove her popularity. Noise, activity, men, provided an
illusion of acceptance. But there was nothing in all this to
help her grow up, and so she stayed the same age as the little
girls. She never learned to do anything more for them than
to shout, as another child would shout, an objection to what
other children happened to be doing.

The caseworker did not hear one thing the woman was
trying to say between the lines. But suppose he had understood, what could he have done? Can we accept antisocial
behavior? A mother who fails to control her daughters? A
woman who entertains men far into the night and stages
noisy parties that get her thrown out of the apartment house?

No, we cannot accept that behavior, of course. But we can
understand that the woman is a small child inside, and a
small child is not going to be able to discipline and control
other small children. A woman who has been devalued by
a husband who preferred a way of life that did not include her
will certainly need to find some proof that she nevertheless
has a value, and the only way that had occurred to this
inadequately educated, untrained, immature woman was
through the attention of other men—and the way to buy
that was with drink and noisy good times.

If we listen, if we pay attention, if we understand, perhaps
this woman will no longer need her defenses of denial and
projection. She might be able to relate to the worker, not
as someone who attacks and criticizes and disbelieves what
she says, but as a helping person who recognizes what she is
going through and who will support her and help her find
better ways to satisfy her need. This woman who has the

biological urges of an adult but the emotional needs of a child will begin to turn to the caseworker as she would have liked to turn to a kindly, wise, understanding parent, for advice not laced with criticism, for help that is for herself and not wholly directed at her daughters.

But how can a caseworker convey understanding and acceptance? We must convey it indirectly. We cannot very well say in so many words, "Yes, I understand. You are really only six years old. You can't be expected to take more responsibilty for your daughters than a six-year-old would." No, that would certainly be an attack, the last thing we want to do. We cannot "explain," nor can we "tell her."

We have to communicate our concern in less direct ways. First, we listen. We follow her lead when she gives us clues. She wants to leave the little girls out of the conversation—so we leave them out and concentrate our attention on her. We let her talk and we do not ask questions which put her on the defensive. We do not scold her and we try to find a way in which she can satisfy her emotional needs in a fashion that is socially acceptable. Our own concern for her, our listening, will of itself be therapy, but of course that will not be sufficient since we cannot be with her enough hours of the week. So we try to find something that will interest her and give her a feeling of accomplishment without damaging the girls. With a woman of her temperament, this would probably be something that involves contact with other people, a lot of people: singing in the choir, sewing with a group of women, going to swimming classes at the YW, joining a parent–teachers group—utilizing whatever interests or skills we can discover. Maybe we can find a job for her where she can be with people—clerking in a store, working in a factory, waiting on table. We get the minister or the priest interested in her, the school, any appropriate neighborhood group.

Involving the community will help immensely, for it broadens our approach, it bolsters our efforts to prove to this woman that she is worthwhile, that she has some importance in her own right. After all, the main purpose of all our casework with people of this sort is to improve their self-image, to give them strength to grow up, or at least to approach a maturity which will enable them to behave in a fashion acceptable to society and give both warm adult love and kindly consistent controls to the children for whom they are responsible. However, we must face the grim fact that it may not be easy to find people in the community who are willing to cooperate. It may be impossible. The client herself will quite possibly make our efforts to help her more difficult. This particular type of woman will probably be amiable, will make promises, will agree to all our suggestions— and will consistently fail to follow through. This will be discouraging enough for the caseworker; the lay helper in the community will be even less able to maintain his interest and his efforts in the face of the lack of visible progress.

This we can be sure of. Such a woman as Mrs. M. can respond only if she is approached as an individual, as a special person in her own right. Only then can she see any point in accepting help. Even after she shows some few signs of emotional growth, she will probably backslide, not once but many times. She will respond again to the worker's efforts, backslide again, say she is sorry, do a little better for a little longer, backslide again, until the worker is frazzled and discouraged. But we must not lose heart. Only if we stand by, bolstering this needful child-woman with our interest and our concern, will she be able to do a little more for her two girls. And remember, we may never quite manage to turn her into a completely moral, right-living citizen. But we may support her and nudge her a little way toward maturity, and every little bit counts toward an adequate, satisfying life for herself and for her children.

Other clients will show different patterns in their futile attempts to cope with a life whose demands are overwhelming. Often these inadequate people who need love and acceptance more than anything else in the world behave so that it is next to impossible really to like them. Sometimes they seem to be making deliberate attempts to aggravate the caseworker and alienate everyone around them. It is as though they had formed a habit very early in life of responding to everything with anger and resentment, and now, even after the source of the original anger has vanished, the response continues. Such people behave almost as though they felt compelled to create situations which will provoke the worker to retaliation so that they can say to themselves, "See, I knew he wouldn't help me. I knew he would never understand. I knew he would be cross with me. I was right to be angry with him." These people will not—in fact, cannot—move even a quarter of the way to meet the worker, and if he does not go all the way to them, they say, "I realize you don't want to help me." They persistently miss their regular appointments, and when the caseworker cannot give them special appointments, they say, "Of course. I knew all the time you did not care whether or not I came." They make excessive demands, and when the worker does not give what is impossible to give they say, "Nobody ever wants to help me."

The caseworker must go out of his way to avoid letting these resistive, defiant clients feel slighted, and when they feel slighted in spite of all his efforts he must not lose patience. He must give and give and give with little or no return from the client. He must recognize that none of these people will ever be completely whole, completely secure within themselves. But if he persists, some of them will learn at last to relate to him in some degree, to accept the strength and support he has been trying this long while to give. Then, if they reach that point, they can be better parents and better citizens, able themselves to give to their children because they have been given recognition and approval for every infinitesimal bit of effort they have made; they have at last experienced a personal concern for themselves as individuals.

At best, this work with immature, resistive parents is slow, draining the caseworker, and sometimes the effort brings no reward whatever. Some of these clients have been so damaged in their own childhood that they can never be whole again, can never respond, can never learn to give. But the caseworker must try. He may never be able really to like the client, but liking has little to do with it. The worker must recognize the need and respond sincerely to the need, in whatever disguised way it is expressed.

XXIV

CLIENTS WITH CHARACTER DISORDERS

It is heartbreaking to see a baby flinch when anyone approaches, grow rigid when someone tries to cuddle him, or remain flaccid and limp like a bag of wet sand when he is picked up. Such babies have had no experience of love. They have learned to expect to be struck or to be roughly handled, or they have learned to expect no human response at all. Such an infant is pathetic. An adult with the same kind of reactions is both pathetic and frightening. Unlike the baby, an adult is expected to assume responsibility for himself and, possibly, for a family, but if his impulse is to flinch when any human contact is offered he will not be able to accomplish much with his life. A baby may stiffen when people come close enough to frighten him, but an adult can do more than that. He can hit back, either with physical blows, or with bitter, accusing words. A baby may let himself go limp because he has no reason to expect anything pleasant from human contact and therefore has no impulse to respond. An adult who feels the same way may not be physically flaccid, but he will be emotionally unresponsive. A child of two may be mad at the world because it has frustrated his every effort to find satisfactions, has rebuffed his tentative offers of friendship, has given him no reason to think anyone will bother to take care of him. Such a small child may bite and kick and scream in rage. An adult who feels the same way for the same reasons will want to do the same things, but he will react a little differently. An adult may want to bite; instead, he uses hostile, biting words. He may yearn for the cherishing and protection he should have had as a small child, but he does not scream in disappointment when life does not proffer it to him. Instead, he somehow manages the situation so that a caseworker is pretty much obliged to take care of him. He develops illnesses, and needs special medicines and nursing care. He loses his job, and the welfare has to provide for him and his family. If the demands of society are just more than he can take, he escapes with the help of alcohol or drugs or sexual promiscuity. A child might curl up and go to sleep, or creep off to play some fantasy game by himself; the harassed adult must find his anodyne in another way.

None of this, of course, is the result of conscious, deliberate planning on the part of the adult who is exhibiting an adult version of childish behavior. The grownup who acts always on impulse without thought of consequences, who does self-destructive things and then blames somebody else, who feels unreasonable anger and hostility against people who have done him no harm, is only behaving as an emotionally undernourished child would behave. That adult is, in fact, an emotionally undernourished child no matter what his chronological age may be.

These impulse-ridden, angry people are said to have character disorders. The particular way in which the disorder is expressed depends on the degree of early deprivation and the time in the child's life when the deprivation occurred. It is possible that as a small, helpless infant a person might have had all the tender loving care he needed, and then when he was three lost his parents, either actually through death, or emotionally through a loss of their interest. If the adults in his life then were overdemanding during his period of discipline, he might grow up with a fair degree of self-confidence but a strong bitterness against authority, whereas a child who had never known love in infancy might spend all the rest of his life trying unconsciously to arrange circumstances so that someone had to take care of him, as though he were trying to make up for what he missed. However, both would be impulsive, resentful, hostile, demanding, and without much sensible relation to the present reality circumstances.

A deprived child can be helped if the assistance comes soon enough, before his poor attitudes are fixed and his self-doubts internalized. But the longer he is obliged to wait before he is given what he needs, the more difficult it becomes for anyone to give enough, or to give in a form which he can trust and accept. The older the deprived individual becomes without help, the harder it is to communicate with him. He will lurk behind a defensive wall which he has built to protect himself from any repetition of the hurts he experienced earlier.

That self-protective wall can be very high and very sturdy. The individual is suspicious, and so almost anything a worker can do will be construed as hurtful. This is frustrating, baffling, and exasperating to the well-intentioned caseworker who sees his client rejecting the very thing he most needs. A deprived person who has never been given any assurance that he can be found acceptable cannot easily believe repeated assurances that he really is a worthwhile person. He is full of anger and resentment at what people did to him when he was a small child, and the anger does not evaporate with time, but continues to seethe inside of him, sometimes spilling over onto the caseworker and others who want only to help. He has had bad experiences with a domineering parent, and so he resents all authority figures, no matter how reasonable the authority may now be in reality. He cannot see today's reality because his vision is distorted by yesterday's events. He once reached out for love from his mother and was rebuffed, so now he does not dare let himself love again, expecting only another rebuff.

It may take long months of patient, unrewarding effort on

the part of some concerned person, but it is often possible to reach a deprived child of three or six or ten or even fifteen, and persuade him that although some people important in his life have failed him everybody will not fail, there are people who will love him, who want things to be right for him and will work hard to make them right. When he has finally learned that not all adults are selfish or domineering and that he can risk responding to people differently, according to what each one really is, he is on the road to recovery from the consequences of his early unhappy experiences.

If a seriously deprived individual reaches adulthood without finding help, it may be almost impossible to communicate with him at all. He responds to every situation as he learned to respond to the hurtful, depriving situations of his childhood:

He is unable to discriminate between his boss, his wife, and a Hitler. This makes him angry, either consciously or unconsciously. Neither can he distinguish between situations in which anger is justified and those in which it is not. Furthermore, his reaction to his own anger is also fixed; he may, for example, react passively to any situation that might elicit his anger. This rigidity or inflexibility, this inability to discriminate among various kinds of stimuli and react to them appropriately, distinguishes the pathological character traits from the normal.[1]

Farther along in the same article, the author gives an example:

Rigidity of response can take any of several forms. There may be a fixed emotional response to a variety of situations. An example . . . is found in the person who reacts to all situations as if he were being humiliated. I recall a woman of this type. If she was accosted by a man, she felt humiliated. If she was not, she felt humiliated. If she was told what to do, it was humiliating. If she was not told what to do, she was being ignored, and this too was humiliating. If she was not able to do something, it was humiliating; if she was, it was humiliating that she had to perform such undemanding tasks.

[1]Merl M. Jackel, "Clients with Character Disorders," *Social Casework,* XLIV (1963), 317.

Regardless of the situation there was only one emotional response available to her.[2]

Somewhere along the line during her early years, this woman had faced so many humiliating experiences that she had come to expect only humiliation, and the response had become fixed until she could no longer differentiate between various kinds of experiences. Caseworkers face this type of individual often, adults who have internalized the habit of suspicion, of self-doubt, of looking for insults, of expecting rejection. All of this has grown to such proportions that an almost impregnable barrier has been built between these people and the rest of humanity whom they see, not in the light of reality, but always in the light of the people encountered in childhood. These are the clients who make insatiable demands that nothing ever completely satisfies because they cannot believe that anyone is ever really trying to satisfy them. The slightest suggestion of rejection from the caseworker will be considered a serious affront—even such an unavoidable incident as missing an appointment because of illness; even such an excusable matter as answering a telephone call during an interview.

A caseworker who attempts to help a family in which the adults show the effects of serious childhood deprivation must discipline himself to be patient, to be long suffering, to recognize that offensive words and behavior are not directed at him personally but against life in general. The caseworker must learn never to expect more from these emotionally underdeveloped people than they can actually produce, and it will not be much. The worker must necessarily set reasonable limits to the demands which the immature grownups make, since it will in any event be quite impossible to fill the bottomless need. But the worker must learn not to blame the childish adult for being childish. Such persons have never been given the emotional nourishment

[2]*Ibid.*

that would have made maturation possible. The worker above all must discipline himself against ever hitting back at these immature adults whose aggravating behavior so often seems deliberately designed to provoke a return blow. To punish such a person accomplishes nothing. It will not teach him to behave like an adult any more than smacking a screaming infant makes the infant stop crying. Punishment or criticism will never seem justified to such a client. It will only confirm his belief that everyone "picks on" him, everyone is out to get him, nothing will ever go right for him.

Beatrice Simcox Reiner and Dr. Irving Kaufman say:

Study of persons with character disorders reveals certain typical features: a history of traumatic episodes, major disturbance in psychosexual development, and a characteristic pattern of ego pathology. The trauma often includes the actual or emotional loss of parents. In our cases, the adult clients reacted as if they had been abandoned by their parents—even though the latter might be dead—and were searching for them. They seemed angry at the loss and did not as a general rule show the usual affective reaction. Instead they denied the feeling of loss while attempting to deal with it in various substitutive ways. We found no overt depression in our cases, but rather a process of denial and a resultant core of anxiety.... The characteristic pathological ego mechanisms which these clients manifested at the time of initial contact were those of denial, displacement, projection, and the repetitive compulsion of antisocial acting out. They denied the affective component of the loss of parents and displaced the anxiety onto other persons—the landlord, schoolteacher, or neighbor. In the displacement they often became involved in intense situations in which all family members took part. Some tried to narcotize the hurt by alcohol, promiscuity, or hyperactivity. The pathology included stealing and desertion. It would seem that the specific choice of symptom depends upon a variety of factors, including especially the level of psychosexual fixations and the client's particular identifications.[3]

Perhaps the characteristic which is most difficult for a caseworker to accept is the unreasonable and unreasoning pro-

[3]Beatrice Simcox Reiner and Irving Kaufman, M. D., *Character Disorders in Parents of Delinquents*, p. 10.

jection onto the worker of a hostility whose basis is actually resentment against the parent. The anger which the client shows is really not related to the worker as an individual, but that is not too easy to remember when a client has written a detailed and circumstantial letter of complaint about the worker's behavior, dress, attitude. When a client with a personality disorder feels this way—and most of them do— then nothing the caseworker does is ever thought to be right, no service he provides is enough; the client accuses him of neglect, of favoritism, of withholding relief checks for his own use, of doing any number of nefarious things, when all he ever wanted to do was offer friendship and help. This hostility may be expressed directly to the worker, or it may appear in the form of complaints to the supervisor, the agency's director, the governor of the state, or to other clients, thus sabotaging a worker's efforts to form a good relationship.

Reiner and Kaufman again say:

Working with clients with severe character disorders calls for special personal qualifications on the part of the caseworker. He must be able to tolerate the tremendous demands that these emotionally needful people make on him. He must be patient and able to curb his own anxiety and resentment and at the same time be constantly aware of his own reactions and feelings. Suppression or denial of feelings will interfere with the fluidity of communication with these clients. It is essential for the caseworker to be able to communicate both verbally and in a nonverbal symbolic way with these acting-out persons . . . . Such communication requires intuition supplemented by technical knowledge about the meaning of behavior; neither one gets far without the other.[4]

An inexperienced caseworker who encounters for the first time the unreasonable and searing hostility of a client with a personality disorder is almost certain to react with answering anger. He may be able to control his words; he may even be able to control the expression of his face, but he is sure

[4]*Ibid.*, p. 14.

to come back to the agency overwhelmed by feelings not conducive to future good work. He will either continue for days to sputter with angry self-justifications of his reactions, or he will be swamped by shame because he believes that good caseworkers never feel wrathful. The latter response probably indicates a better prognosis for a career as a helping person, but it still is not good. Of course caseworkers feel anger. And discouragement. And distaste for the less likable clients. Caseworkers are human, fortunately. It is far better to admit the resentment than to try to deny its existence, pushing it down into the subconscious where it will boil on anyway, blocking communication in ways of which the worker will not be aware. So what if the caseworker does feel angry? That may make it a little more difficult for him, but by no means impossible. He can still follow through with good casework planning. Let him admit to himself that he is upset, let him control all overt expression of his negative feelings, and then let him stop thinking about himself and put all his attention on the client. What happened to that client years ago that he should behave so unreasonably now? What suspicion and hurt and insecurity are interfering with the client's ability to see what people are really trying to do for him? We cannot easily be fond of such a client but we can be sorry for his pervading unhappiness. He is no less miserable because he is bringing it down on himself by his own attitude. Fondness is beside the point. A physician need not be fond of a difficult, uncooperative patient, but he can still try to cure the disease which is making the patient difficult. So we can handle our own impatience, our own responsive anger, and go ahead doing our best to cure, or at least to lessen, the client's personality disorder.

We have said that the manner in which a character disorder is expressed depends in part on the time in the individual's life when the deprivation was suffered. Reiner and

Kaufman say of the person whose deprivation came during the stage of dependency:

The person... presents problems to everyone. To himself he presents the problems of depressed feelings, a haunting sense of childishness and failure, and a feeling of being an outcast. He gives inconsistent nurture to his children when they are young and is unable to help them with their later problems of development. He offers them a faulty ego ideal since his own weak ego results in lack of impulse control and confused perception of reality.

These persons present problems to the community. They often need financial assistance and free medical care. They are in conflict with various community standards and frequently they themselves and their children come to the attention of the courts. They present special problems to the social worker who attempts to help them with any of these problems. They are difficult to engage in a relationship and when a relationship is established considerable time and patient work are required before their patterns of behavior begin to change. Agencies are in a difficult position in dealing with their disturbed behavior since it not only creates many real difficulties but often tends to provoke retaliation on the part of the staff who may exhibit ... punishment in ways which recapitulate the pathology rather than working it through.[5]

However, if the caseworker has the patience and self-control to follow a few rules there is some chance of eventually helping such an immature adult begin to feel, think, and behave somewhat more like an adult human being. An individual who has been deprived in babyhood and who has had nothing during childhood to help him catch up with what he missed earlier may never really function like a completely adequate person, but perhaps he can be helped to take a step or two toward the kind of behavior which will enable him to hold a job, avoid such obvious traps as alcoholism, and relate in some sort of acceptable fashion with his own family.

Here are some of the rules, and they are not easy to follow:

1. The caseworker must not let such a client feel abandoned.

[5]*Ibid.*, p. 36.

Since he is inclined to feel that way with or without reason, this takes unremitting, alert attention on the part of the caseworker, who must avoid giving the slightest excuse for the client to think himself deserted. Never permit too much time to elapse between contacts. Make frequent appointments, and keep them without fail. Missing an appointment, no matter how valid the excuse, will certainly be construed by the immature client as desertion. It may take weeks of careful, attentive relationship to rebuild the shaken confidence after one missed appointment. If the client himself misses an appointment, as he certainly will, and often, the worker should telephone or visit him soon afterward, not to scold him for upsetting the schedule, but to reassure him of continued concern and interest.

2. If such a client shows an inclination to pour out emotional material, the caseworker must be noncommittal. Any individual whose unhappy early experiences have taught him to be skeptical of everybody's good intentions may well be frightened after he has opened the way for a close relationship. So be interested, but not too much so. Be casual and matter-of-fact until the client himself shows that he no longer fears that his confidences will be used as a basis for jeering at him or hurting him again as he has so often been hurt before. On the other hand, of course, his expression of emotion should not be cut off. That would be considered rejection. And do not be surprised if the client withdraws into his shell for weeks after he has poured out confidences. Do not bring up the confidential material but maintain a steady, matter-of-fact concern for him and let him come back at his own pace.

3. The caseworker should participate actively in helping to solve reality problems, such as housing, employment, medical needs. This may involve actually making appointments with an employment agency, with a doctor or a clinic, and perhaps going with the client if he seems confused or unsure of himself. Remember, this type of client is no more able than a

small child would be to plan wisely or operate independently. These insecure, angry people have been given no assurance when such assurance would have counted most.

4. The worker should share the client's interests whatever they may be—sports, politics, pets, sewing, dress style, physical symptoms, anything.

5. The worker must be patient with the "demand feeding" but necessarily hold within the framework of what is realistic. Avoid the fantasy of being the all-giving. One demanding client can take a disproportionate amount of any caseworker's time and can be a tremendous drain on any caseworker's emotional energy. A practical balance must be found between the needs of this client and the needs of all the others on the caseload—and the perfectly justifiable need of the caseworker to find some opportunity to recharge his own batteries.

For caseworkers attempting to help people with character disorders it is a long, hard pull, sometimes with little or no visible reward. Often it is only through indirect hints that the worker can see that he is achieving some small success in his efforts to build a relationship through which he can help. Reiner and Kaufman give a few suggestions of how we may see that success is on the way:

The signs differ with different clients, but one or more of the following actions or attitudes on the part of the client will indicate that there have been some significant gains in the relationship.

A request for help in some reality issue

Evidence of caring about what the caseworker thinks

Quoting the caseworker (either explicitly as "As you said" or implicitly in a dialogue with someone else)

Ability to tolerate the caseworker's encouragement to look at reality

A more relaxed and less guarded attitude—possibly venturing some humor

Admission that he could be wrong (even if he doesn't mean it completely)

Entrusting the caseworker with a confidence

Willingness to begin to give background information (which he withheld before)

Coming to the appointments more regularly and on time.

Any of these signs means that the client has begun to avail himself of the ego-nourishing supply offered by the caseworker who has tried to convey "You matter to me" and "You will not be left to cope alone." The shift means that the client has sufficiently relaxed his fears of closeness, trusting, or dependency, to begin cautiously to resume the process of growth and maturation through a relationship with a substitute parent figure.[6]

[6]*Ibid.*, p. 93.

XXV

MANAGEMENT OF MONEY

A large proportion of social work clients find themselves involved in money problems — either lack of sufficient cash to meet the rising cost of living, or inefficiency in handling what resources are available, or both. Automation or a change of industrial procedures may put employment out of the reach of an older man. Inadequate training or education may close the labor market for others, young or old. Mental slowness, physical disabilities, or emotional maladjustment may put still others out of the running.

Whether or not delinquency, marital discord, poor health, alcoholism, or other personality problems are the results of economic insufficiency or the cause of it, the fact remains that money problems inevitably aggravate whatever other difficulties exist. So help toward the wise handling of money becomes one of the tools of casework in handling situations that are not purely financial.

The first step is for the social worker really to understand what the client is facing, and that is not always easy. Understanding must go deeper than an awareness of the need for more food or better housing. In general, caseworkers come from the middle and upper-middle economic brackets. Many of them have been brought up in families that may have thought twice before buying a second car or planning a European tour, but usually the father had a steady income, there was never any real doubt but that payments would be made on the home, or that the table would be set with three nourishing meals a day. Because there might have been an hour or two of tension on the first of the month when father went over the bills, these workers may feel that they know what money problems are, but they are actually a long way from any true empathy with the chronically impoverished. Another, smaller, group have really felt an economic pinch. Perhaps they worked their way through college and had to forego fraternities and social clubs, movies and dinner dates. These come closer to a realization of the effect that low income may have on one's way of life, but there is still an important difference between these workers and their impoverished clients. The workers had strong motivation, and they had skills adequate to getting the utmost out of every penny spent. So these workers, too, have much to learn about the situation, the feelings, the attitudes of the client group that lacks both skill in management and motivation to endure.

A few years ago a newspaper reporter became exercised over publicity concerning the meager welfare grants in his city. He set out to prove whether or not a family could live on a welfare grant. He put his family on the same food budget which the agency gave to families of similar size, and for two weeks his paper published the daily menu that his wife prepared, and the cost. At the end of the time he felt that he had proved that meals on a welfare budget would be adequate, healthful, and appetizing, with enough variety to avoid monotony. I do not remember whether he started his experiment without a supply of staples, such as sugar and flour, but I hope he did, for clients have no backlog of such items to rely on. I do not know whether he figured in the gas bills and the cost of refrigeration. I cannot remember whether he carried on his experiment in summer when fruit and vegetables are comparatively cheap, or in the winter when clients who live in ramshackle cold-water flats need extra nourishment to maintain body heat. But I do know that he failed to take into consideration several items which affect the client group.

First, his wife probably had more facilities for economical shopping and meal preparation than housewives who have to walk, not drive, to the stores, dragging one or two or three preschool children with them. She surely possessed more skills than clients whose grade-school education has not equipped them to compute prices quickly as they select food from the shelves, who have no training in dietary needs, and who have to struggle with feeble refrigerators, balky stoves, and pots and pans of poor quality.

Second, the reporter's family accepted the welfare budget voluntarily, as an experiment. The welfare family is not where it is by choice, and may well be overwhelmed by bitter feelings of resentment, anger, hate, and hopelessness which sap emotional energy.

Third, the reporter's family went on the welfare budget after a life of comparative comfort. They were all aware that they could drop the experiment whenever they wished and would certainly drop it in a few weeks. This puts quite a different color on the whole affair. A welfare family may never have had the slightest leeway in money matters, and know that they are not likely to have as long as they live. There must always, day after dreary day, be cautious, calculated shopping, extreme economy in meal preparation with never a slip, never a moment of relaxing the watchfulness. It must go on—and on—and on. This inevitably produces a completely different mood.

Fourth, I do not know how the reporter explained things to his children, but even if he held them firmly away from movies or any other entertainment that cost money, refused to allow candy or snacks, they must have known that it would all be over in a short while, and they could look back on the experience and make it a conversation piece. It is not a conversation piece for welfare kids who never have enough money to justify indulgences. A Saturday afternoon movie, even an ice cream cone, means that much less to spend for required nutrition. Parents on welfare have to say "No" and "No" and "No" over and over to children who find it difficult to understand why they cannot do what their companions do. This can never be easy, and may be impossible for parents, themselves emotionally immature, who lack the strength to be consistent with themselves, let alone with their children.

These comments are presented, not as a criticism of the reporter's well-intentioned and useful test, but to point out to social workers the areas which such an experiment does not touch.

Again, before any social worker can help a client, he must have some understanding of what the client is struggling with, his inner as well as his external problems. Schneiderman points out the differences between the life style of the impoverished and that of middle-class society. The two groups think and feel and act from divergent premises:

The study suggests ... that the public school teachers and social workers who serve the impoverished may be engaged in an intercultural enterprise and that the problems in communication and joint goal setting are to be expected as a consequence of beginning from different first assumptions about life and its major themes and organizing values. The points of significant differentiation of the culture of poverty from that dominant in the general community include (1) an inclination to subject oneself to, or to live in harmony with what is seen as natural or given in life, as opposed to the view of man as master over the forces of his social and physical world that has characterized American life; (2) an inclination to focus on activity as a relatively free expression of what is conceived as given in human personality, stressing spontaneous nondevelopmental conception of activity in contrast with the doing, accomplishing go-getting attitudes so valued in American life; and (3) an inclination to emphasize present time and present concerns over the requirements of either past or future in contrast to the typical American concern for future planning.[1]

[1]Leonard Schneiderman, "Value Orientation Preferences of Chronic Relief Recipients," *Social Work*, IX, No. 3 (1964), 13.

What this means to the caseworker is that he must understand that more often than not the family which has been poor all its life will see no possibility of ever being anything but poor, and therefore will see no value in making any effort toward improving its circumstances. This chronic hopelessness, this accepting as inevitable what now is, can be expected to affect behavior. Why struggle, why make sacrifices today if tomorrow will be just the same no matter what one tries to do now? Why plan, why scrimp and save when life will certainly come crashing down on one's head tomorrow as it has all of one's yesterdays? Why not go to the movies today and eat popcorn and ice cream today? Tomorrow we may be dead or in jail.

Most caseworkers come from a culture that operates from a different major premise. They have learned from infancy to look toward the future: "Better not eat that chocolate now. You can have two chocolates after supper." "Do your homework now. Then you can go out and play without having to worry about it." "Study hard this year and you have a good chance to win a scholarship." "Plan on college. You can get much better jobs with a college degree." "Save a little each month and you'll have enough for a down payment on a home of your own."

People who have spent their childhood in families with no habit of thinking toward the future, with no special motive for controlling immediate impulses and desires, will not easily acquire a new life style in adulthood. This does not mean that it is hopeless for a caseworker to attempt to help these clients to plan. It does mean that before any success can be achieved, the caseworker must have some feeling for, some awareness of, the client's life style, the premises from which his attitudes and behavior stem.

It is worse than useless for a caseworker to go into the home of the impoverished and say, "You must stop spending your money for beer. You must pay your light bills and the rent." In one form or another, in behavior if not in words, the client will retort: "You don't understand. You don't know how we feel. We *need* the beer. The kids have to have candy — or the movies — or a television set. They have to have *some* fun. What would life be without it? If we get evicted, so what! This flat isn't so much anyway. There's cockroaches in the sink, and the toilet won't work half the time and landlord doesn't come to plaster the ceiling. If we get thrown out we'll find something else. What have we to lose? Let's have a little fun today."

The caseworker's first task is to try to give the client sufficient motivation to make an effort toward planfulness, toward thinking of the future as a time when things will be better, toward making sacrifices today gor the sake of to-morrow's reward. The worker must be practical and realistic. Because the client has no pattern of hope it is no easy matter to provide him with any solid reason for planfulness. It is a little less difficult if the client has known better times in the past. Perhaps this man once when he was a boy had a paper route and enough money to spend as he wished; perhaps this woman once enjoyed a holiday on a farm and can recall what a well-ordered household is like. If there is any experience in the past worth clinging to, the caseworker should search it out and help the client cling.

The caseworker must allow for individual habits and tastes. Country people, transplanted to the city from a farm where whole milk was plentiful, will not take kindly to the less expensive evaporated product. It takes patience to per-suade them to try it. Housewives from old Italy will not willingly give up using imported olive oil. Jewish people must have Kosher food although sometimes it is more expensive.

It is easier to work out a budget on paper than it is to translate it into practice, and the caseworker must be at all times sensitive to the meaning to the client, both of money itself as a symbol and of the particular items for which the money is being spent. Frances Feldman says:

Money itself does not bring happiness. Nor does its limited availability inevitably bring unhappiness. Its absence may produce anxiety and tension . . . . Money is a powerful symbol, representing both love and protection and the gratification of normal dependency needs. It is an equally powerful means of gratifying infantile wishes and of expressing hostility.[2]

Again, she says that "what seems on the surface to be self-indulgence may be a gratification of dependency needs" or, for that matter, of a strong urge to establish status that will augment the ego image.

Rhys Davies[3] tells a story about the wife of a Welsh miner who nagged her husband into buying an organ which nobody could play so that she could brag that her house had the only organ in the row. I myself knew a farmer in a remote region who went to considerable financial sacrifice to buy a refrigerator as a special gift for his wife although there was no electricity in his home and no prospect of electric lines running in.

Sensible? Certainly not. But humanity is not noted for being sensible, and motivation based on emotion is far stronger than any based on common sense. There are times when a caseworker must give priority to the items which are important to the client even at the sacrifice of something which seems to the worker eminently more desirable.

A family applied for relief, claiming that the man's income was insufficient to pay the rent and provide food. It was found that they had recently purchased — on time, of course — a new bedroom suite, an overstuffed sofa and two chairs, a rug, and a television set. Monthly payments to the finance

[2]Frances Lomas Feldman, *The Family in a Money World,* p. 32.
[3]Rhys Davies, "Mrs. Evans, Number Six," in *A Pig in a Poke,* p. 145.

company used up so large a proportion of the pay check that there was not enough left for necessities. Because the man's income was sufficient to meet the family's basic budget for food, rent, and clothing they were not eligible for assistance from a public agency, but they did need counseling. It took a number of interviews with a patient, tactful intake worker before the family could be nudged into recognition that they were paying far too high a price for the status they enjoyed with their new furniture, considering the interest charges of the finance company, the anxiety and tensions created by the money shortage. Of course, the family brought up the matter of losing the money already paid for the furniture, but in the end they were persuaded to allow the finance company to repossess the bedroom suite, the rug, and the chairs. They clung to the sofa and the television set. They replaced their sacrificed furniture with usable secondhand pieces and with the help of the intake worker drew up a budget which permitted them to make the payments they had to make and still have enough left for food and rent.

Sometimes it is easier for the caseworker to help than it was in the case of this family. It depends on the client's motivation. A mother had become aware that her children suffered from too many upper respiratory infections. The visiting nurse told her that they would have more resistance if they had a better diet. But, the mother wept as she talked to the caseworker, how could she manage to buy orange juice and more milk and high-protein foods on her welfare allowance? Each month her check went to pay the rent and last month's grocery bill, and then she had to rely on credit again until the next check came. The grocer did not like to charge expensive items like fruit juice and ground steak. In this case the mother had strong motivation in her sincere desire to keep her children healthy. The worker had no need to persuade. He had only to work out the means. He arranged for free milk from the school once a day for the children, went with the mother to the grocery store, and helped her make out a practical shopping list that included fruit, chopped meat, and high-protein cereals but omitted cookies, cupcakes, and pop.

Another family was threatened with eviction for nonpayment of rent. They did not want to move because the children were getting on well in school for the first time and it would be, they said, a shame to take them out now and make them start all over some other place. The worker figured out a budget that allowed for a small payment each month on the back rent while keeping up with current expenses, and he persuaded the landlord to accept the arrangement. The implementation of this plan involved frequent visits by the caseworker to the family to encourage them to stick even approximately to the difficult budget. But in this situation, too, the family had motivation that kept them trying.

The help which the caseworker provides must be practical, specific, and realistic, sometimes going beyond the more obvious call of duty. A widowed father whose twelve-year-old daughter was living in a group home wanted to buy a pair of fancy party shoes for her. He visited her every Saturday afternoon but never managed to hang on to enough money from his Friday pay check to get the shoes. He told the caseworker that he always went straight home from work on Fridays, paid the landlord for his next week's board, and then went out "with the boys." Somehow the money was always nearly gone by the next day. So the caseworker suggested that if he really wanted to save for the shoes he should stop in at the office on his way home from work on Fridays and leave what he thought he could spare, taking the rest to pay for his board and his Friday night spree. The caseworker would hold the money for him. The father agreed, and the plan worked. He not only saved enough for the shoes but over the weeks deposited enough with the caseworker to buy a number of pretties for the daughter and even a new suit for himself. For the worker, this involved waiting a half hour after work every Friday, but it was worth it to see the father's pride when he was able to get things for his daughter.

If clients, like this father, are already strongly motivated to handle money, the battle is more than half won. Nevertheless, the other half may involve patience, sympathy, and understanding on the part of the worker. He must never expect too much. A woman who is overweight, has varicose veins, badly fitting shoes, and no bus fare, is not going to get herself to a supermarket six blocks from her home. She will shop in the neighborhood store even though prices are higher. A woman who can barely read will not write out menus for a week in advance, nor will she follow a shopping list unless the caseworker is able to go to the store with her many times to teach her how to select the proper food. A man who knows he has not enough money to buy all the food he would like to have will choose potatoes or something cheap and bulky that will fill his stomach for less outlay of cash. A mother overburdened with the care of too many children in too small a flat, too much work to do with too little equipment, will select foods that can be prepared fast with the least labor—cold cereal, hot dogs.

Keep the goal close, not too far in the future. Clients who are not accustomed to thinking about tomorrow can hardly be expected to visualize next year. Cold beer and an air-conditioned movie have more appeal in July than the winter coat which will be needed next December. Today's temptations will override a reward too far removed. So talk about the socks and underclothes the children need today.

Most clients with money problems will think that they are already doing everything that can be done to make their allowance stretch. Probably a great deal of their energy will go into bewailing their unhappy lot, or blaming society, or the welfare, or the company boss, for not making an easier life possible. The worker must listen to their complaints without argument, and stand ready to redirect the conversation if the complaints seem to be going round and round and never coming out anywhere. Perhaps the worker can interject some such remark as, "Well, I know how you feel, but we have to live with things as they are. Suppose you and I see what we can do to make things easier for you right now."

In any event, the caseworker must see the client's point of view; for almost certainly the client is struggling with problems, social, economic, emotional, which the caseworker has never faced, but which he can imagine if he makes the effort.

XXVI

COUNSELING THE FAMILY OF A MENTALLY RETARDED PERSON

Mental retardation is a condition in which the brain is either arrested in development (as in Mongolism) or damaged for many other known or unknown causes and therefore is unable to function to its fullest capacity. Mental retardation is not a disease, contagious or otherwise. It is not to be confused with mental illness. The person afflicted by mental retardation has no special behavior characteristics per se; that is, he is not emotionally disturbed, a sexually deviant, delinquent, abnormally fat, and so forth, merely because he is retarded. However, he may become any one of these through environmental influences. He differs from the normal population primarily in his mental slowness and in his lower level of competence. Mental retardation is not necessarily inherited though it may be due to inherent factors.

According to the report to the late President Kennedy, there are some 5.5 million retardates in the United States and approximately 126,000 retarded babies are born each year. Much has been done to decrease the number of mentally retarded and the degree of involvement through prevention and control of known causes. Early detection is tremendously important. Today an operation can eliminate or alleviate the damage done by hydrocephaly; a properly adjusted diet will minimize the damage caused by phenylketonuria; and proper prenatal and postnatal care will prevent or lessen the damage caused by lack of oxygen, excessive drugs, harmful drugs, blood incompatibility, over-exposure to X-rays, or caused by specific diseases to which the expectant mother is exposed. Also, a great deal is being done to improve the performance of the child who is a retardate because of social and cultural deprivation.

Unfortunately, all the causes of mental retardation have not yet been discovered, nor is it possible to eliminate all that are already known. It is estimated that 15 percent of our population are afflicted by mental retardation; this condition respects neither race, color, nationality, creed, nor social or economic background. Rare indeed is the case-worker who will not at sometime need to counsel a family or an individual affected by this condition. He will find that counseling in this situation will be probably more difficult than counseling when other handicaps are present, though it will be similar. This is so because this particular handicap is not only lifelong, but generally incurable and pregnant with the emotions of guilt, shame, antagonism, and fear—all of which are caused by misconceptions regarding retardation, the attitudes and behaviors of society, and the universal adulation of intelligence. The parents of a retardate, having been rebuffed, or misdirected, or finding all doors closed, and having the need for a scapegoat, will often direct their hostitily toward the caseworker. He must be aware that this attitude is not necessarily personal, and he must be mature enough and skillful enough to handle it.

The knowledge that the baby so long anticipated with joy and high expectations is retarded, that their dreams and hopes are for naught, is a disastrous, traumatic and unacceptable experience to any parent. Following this shock comes the threat to the personal image of self-worth held by each parent. The degree of humiliation and guilt which ensues is determined by the individual's background and adjustment. This experience will produce far greater anxiety in a college professor, for instance, than in a school dropout. The resistances to these threatening and fearful feelings are expressed by laying the blame elsewhere. Simultaneously, several reactions take place. The parents are certain that the doctor or the hospital was either negligent or wrong, so a "shopping" tour is undertaken to find someone who will say that the first diagnosis was inaccurate, or someone who will have a miracle cure. These avenues being exhausted, often even God becomes the scapegoat. The unanswerable question is, "Why me? I don't deserve it. He can't do this to me!" Even the mate may be blamed as the source of the tragedy, causing untold damage to the marital harmony, and thus affecting the entire home atmosphere. If the parent or parents arrive at this crisis with poor background (see Chapter XI), defeat can be complete, and the family will be totally disintegrated.

Mr. and Mrs. X. present an excellent example of such inadequacy. Mr. X. had been raised by an alcoholic mother who spent so much money on liquor that her children went hungry and poorly clothed. In his childhood Mr. X. had been picked up by policemen a number of times for selling newspapers long after normal curfew hours for little boys. Mrs. X. was raised by an inadequate father who rationalized his financial incompetence by asserting, "God will provide." After his death, her family lived on welfare until her mother remarried. Unfortunately, she and her stepfather deeply hated each other. Her marriage was an acceptable method of "getting out." After their marriage these two insecure, immature adults, of the Jewish faith, moved into what they decided was an anti-Semitic neighborhood, and although they formed several close associations they continued to feel rejected. Two boys were born to Mr. and Mrs. X. Finally, with much personal sacrifice and determination, the X.'s were able to buy a home in a status-satisfying suburban area. They gained even greater status by joining a prestige Temple. Six months later a microcephalic son was born to them. By the time this retarded child reached two years of age, the father was about to be fired from his position; the mother was on the verge of a nervous breakdown; and the two brothers were having difficulties with the school authorities because of their poor academic performances, despite their high IQ levels, and because of poor personal adjustments to others. The family used the retarded child as the "whipping boy." It was only by removing this child from the home, and persuading both parents to accept psychiatric therapy voluntarily, that the immediate social and physical pressures were relieved.

If the caseworker enters into a counseling role after the original reactions have become rationalized, and after interpersonal behavior patterns have become habitual and subconscious, he may find that the inadequate mother, or the mother who has lost her self-image, has done nothing for her child except, possibly, provide good custodial care. The mother who has refused to recognize her child's condition will have rationalized that he is an infant, and she will keep him so; or she will make excessive demands of him which will create frustrations and confusion in the child, and will increase her hostility for what she labels "laziness" or deliberate resistance. The mother who has rejected this child will have buried her antagonism very deeply and will present an image of a very concerned, self-sacrificing parent who is to be highly commended.

Extreme overprotectiveness may be one of the visual evidences of this reaction. At the time the agency became active in the case of the Y. family the retarded daughter was fourteen years of age, about 5′ 3″ tall, and weighing 134 pounds. This girl slept in a very low double bed with specially constructed sides, in the manner of a crib, to protect her from injury should she fall out of bed. A gate, such as those used to confine babies and puppies, was placed across her bedroom doorway so that if she should get out of bed during the night, she could not wander into some other part of the house and get hurt. The top of this gate was thickly padded as a further protection should she fall against it. The parents never left her, going out only to places where they could take her. They had had an occasional babysitter until she was eight years old. At that time, the sitter was dismissed because she had dared to encourage the child to get into a chair by herself. Mrs. Y. was horrified at the potential danger to her child. Having fired the sitter, Mrs. Y. has never hired another since no one can be trusted to give her child the solicitous care she feels is needed. Though the girl has the neccessary mental and physical capacity to perform many independent acts, Mrs. Y. still feeds her, bathes her, and dresses her. Mrs. Y.'s first comment to the counselor in her home was, "My friends think I am foolish to have you come. Since I take such good care of my daughter, I should be teaching you."

While this is only a partial delineation of the emotional reactions and some of their ramifications, one can readily understand the need of parents of a retarded child to have a supportive, nonjudging, understanding friend. They need help for their catharsis. The verbalization of their guilts, shame, and fears is necessary before comfortable inter-personal relationships can be established in the family. *Any attempt to belittle or ignore the impact of a retarded child on a family would be a foolish mistake.*

Much has been done for retardation in the past ten years. A family given knowledge of what retardation is, what its implications and limitations are, what its future holds, and what can be done about it now, will be able to help their child attain his maximum growth. Nor will they need to feel rejected by their God or their society. It is possible for a retarded child to fit into his relative place within his family hierarchy without a disproportionate amount of concern and care at the expense of his siblings. This can only be done, however, when healthy, positive attitudes of expectation and understanding are consistently maintained.

How does a caseworker do this? First, he must induce catharsis by whoever is involved. Second, he must interpret retardation and impart knowledge of what is to be done. Third, he should provide the family with an opportunity for association with other families of retarded children because of its therapeutic value.

In addition, the family must be given continual support and specific activity to perform. Knowing that this retarded child is more like other children than he is different from them and that he follows the exact patterns and stages of development that other children do is not sufficient. Nor is it sufficient to recommend the use of good common sense adapted to the needs of the retarded child. The parents must know that this child will not reach out for the world, it must be brought to him. A child who spends all of his time in a crib on his back will be further delayed in his development. Informed parents can and do have relaxed, happy, contributing families. They know that today's knowledge finds the retardate performing far beyond what was previously believed possible. However, experience proves that achievement does not occur in a negative atmosphere. Attitudes of the "poor-little-thing" variety only serve to undermine the child's self-image. It becomes mandatory to stress the child's similarities to other children and his need to adjust his differences. Unfortunately, too often parent and teacher alike point up these differences by permitting unsatisfactory personal appearance and by accepting a poor performance without providing opportunity to improve either. Then too, "readiness" has been improperly accepted as a primary factor in learning. As a result, no opportunity for development has been offered while waiting for this maturation. Lost and forgotten has been the fact that readiness is also the result of learning and that basic preskills and knowledge must exist before readiness is activated. For example, a child who is kept in a crib will not crawl; a child who is never offered a spoon will not feed himself, nor will a child who has not been taught such matters toilet-train himself. Furthermore, the child whose gutteral mutterings and gestures are always understood will have no motivation to undertake speech.

Over and above this, the retarded child must also be trained with gentle firmness to conform to specific rules and limitations if he is to be acceptable to, as well as accepting of, his society. He blooms in an atmosphere of praise, though he learns well by failure too. Consistent discipline is essential to this child's development. Discipline is not simply a question of "to spank or not to spank"; it is one method of setting acceptable patterns of behavior. The retarded child learns rules and limits best when privileges are withheld and objects that cause frustration and anger are removed. Since he is generally a gregarious person, effective methods of control are established by ignoring or isolating him. Parents need interpretation to understand that a child of five or six years of age cannot be allowed to continue at the two to three year level of behavior, although he may only have the mental age of two to three years. Barring physical or pathological complications, a six-year-old retarded child can be expected to be ambulatory, toilet-trained, and able to make his wants known. He should have mastered many self-help skills in eating and dressing. He should have learned to recognize possession (mine and thine) and abide by realistic rules of right and wrong. By the same token, however, this child must not be exploited nor allowed to become the scapegoat of all the ills and failures of his family.

What of the sibling of a retardate? Where does he fit in the family? Public misconception holds that he is destined for delinquency, maladjustments, and substandard performance. While it may be true that he can be filled with anger, frustration, and shame, these are not necessary reactions to retardation. As with anyone, it is his environment that makes him so.

It is the experience of the author that families, relatives, neighbors, and friends reflect the attitudes of the parents (usually the mother's) toward the retarded child. The belligerent parent will look for evidence of nonacceptance. Rejection is seen in what may be no more than reluctance to intrude on the family's privacy. The unrealistic parent will be offended if her child is not accepted, regardless of his behavior. More often than not, unfair demands of high performance are made of the sibling. No wonder he becomes frustrated and confused. However, the home in which the retarded child is recognized as being only one member, and is kept in his rightful place in the family hierarchy, has no "problem" siblings. Neither does the sibling have difficulty if realistic attitudes and acceptance are established, and if his responsibilities are not too great. In the home that draws the sibling into this problem and receives from him some help with it, and also experiences community acceptance, the total family unit becomes strengthened and enriched. The problems of the family, if any, stem from family weakness or environmental causes rather than from living with a retarded child.

One cannot at this point overlook the continuing need for residential custodial care for some retardates despite its excessive cost and the documented superior performance produced by at-home care. This group of retardates will include the profoundly retarded person whose performance at best will be minimal; the burden of his care becomes physically and

emotionally impossible for the whole family. It will also include the orphaned retardate for whom the sibling, if any,
has no legal obligation. It will also include the retardate whose
family is characteristically weak and whose mental health is
so poor that his continued presence in the home only produces further anxiety. This family must be relieved of this
added pressure, if only on a temporary basis. However, this
is easier said than done. By implication, our culture regards
institutionalization as the complete negation of family love
and responsibility. At the very least, the institution is regarded
as a "black hole of Calcutta" and its inmates as doomed to a
living death. The total family needs interpretation of the
institution as a residential care and training center wherein
a retardate receives better care and training than his home is
equipped to give.

The institution must be seen as a place wherein the retardate has twenty-four-hour supervision in an accepting atmosphere. The institution also offers him additional opportunity for association and competitive activities at his level.
Parents should be encouraged to visit the institution and
helped to understand that the degree of whiteness of the
linen is relatively unimportant. By contrast, judgment should
be made of the interrelationships of staff to retardate, retardate to staff, and retardate to retardate in this setting. Because of the subconscious attitudes created by our society
regarding the out-of-home placement, the caseworker must
never make the mistake of emphasizing the advantages of this
plan for either the parent or the other siblings. This again
will increase the ambivalence of the family. Strangely enough,
regardless of religious background, most families will more
easily accept placement in a Catholic institution. This too is
a culturally borne attitude because nuns are seen as dedicated
by vocational choice to serving their fellow man.

In conclusion, several points should be noted: One must

not forget the importance to the retardate of acquiring skills that will enrich his leisure time. A number of studies of retardates returned from institutions to jobs in their community show that the usual reason for failure to adjust is not job incompetence, but difficulties created during the retardate's free time.

A family should be urged to seek legal advice in making a will. Many a time the settlement of an estate has been prolonged and unsatisfactorily adjusted because a retardate has been adjudged incapable of making sound decisions in his own self-interest.

Finally, a caseworker who counsels the family of a retardate must keep abreast of what is happening in this field. Interest and research have become tremendously accelerated, and no one, not even the "expert," is certain what tomorrow will bring. Regardless of the future discovery of cures for retardation, the retardates in our society today will remain with us, and the caseworker should conscientiously attempt to alleviate the social, changing, lifelong problem of the family of a retardate.

Above all, one must not forget that the retardate, even more than the normal child, is uncanny in his sensitivity and will respond to the expectations held for him.

XXVII

NEW SUPERVISORS

Any social worker who moves from the position of caseworker to that of supervisor faces personal adjustment which for some is very difficult and for all demands self-awareness. As a caseworker, he has had direct, face-to-face contact with the client. He has seen with his own eyes the client's response; he has applied his own intuitive powers as well as his experience and knowledge in determining the client's emotional needs, in sensing the client's ability to use help, in recognizing the moment when the client is ready to move along independently. To a caseworker, much of the reward for the daily expending of emotional energy comes from actually seeing the growth of internal strengths in the client, of actually feeling the importance of the client–worker relationship which has made the growth possible.

To a supervisor, none of that is directly available. There are compensations, of course, but there is an unavoidable loss of contact with the client. This the newly appointed supervisor must recognize and accept. He must resolve his feelings about "losing the client."

From the moment that the new appointee takes his chair behind the supervisor's desk he must learn to work through a third person. He must make it very clear to his former clients that he is no longer the one with whom direct contacts are to be made, to whom information of any new developments is to be given. The supervisor must resist the temptation to accept telephone calls from clients or interview those who drop in without appointment. The new supervisor must not have direct contact with a client unless a real emergency comes up when his caseworker is not available, and even then the supervisor must make it clear that the message will be relayed to the worker, who will continue with the case. For some new supervisors this renunciation is not easy, especially if the client is one with whom he has worked previously. All sorts of rationalizations will come to mind. One cannot be rude to a client. One must not let a client feel rejected. The caseworker is inexperienced and cannot handle the situation. Nevertheless, transferring a case can and must be done without rudeness or rejection. It is the agency which must not reject a troubled client, and the new supervisor must learn to accomplish the agency's objective through a third person. Any interference on the part of a supervisor, no matter how well meaning, will decrease the strength of the new caseworker's relationship with the client, will tend to weaken that worker's confidence in himself, and will threaten his initiative. Since so much of effective casework depends on the use of relationship, nothing must be permitted to dim that relationship for the caseworker who is now doing the direct casework.

The supervisor must learn to see the client's situation through the eye of his worker. The diagnostic skills which made him a good caseworker must now be applied to the task of understanding the caseworker. The satisfactions he had from seeing the client develop strengths must now be earned through seeing the caseworker develop skill and initiative. The supervisor must avoid trying to make the caseworker a replica of himself. He must understand the effect that the worker's unique personality is having on the client. The supervisor must adapt his demands, his guidance, his teaching, to what the caseworker needs in order to do the best job of which he is capable.

A casework supervisor in a welfare agency has threefold obligations:

Administration. — The supervisor must see to it that the standards of the agency are maintained and that the services for which the agency is responsible are adequately provided. Because supervisors should have very little direct contact with the client, this obligation must be met indirectly, through a third person, the caseworker. Since the over-all agency control of its coverage depends on the administrator's acquaintance with reports and statistics, the supervisor must make certain that these are made out accurately by the worker and submitted on time. Visits to clients must be frequent enough to make worker and supervisor aware of any changes in the client's situation. Records must be dictated and kept up to date. For all of this the supervisor is accountable, and this necessarily involves a certain amount of checking up on the performance of workers who may forget or procrastinate or just plain not know what needs doing or how to do it. A supervisor's job frankly has policing in it — perhaps one percent of policing to 99 percent of other duties. The policing aspect should be admitted and openly discussed between supervisor and worker. It will be more acceptable to the worker if he is aware of it from the outset, and it will be far less frightening than it would be did it not filter down from top-level administration through the supervisor.

Evaluation. — The supervisor has a responsibility to the client, but again, since he works through a third person, there must be a repeated taking stock of where the worker is and where he is going in his professional development. The supervisor must take continued inventory of the worker's strengths and constantly study devices for building up those strengths. This, in turn, involves the establishing of a smooth, friendly working relationship between worker and supervisor. The final goal of the evaluative process is to encourage self-awareness on the part of the worker, a self-criticism possible only if there is mutual respect, honesty, and liking between supervisor and worker. Without these, the worker's defenses will surely come up, and the supervisor will be faced with a solid wall of denial, projection, or rationalization. Every supervisory conference should include something of the evaluative process. By a frequent sharing of evaluation, whether favorable or negative, the supervisor provides the worker with an opportunity to know what is expected of him and how he is measuring up, and it gives the supervisor a chance to see how the worker reacts to praise or criticism. When comments are negative, does the worker deny, project, become crushed and hopeless, or does he accept them and figure out how to improve? Repeated evaluation of small areas of the worker's performance can help to bring home to him the fact that he is not expected to be perfect immediately and that he is expected to continue to grow and develop and learn. If the evaluation has been on-going, the caseworker need not be surprised or upset at the end of the trial period when the formal written evaluation is presented. And do not forget that evaluations can be positive, too, providing satisfactions for work well done.

One useful device for making the evaluation meaningful to the worker is to have him write out his own evaluation, to be discussed along with the supervisor's evaluation. Doing this promotes self-awareness and encourages the worker to study and assess his own progress. Long before the end of the probationary period the worker should have a pretty clear idea of what is expected of him and should be able to note his performance against the agency standard. Before he can do this, however, the supervisor must have been able to show the worker that his individuality is accepted, that perfection is not expected, that he can learn from his own mistakes.

Teaching. — Although this aspect of a supervisor's job can and should overlap the other two areas, it might be termed the most important part of supervision. A new worker must be provided with the factual tools of his trade—knowledge of the welfare law, agency policies, and the responsibilities and legal limitations of the agency. He must learn about agency and community resources. These are specific matters which the supervisor will tell the worker about and will explain, probably several times over since it is not to be expected that a new worker plunged into the complications of a social work job will remember all the details from hearing them once. On the other hand, a supervisor must walk a careful line between exasperating the worker by belaboring things he already knows, and taking for granted that he knows when he does not, thus leaving him confused and insecure.

Of even more importance than the factual information which a supervisor must impart is the attitude, the point of view, the feeling tone, which it is his responsibility to relay. He must help the worker systematize ideas, develop disciplined ways of thinking; above all, he must nudge the worker gently toward those attitudes and feelings which will become the foundation of good casework and without which all the techniques in the world would be useless.

It is this third aspect of supervision, the teaching, with which this chapter is largely concerned.

There are some qualifications which a supervisor should be able to find in anyone who has accepted a social work job. The caseworker should have *good manners*. Certainly a supervisor should not be obliged to teach a worker the rudiments of courtesy and consideration for others.[1]

The caseworker should have the *ability to express himself.*

[1]An article which is a helpful reminder to caseworkers is Elizabeth de Schweinitz, "Courtesy—a Requirement for the Social Worker," written for new staff members and students of the Board of Public Welfare, Washington, D.C., in 1948. Some state departments have received permission to reproduce it, and it is probable that any agency could secure similar permission to copy and use the article.

There will, of course, be a wide variation here, depending on home training, type of schooling, and native abilities, but a caseworker must be able to make himself understood, and the supervisor should not have to teach him the basic rules of grammar.

The caseworker should have *freedom from the more flagrant prejudices*. Again there will be wide variations. Every caseworker arrives at his first job trailing some residual prejudices, but these will diminish as his reading and his experience broaden his horizon, and as he comes into contact with clients from many different walks of life. If the prejudices do not diminish after a reasonable time, we may have a neurotic individual who should be helped to see that he is in the wrong line of work.

Every new caseworker comes to his agency with an *eagerness to do a good job* and wants only to find out how to do it. Most new caseworkers are convinced that they want to help people. It is possible that later the grim realities of the job may make it less rewarding than they had hoped, but at the start the sincere wish to help is an asset on which the supervisor can build if he starts quickly. The momentum may carry the worker through his first attack of doldrums. Even if the new worker has not thought through his career plans sufficiently to know whether or not he has any real urge to help humanity, he will certainly want to win the approval of his colleagues by doing efficiently whatever is expected of him, and he will want to visualize himself as a success in his new undertaking. This will supply sufficient motivation to make a new caseworker ready to learn and to work hard. After all, nobody thinks of social work as an easy job, and nobody will go into it expecting it to be a snap. The wise supervisor will take advantage of that initial momentum and will attempt to establish good work habits before a possible discouragement and disillusionment make the worker slack off.

There are some other attitudes not really compatible with

good casework practice which are nevertheless so often found in new and inexperienced caseworkers that we can only be astonished if they are not manifest:

Anxiety. — An inexperienced worker will feel uneasily that he does not know enough, has not enough skill, to do what is expected of him. Most new workers will frankly admit their feelings of inadequacy; a few, unable to face their own anxiety, may swing into reaction formation, deny all trepidation, avoid asking for help or advice, and try to "bull it through" alone. If this attitude is the result of discomfort with their anxiety and a wish to find comfort by denying anxiety, it will probably decrease as the workers become more secure, as their fund of information and experience grows. If it is a manifestation of a deep-seated resistance to all authority, it may never disappear and will be a serious obstacle to growth. But at first a supervisor should be patient, both with the expressed anxiety and with the denial of anxiety. Eventually, the supervisor will have enough evidence to know the dynamics that motivate the behavior.

Dependence. — Out of a new worker's inexperience and lack of knowledge grows a natural tendency to ask for constant support and reassurance from the supervisor. Many novice workers openly admit this dependence and turn to the supervisor for help before each new client contact, and for reassurance after the contact has been made: "Do you think I said the right thing? Maybe I should have handled it some other way?" If at all possible, the supervisor should make himself available to the new worker at any time that he is needed, following a "demand-feeding" routine. Some workers — in fact, perhaps most workers — are ambivalent, longing to feel that they can dare to be dependent, wanting also to think of themselves as adequate, not in need of any "parental" support, and this attitude too the supervisor must be able to recognize and accept.

The initial anxiety, with its initial dependence, should be relieved as quickly and painlessly as possible, and this can best be done by promptly giving to the worker the tools of his trade. Some type of orientation to the agency should be provided just as soon as possible, either by the supervisor himself or by in-service training. If the period of anxiety is unduly prolonged, the worker may develop the habit of clinging to rules and routines in order to avoid complicated issues, or he may turn to colleagues for advice, possibly getting wrong information and certainly reducing the chances for a good supervisory relationship.

A worker's failure to use information which the supervisor has provided may be due to his having been given too much too fast, with no opportunity to digest or to apply what has been poured into him. Or it may be due to the supervisor's failure to provide a central point of interest. A great mass of undifferentiated material can only confuse. To avoid this difficulty, the supervisor should impart first the type of information that can fire the worker's imagination. He should not sit the worker down in front of a manual or a weighty record. Perhaps the best initiation to agency work is by means of a case situation presented verbally by the supervisor, who can make the clients come alive as real people. Then, after talking about the people and the problems involved, the worker may be able to read the record with some understanding.

Information should be given as fast as the new worker can absorb it, but never one bit faster. This takes skillful timing on the part of the supervisor, for workers differ widely in the speed with which they can grasp a new job. Moving too slowly will leave an active, quick worker bored, and will open the way to bad work habits. Moving too rapidly will leave a slower individual confused and discouraged.

If at all possible, a tyro should be sent out for his first client contact into a situation that calls for asking questions rather than answering them, for making observations rather than making suggestions. The supervisor can help him in advance by discussing with him what he should look for, what he should notice, what questions he should ask, and can re-assure him that if the client asks questions which he cannot answer he should feel free to say that he is new on the job, he does not know, but he will find out. Then, when the worker comes back from this first visit, the supervisor should be on hand to talk it over with him, to discuss what his observations meant, to ask questions which may point up areas which the worker missed.

Routines should be taught only as they are needed, and only as they can be applied to specific cases. Every bit of infor-mation should be tied to a case with which the worker will be occupied at once. This will give him some feeling of com-petence, and will help to fix the information in his mind.

Because a worker coming to an agency job for the first time must absorb such a vast quantity of information about rou-tines, policies, requirements, a supervisor must expect to repeat many times. No worker can grasp it all the first time nor remember from a single telling. But eventually the worker should show encouraging signs of being able to carry over from one case to another. If it is the policy of the agency to have a child visit his dentist twice a year, the worker must be told this fact when he arranges the visit for the first child on his caseload. The supervisor must expect to remind him when visits are due in another family; perhaps tell him when appointments fall due for the third family, and even for the fourth. But by this time he should be able to remember and accept this routine, and himself arrange for the next trips for the next family. It is a danger signal if the worker remains too long in the initial stage of depending on the supervisor to remind him of every move to make, and this prolonged dependency should sooner or later be brought out in supervisory conferences as part of the ongoing evaluative process.

If possible, the teaching should be tied in with the worker's past experiences, with his college record, any previous jobs, any summer employment as camp helper, scoutmaster, group leader, or whatever: "Talking to this child won't be much different from talking to children in homes where you were baby sitting." And, of course, in each repeated procedure should be tied in with the previous occasions when it was used.

So much for the new worker's anxiety, insecurity, and dependence. There are still other characteristics which are commonly found in inexperienced workers.

The fantasy of being the good parent. — A characteristic often found in a well-meaning but inexperienced caseworker is the delusion of himself as the all-giving, the all-powerful parent who rescues the downtrodden from the ogre of social ills. As a matter of fact, this attitude may be an indication of good potential for the future, but it presents fairly serious hazards at the outset, chief among which is a blindness toward reality situations. Sooner or later such a worker faces bitter disillusionment as he sees the results of his own poor judgment (which he is loath to admit); the frequent resistance of the client to being rescued (which he cannot understand); the indifference of schools, employers, neighbors, to helping in the way he thinks they should help (which infuriates him); the limitations of the agency and of community resources (which he resents and feels somebody should do something about right away). At this point the worker is in danger of becoming so discouraged that he does not want to continue in social work. If he can be brought through these initial disillusionments, can be helped to accept limitations and work within reality situations, he will probably be a first-rate caseworker. But he may need a great deal of comforting and interpretation from the supervisor at the start.

Judgmental attitudes. — Many workers, in spite of sincere efforts to rid themselves of prejudice, will bring to the first job, as a result of home training, a judgmental attitude in any number of areas — sexual promiscuity, personal uncleanliness, drunkenness, avoidance of family responsibilities. It is not to be expected that young workers can see such behavior as symptoms of emotional illness. To the young, it always looks as though that man could stop drinking if he only tried, as though that mother could keep her home cleaner and get meals on time if she really wanted to. It is inevitable that until experience broadens their view, they will apply their own standards and their own values to every client. Also, some young workers have a physical aversion to certain types of impairment — mental retardation, spastic conditions, epilepsy — or they have a fear of possible physical attack, or of contagion. It takes time, experience, and help from a supervisor before a worker can see these unpleasant conditions as illnesses which he must help to minimize just as doctors try to ameliorate crippling physical conditions no matter how unpleasant the patient's body and behavior may be.

These judgmental attitudes must be handled, but probably the supervisor should wait until the worker has some feeling of identification with the agency, and has a secure relationship with the supervisor. If the prejudice, the learned fears and aversions, have come from the influence of the worker's own parents, they will not be easy to change before the worker has separated himself emotionally from his parents and identified with his new status on the job.

The teaching which a supervisor provides can never be divorced from a constant awareness of the kind of person he is instructing, and how that person is reacting to the learning experience. A caseworker's response to new knowledge is affected by his own individual background, the social and educational experiences he has had, his moral, religious, and racial norms. The supervisor should be conscious of all these, and also alert to the worker's individual speed of learning, his special defenses, his pattern of reaction to trying situations, his personal methods of relating to people, his system for establishing communication with people. A supervisor must guard against any temptation to force a worker into performing in exactly the way the supervisor would, no matter how successful his own system has been for him. If a caseworker produces good results, then for him his own ways are best.

If a new worker makes a mistake in handling a case, the supervisor must decide whether the error occurred because the worker did not know what he was supposed to do, because he knew but lacked the skill to do it, or because he was blocked from doing it by his own emotional make-up. This cannot be determined at once, but probably the supervisor should start off with the supposition that the worker did not know. So the supervisor gives all the necessary information all over again. If he finds that the worker knew but lacked the skill, then it is up to the supervisor to teach—not tell. And only when it becomes clear that this lack of skill did not account for the error must the supervisor come reluctantly to the conclusion that there is an emotional block on the part of the worker. Even then, he need not give up, for a supervisor's psychological support and help toward self-awareness may turn rationalization into at least an approximation of sublimation.

The true teaching of casework skills cannot be done by telling a worker what to do. Learning can best be accomplished if the learner can move from the familiar into the new, from the simple to the more complex. Probably the ideal method is to provide a new caseworker with a protected experience, assigning initially cases that are simple, and moving into depth only as the worker is strong enough to use the more difficult cases in his learning. Unhappily, this is all too seldom possible in the busy public agencies, and too often inexperienced caseworkers must be given a heavy, unselected caseload almost at once. If this is the situation, then the supervisor must partialize the learning for the worker, selecting the aspect of casework which the worker is ready to use for the *teaching*, but *telling* him what to do in other situations. However, the supervisor must be careful not to continue the telling one minute after the worker is ready to use teaching. This takes self-discipline on the part of the supervisor; for telling a worker what to do in an emergency situation takes less time than the slower, but infinitely more valuable, teaching.

A supervisor, observing a worker's activities with a client, will see that sometimes the worker has said or done exactly the right thing but cannot explain why he did it. This sort of intuitive response will happen at times to any untrained and inexperienced worker who has selected the right profession. It is an unconscious understanding of the client, born of common experiences, of having traveled the same road toward growth. The supervisor should pay special attention to the type of situation which a worker handles well by intuition. He will thus get a picture of the individual worker's pattern, growing out of that person's personality and special endowments. But intuition is not enough. It cannot be counted on, and so the supervisor should press the worker to analyze the steps he took correctly. Why were they right? Why did they succeed? Such an analysis of the things well done can bolster a worker's self-esteem, develop his security, make him more able to face possible adverse criticism when that becomes necessary.

Caseworkers must become professional people, knowing all the time what they are doing and why they are doing it. That is where the analysis of the "why" is so beneficial to the worker's professional growth.

At the same time, the supervisor must use some moderation, for too much analysis can stifle spontaneity. Emphasis should be put on how the client felt rather than on how the worker felt. Not "Why did you do this?" but rather "How did the client feel when you did this? Why do you think he felt that way?" If the worker's attention is centered too much on himself he may become immobilized through self-consciousness, with his efforts to observe and control himself, so that he has little attention left over for the reaction of the client. So we always focus attention on the client. When the worker has done something good by intuition there is not much use in asking him why he did it. He probably does not know anyway. We say, "The client's response to what you did was good. Why?"

The supervisor's teaching job is always directed toward helping the worker reach a deeper understanding of the client. Help the worker read a record or a referral summary, looking for clues to the client's needs. Help the worker recognize what the client is really saying, really asking for, behind his words.

The supervisor should make the caseworker think. If he is trying to understand the dynamics behind a client's behavior, the supervisor should never explain to him, even if it is all perfectly obvious. The supervisor should not let the worker maneuver him into doing all the talking, or making all the decisions. The supervisor does not accept the first interpretation offered by the worker even if it is probably the right one. Instead, all possible interpretations are discussed discarding them one by one until only the most likely one is left. If the worker is trying to plan for a client, he should not be told what to do. Nor should the first plan he suggests be accepted. Instead, alternatives should be discussed and what might result from each one, discarding some, retaining the best. This, of course, is the *teaching* technique. While the worker is still very new and inexperienced the supervisor will be *telling* him what to do about some of his cases and will be using the teaching approach only with a few of the cases.

This way of handling a worker's learning needs will take time in a supervisory conference, but it has advantages:

1. It will persuade a worker to think instead of jumping into half-baked plans without considering possible alternatives.

2. It will improve his casework skills because the supervisor's tolerance for the client, his efforts to understand the client's motivations, will condition the caseworker's own attitude toward the client.

3. The supervisor's efforts to look at all sides of a situation will increase the worker's confidence in his superior's tolerance toward any mistakes he might make, and give him more freedom in talking frankly about any areas of doubt he may have concerning his own work. This provides a better opportunity to help him.

4. A serious effort to analyze the reactions and motivations of the client indirectly helps the worker understand himself and may go a long way toward overcoming any emotional blocks he may have that prevent him from doing the best casework jobs of which he might be capable.

A supervisor quite early in his relationship with a new worker must decide what the worker needs from him. Support and encouragement? Discipline to stand alone? Grasp of the dynamics of human behavior? Tolerance for human error? Help in organizing his week's work? Guidance in establishing relationship with the Client? Guidance in directing and controlling an interview? Awareness of the need for a casework goal? Then, having determined what the worker needs, he selects the goal toward which he should move first and builds every supervisory conference with that goal in mind. And he does not let the worker distract him.

In every supervisory conference:

The supervisor *listens* to what the worker has to say and hears him to the end with full attention.

The supervisor *supplements* what the worker brings, by adding information, knowledge, or focus.

The supervisor *questions*, bringing out the why, stretching the worker's thinking, broadening his perspective, stimulating him to new ideas.

The supervisor *evaluates*, making every conference an occasion for a partial evaluation of how the worker operates, sharing his thinking with the worker so that the worker knows how he stands.

The supervisory conference should be a planned affair, with both worker and supervisor participating in the planning. One good technique is for the worker to select cases to be discussed and to notify the supervisor at least a day in advance of which cases he would like to have on the agenda. The supervisor, of course, must watch for any tendency on the part of the worker to present only cases of a certain type, or only the easy, successful cases — or, for that matter, any tendency to bring in only the poorly handled cases. Sometimes the supervisor will want to discuss a case situation in which the worker has failed to see the implications. But in general it is healthy for the worker to select the cases he wishes to present.

Sometimes a new supervisor will find himself confronted with caseworkers older in experience than himself, even workers who have been his colleagues and who might not be too happy about his promotion. Then the supervisor–worker relationship is of the utmost importance and may present some difficulties. Establishing a good working relationship is so much a matter of the individual personalities involved, the training, the work experience, and the previous attitudes that it is almost impossible to offer much advice. But here are a few hints:

The supervisor must not "throw his weight around."

He must give all possible credit to the worker's background.

He must never downgrade the worker.

He must give the caseworker every opportunity to make suggestions. If it is not possible to accept his suggestion, the supervisor must be very certain to discuss it thoroughly, pro and con.

Sometimes a supervisor finds himself with a worker who has "gone stale," who has carried the same cases so long that he can no longer see them with any vividness. If it is not possible or practicable to give him new cases, the only recourse is for the supervisor to read the records and find a fresh approach. There ought to be one case on his caseload which will benefit by a more dynamic approach, or by a change of casework goal. No case remains static and unchanged. Clients grow older. Health conditions vary. Neighbors move out and new neighbors come in. Somewhere there must be lurking a fresh viewpoint. Or the supervisor might ask the worker to make a detailed report on the case movement. That should recall to mind the original case goal and provide an opportunity to see whether or not it was realistic and to what extent there has been movement toward that goal.

What makes a good supervisor?

A good supervisor must be able to organize his work so that he can deal with a number of varied duties without confusion to himself or his workers.

He must know his agency, its policies, its resources, its limitations, and be able to convey this information to his workers in a way they can grasp and will remember.

A good memory helps, since the supervisor must have a working acquaintance with all the cases carried by all his workers. But lacking the memory, a good system of note-taking and card-filing may be the best substitute.

He must have an understanding of the individual needs

of each caseworker for security, stimulation, encouragement, which must be met before the worker can function up to his potential.

He must have sufficient diagnostic skill to recognize the point which each worker has reached in development, and meet the worker at the point where he is, not expecting too much from the frightened beginner, not oversupervising the more experienced.

Above all the supervisor must be able to convey to all workers a feeling of hope and optimism tempered by reality, an acceptance of people, a dedication of helping.

I once asked a group of very new workers to write out their ideas of how a supervisor could best help the caseworkers. I shall close this chapter by quoting one worker's description of the job of a supervisor:

> Because this job so seldom deals in blacks and whites, and so often in the various gradations that lie between, the ideal supervisor must be able to direct the starry-eyed new worker away from her own moral values, away from her Sunday School texts, and turn her toward the less judgmental. This is a big hump to cross, and the changeover from the judgmental to the evaluative approach cannot come without some heart searching and the help of a firm guiding hand. The ideal supervisor is one who can channel the boundless energy and enthusiasm of the new worker into constructive paths, and protect the client until this energy is tempered with some degree of objectivity. This is an important task, as with the large turnover in a public agency there seems to be a preponderance of the starry-eyed.
>
> The supervisor serves also as a sounding board for plans, ideas, and gripes. As such it is important that she be experienced in working with the tools realistically available, as there is often a large gap between "what we wish could happen" and "what usually does happen."
>
> The supervisor cannot allow a worker to concentrate all her attention on the three appealing children in her caseload to the exclusion of "Little Miss Retarded" or "Young Master Defiant." To avoid this the supervisor must keep current on all cases under her

care and aware of the total picture. This takes a good deal of concentration, an organized mind, and a system.

The supervisor must be able to understand what both the new worker and the old worker are feeling. The new worker comes with a certain dedication, and this must be channeled. The old worker has become channeled and must be rededicated. Both tasks take a lot of tact, a good knowledge of the problems to be faced, a working relationship with people. This last may be the most important.

The supervisor must achieve and maintain good communication between worker and herself. The supervisor must be sensitive to the needs of each worker. She must be able to ease up or bear down in relation to the worker's ability and training.

A supervisor must have a real interest in people and in her job of arranging that people be helped. Promotion seems to be a mixed blessing as with the increased responsibility there comes a loss of direct contact with the clients. This is coupled with the necessity to work through another individual, the worker who is supervised, in order to achieve goals which the supervisor sees but which may not be too clear to the worker. This must present problems which have to be handled with tact, for in pointing out weaknesses in the casework the supervisor must avoid emphasizing weaknesses in the worker, lest she destroy both case and worker.

In summary, the supervisor must combine conviction, tact, interest, dedication, organization, the ability to individualize, experience in the field and objectivity, all in a physique of considerable ruggedness. She must be a Grandma Moses, and a Jack LaLane, with touches of Spock, Fraiberg, Baruch, Ribble, and the Cleveland Public Library.[2]

[2]Linda Scott, 1963.

BIBLIOGRAPHY

Abrahamson, Arthur C. Group Methods in Supervision and Staff Development. New York, Harper and Brothers, 1959.

Ackerman, Nathan W., Frances L. Beatman, and Sanford N. Sherman. Exploring the Base for Family Therapy. New York, Family Service Association of America, 1961.

Aldrich, C. A., and M. M. Aldrich. Babies Are Human Beings. New York, Macmillan Co., 1938.

Allport, Gordon Willard. Pattern and Growth in Personality. New York, Holt, Rinehart and Winston, 1961.

American Public Welfare Association. Guide Statement on Protective Services for Older Adults. Chicago, the Association, 1962.

—— The Newcomer – Public Welfare's Challenge. Chicago, the Association, 1962.

—— Public Welfare Service and Aid to Dependent Children Chicago, the Association, 1961.

—— The Supervision of Caseworkers in the Public Welfare Agency. Chicago, the Association, 1958.

Archer, Jules. What Should Parents Expect from Children? New York, Public Affairs Pamphlets, 1964.

Auerbach, Aline. The Why and How of Discipline. New York, Child Study Association of America, 1957.

Austin, Lucille, and colleagues. Techniques of Student and Staff Supervision. New York, Family Service Association of America, 1950.

Averton, Alice, Katherine H. Tinker, and associates. Casework Notebook, Minnesota Family-centered Project. St. Paul, Minn., Greater St. Paul Community Chest and Councils, Inc., 1957.

Baker, Inez, *et al.* Administration of Public Welfare Services in Unmarried Parenthood and Adoption. New York, Child Welfare League of America, 1956.

Balint, Alice. The Early Years of Life. New York, Basic Books, 1954.

Baruch, Dorothy W. How to Live with Your Teen-ager. New York, McGraw-Hill Book Co., 1953.
—— New Ways in Sex Education. New York. McGraw-Hill Book Co., 1959.
—— One Little Boy. New York, Julian Press, 1952.
Baum, Marion. Some Dynamic Factors Affecting Family Adjustment to the Handicapped Child. Washington, D.C., Council for Exceptional Children, 1962.
Begab, Michael J. The Mentally Retarded Child. Washington, D.C., U.S. Department of Health, Education, and Welfare, 1963.
Bell, Norman W., and Ezra F. Vogt, eds. A Modern Introduction to the Family. Glencoe, Ill., Free Press, 1960.
Benson, Rubye G. An Intensive Casework Program with Families. Chicago, American Public Welfare Association, 1960.
Berg, Robert, and Callman Rawley. Planned Observation in Parent–Child Counseling. New York, Child Welfare League of America, 1958.
Blackey, Eileen. Services in the ADC Program. Washington, D.C., U.S. Department of Health, Education, and Welfare.
Blatt, Marianne, *et al.* Brief and Intensive Casework with Unmarried Mothers. New York, Child Welfare League of America, 1963.
Block, Babette. Foster Family Care for Unmarried Mothers. Washington, D.C., U.S. Department of Health, Education, and Welfare, 1953.
Boardman, Helen E., *et al.* The Neglected Battered Child Syndrome. New York, Child Welfare League of America, 1963.
Bork, Kathryn A. "A Staff Examination of Recording Skill: Part I," *Child Welfare,* XXXII' No. 2 (1953), 3–7; "A Staff Examination of Recording Skill: Part II," *Ibid.*, XXXII, No. 3 (1953), 11–14.
Born, Ronald H. Rehabilitation for Independence. Report of the Family Rehabilitation Program. San Francisco, San Francisco Welfare Department, 1962.
Bowlby, John. Child Care and the Growth of Love. Baltimore, Penguin Books, 1957.
—— Maternal Care and Mental Health. Geneva, Switzerland, World Health Organization, 1952.
Bristol, Margaret Cochran. Handbook on Social Case Recording. Chicago, University of Chicago Press, 1936.
Buell, Bradley, and associates. Community Planning for Human Services. New York, Columbia University Press, 1952.

Burgess, Margaret Elaine, and Daniel O. Price. An American Dependency Challenge, Chicago, American Public Welfare Association, 1963.

Butcher, Ruth, and Marion Robinson. The Unmarried Mother. New York, Public Affairs Pamphlets, 1959.

Butts, Sarah H. Casework Services in Public Assistance Medical Care, Washington, D.C., U.S. Department of Health, Education, and Welfare, 1962.

Carbonara, Nancy Trevorrow. Techniques for Observing Normal Child Behavior. Pittsburgh, University of Pittsburgh Press, 1961.

Cassatt, Anna. Recording in Public Welfare. Raleigh, North Carolina Board of Public Welfare, 1948.

Chance, Erika. Families in Treatment. New York, Basic Books, 1959.

Charnley, Jean. The Art of Child Placement. Minneapolis, University of Minnesota Press, 1955.

Chaskel, Ruth. Assertive Casework in a Short-Term Situation. New York, Family Service Association of America, 1963.

Child Welfare League of America. Standards for Services to Unmarried Parents. New York, the League, 1960.

—— Unmarried Mothers. New York, the League, 1963.

Choate, Reba E., and Ursula M. Gallagher. Unmarried Parents. Washington, D.C., U.S. Department of Health, Education, and Welfare, 1961.

Cohen, Nathan Edward. Social Work in the American Tradition. New York, Dryden Press, 1958.

Cowgill, Ella Lee. A Guidebook for Beginners in Public Assistance. New York, Family Service Association of America, 1940.

Davis, Annie Lee. Children Living in Their Own Homes. Washington, D.C., U.S. Department of Health, Education, and Welfare, Children's Bureau, 1953.

De Francis, Vincent. Special Skills in Child Protective Services. Denver, American Humane Association, 1958.

DelliQuadri, Fred, ed. Helping the Family in Urban Society. New York, Columbia University Press, 1963.

De Schweinitz, Elizabeth, and Karl De Schweinitz. The Content of the Public Assistance Job. New York, National Association of Social Workers, 1948.

Dittmann, Laura L. The Mentally Retarded Child at Home. Washington, D.C.' U.S. Department of Health, Education, and Welfare, 1949.

Douglas County Welfare Department. Family Rehabilitation Program. Douglas County, Nebr., the Department, 1962.

Du Bois, Rachel D. and Mew-Soong Li. The Art of Group Conversation. New York, Association Press, 1963.

Eisenberg, Morton S., M.D. Some Psychodynamic Aspects of Casework with the Unmarried Mother. The author, 1956.

Ellsworth, Dorothy. Precocious Adolescence in Wartime. New York, Family Welfare Association of America, 1944.

English, O. Spurgeon, M.D., and Gerald H. J. Pearson, M.D. Common Neuroses of Children and Adults. New York, W. W. Norton, 1950.

——The Emotional Problems of Living. New York, W. W. Norton. 1945.

Erikson, Erik H. Childhood and Society. New York, W. W. Norton, 1950.

——Identity and the Life Cycle. New York, International Universities Press, 1959.

Espy, Hilda Cole. "The Tragic Problem of Dropouts in Our Schools," *Woman's Day*, August, 1964.

Faber, Bernard, William Jenne, and Romolo Torgo. Family Crisis and the Retarded Child. Washington, D.C., Council for Exceptional Children, 1960.

Family-centered Project. Families in Trouble. Minneapolis, Family-centered Project, Greater St. Paul Community Chest and Councils, 1958.

Family Service Association of America. "Family Casework in the Interest of Children," *Social Casework*, XXXIX (1958), 61–182.

——The High Cost of Unhappy Living. New York, the Association, 1953.

——New Emphasis on Cultural Factors. Reprints from *Social Casework*, 1946–48. New York: the Association.

——Supervisory Techniques in Public Assistance Agencies. Reprints from *Journal of Social Casework*, 1944–46. New York: the Association.

——Understanding the Psychology of the Unmarried Mother. Reprints from *Journal of Social Casework*, 1945–47. New York: the Association.

Family Welfare Association of America. What Social Workers Should Know about Illness and Physical Handicap. New York, the Association, 1937.

Farnham, Marynia. The Adolescent. New York, Harper and Brothers, 1951.

Feldman, Frances Lomas. The Family in a Money World. New York, Family Service Association of America, 1957.

Felix, Robert H., M.D., *et al.* Mental Health and Social Welfare. New York, Columbia University Press, 1961.

Fenlason, Anne F. Essentials in Interviewing. New York, Harper and Brothers, 1952.

Fenton, Norman, and Kermit Wiltse, eds. Group Methods in the Public Welfare Program. Palo Alto, Calif., Pacific Books, 1963.

Fine, Roswell H., and James C. Dawson, M.D. A Therapy Program for the Mildly Retarded Adolescent, *American Journal of Mental Deficiency,* LIX (1964), 23–30.

Fraiberg, Selma H. The Magic Years. New York, Charles Scribner's Sons, 1959.

— Psychoanalytical Principles in Casework with Children. New York, Family Service Association of America, 1955.

Frank, Lawrence. The Adolescent and the Family. Chicago, National Society for Study of Education, 1944.

— The Fundamental Needs of the Child. New York, New York State Society for Mental Health, 1938.

Frankiel, Rita V. Review of Research on Parent Influences on Child Personality. New York, Family Service Association of America, 1959.

French, Thomas. The Importance of the First Interview with the Unmarried Mother. Washington, D.C., U.S. Department of Health, Education, and Welfare, 1952.

Freud, Anna. The Ego and the Mechanisms of Defense. New York, International Universities Press, 1946.

Freud, Sigmund. An Outline of Psychoanalysis. New York, W. W. Norton, 1949.

Friedlander, Walter. Introduction of Social Welfare. Englewood Cliffs, N.J., Prentice-Hall, 1955.

Galbraith, John Kenneth. The Affluent Society. New York, Houghton Mifflin, 1958.

Garrett, Annette. Interviewing: Its Principles and Methods. New York, Family Service Association of America, 1942.

— Learning through Supervision. Northampton, Mass., Smith College Studies, 1954.

Geismar, L. L., and Michael A. LaSorte. Understanding the Multiproblem Family. New York, Association Press, 1964.

Gennaria, Marion R. Pain; a Factor in Growth and Development. New York, Child Welfare League of America, 1943.

Gesell, Arnold L. How a Baby Grows. New York, Harper and Brothers, 1945.

Gesell, Arnold L., *et al.* The Child from Five to Ten. New York, Harper and Brothers, 1946.

Gill, Judge Thomas. "The Legal Nature of Neglect." *National Probation and Parole Journal*, VI, No. 1 (1960).

Gjenvick, Rev. Benjamin A. "The Worker's Position with Respect to Client Self-Determination and Christian Responsibility," in Casework Papers 1959, pp. 31–35, New York, Family Service Association of America, 1959.

Glasser, Paul, *et al.* Group Methods and Services in Child Welfare. New York, Child Welfare League of America, 1963.

Glickman, Esther. Child Placement through Clinically Oriented Casework. New York, Columbia University Press, 1957.

Gordon, Henrietta. "Protective Services for Children," *Child Welfare League of America Bulletin*, XXV, No. 5 (1946), 1–5.

Greenfield, Margaret. Self-Support in Aid to Dependent Children. Pasadena, Calif., University of California Bureau of Public Administration, 1956.

Groves, Ernest R. Conserving Marriage and the Family. New York, Macmillan, 1944.

Gruenberg, Sidonie M., and Benjamin C. Gruenberg. Parents, Children, and Money. New York, Viking, 1933.

Hamilton, Gordon. Principles of Social Case Recording. New York, Columbia University Press, 1946.

—— Psychotherapy in Child Guidance. New York, Columbia University Press, 1940.

—— Theory and Practice of Social Case Work. New York, Columbia University Press, 1940.

Hamilton, Gordon, and Hyman Grossbard. Developing Self-Awareness. New York, Family Service Association of America, 1954.

Hancock, Claire. Children and Neglect . . . Hazardous Home Conditions. Washington, D.C., U.S. Department of Health, Education, and Welfare, 1963.

—— Protective Service in Practice. New York, Child Welfare League of America, 1948.

Harrison, Emma. Public Welfare. New York, Public Affairs Pamphlet, 1963.

Hill, Reuben L. Families under Stress. New York, Harper and Brothers, 1949.

Hillyer, Cecile. The Evolving Concept of Rehabilitation. New York, National Association of Social Workers, 1961.

Hollingworth, Letas. The Psychology of the Adolescent. New York, Appleton-Century, 1930.

Hollis, Florence. Casework—a Psychosocial Therapy. New York, Random House, 1964.

Houwink, Eda. The Place of Casework in the Public Assistance Program. Chicago, American Public Welfare Association, 1941.

Hunt, Joseph McV., and Leonard S. Kogan. Measuring Results in Social Casework. New York, Family Service Association of America, 1950.

Hurlock, Elizabeth B. Child Growth and Development. New York, McGraw-Hill Book Co., 1949.

Isaacs, Susan S. The Nursery Years. London, George Routledge and Sons, Ltd., 1938.

Jackel, Merl M. "Clients with Character Disorders." *Social Casework*, XLIV (1963), 315–22.

Jenkins, Gladys, Helen Shacter, and William Bauer. These Are Your Children. New York, Scott, Foresman and Co., 1953.

Jeter, Helen R. Children, Problems, and Services in Child Welfare Programs. Washington, D.C., U.S. Department of Health, Education, and Welfare, 1963.

—— Children Served by Public Child Welfare Programs. Washington, D.C., U.S. Department of Health, Education, and Welfare, 1958.

—— Services in Public and Voluntary Child Welfare Programs. Washington, D.C., U.S. Department of Health, Education, and Welfare, 1962.

Jolowicz, Almeda R. "The Hidden Parent," in New York State Conference on Social Work, pp. 13–27. New York: the Conference, 1946.

Josselyn, Irene M., M.D. The Adolescent and His World. New York, Family Service Association of America, 1952.

—— Cultural and Emotional Factors in Their Relation to Unmarried Parents. New York, Episcopal Service for Youth, 1947.

—— Emotional Problems of Living. Chicago, Science Research Associates, 1953.

—— The Happy Child. New York, Random House, 1955.

Josselyn, Irene M., M.D. Psychosocial Development of Children. New York, Family Service Association of America, 1948.

Josselyn, Irene M., M.D., and Ruth Schley Goldman. "Should Mothers Work?" *Social Service Review*, XXIII (1949), 74–87.

——"What We Know about the Unmarried Mother." Paper, National Conference of Social Work, 1953.

Kahn, Robert L., and Charles F. Cannell. The Dynamics of Interviewing. New York, John Wiley and Sons, 1957.

Kaplan, Saul. Support from Absent Fathers of Children Receiving ADC. Washington, D.C., U.S. Department of Health, Education, and Welfare, 1960.

Kasius, Cora, ed. Family Casework in the Interest of Children. New York, Family Service Association of America, 1958.

——Goals and Methods in Public Assistance. Reprint from *Social Casework*, 1955. New York, Family Service Association of America, 1955.

——Principles and Techniques in Social Casework. New York, Family Service Association of America, 1950.

——Relief Practice in a Family Agency. New York, Family Welfare Association of America, 1942.

Kasman, Saul, ed. Selected Readings for the Public Assistance Worker. Chicago, Illinois Public Aid Commission, 1953.

Keith-Lucas, Alan. Some Casework Concepts for the Public Assistance Worker. Raleigh, N.C., University of North Carolina Press, 1957.

Kline, Draza. Services to Parents of Placed Children: Some Changing Problems and Goals. New York, Child Welfare League of America, 1960.

Koos, Earl Lomon. Families in Trouble. New York, King's Crown Press, 1946.

Kurtz, Russell H., ed. The Public Assistance Worker. New York, Russell Sage Foundation, 1938.

Leyendecker, Hilary M. Problems and Policy in Public Assistance. New York, Harper and Brothers, 1955.

Littner, Ner. Primary Needs of Young Children. New York, Child Welfare League of America, 1959.

——Some Traumatic Effects of Separation and Placement. New York, Child Welfare League of America, 1956.

——The Strains and Stresses of the Child Welfare Worker. New York, Child Welfare League of America, 1957.

Loyola Graduate School of Social Work. Profile of Children in Foster Care. Chicago, the School, 1964.

McCormick, Mary J. The Role of Values. New York, Family Service Association of America, 1961.

McDonald, Eugene T. Understand Those Feelings. Pittsburgh, Stanwix House, 1963.

MacFarlane, Andrew. The Neverland of the Neglected Child. Toronto, Department of Public Welfare, Ontario, Canada, 1958.

McKeany, Maurine. The Absent Father and Public Policy in the Program of Aid to Dependent Children. Berkeley, Calif., University of California Press, 1960.

Manning, Helen. The Nature of Service in Public Assistance. Washington, D.C., U.S. Department of Health, Education, and Welfare, 1958.

Martz, Helen E. "Illegitimacy and Dependency," *Health, Education, and Welfare Indicators*, September, 1963. pp. XV–XXX.

May, Edgar. The Wasted Americans. New York, Harper and Row, 1964.

Meade, Margaret. A Creative Life for Your Children. Washington, D.C., U.S. Department of Health, Education, and Welfare, 1963.

Mencher, Samuel. "The Concept of Authority and Social Casework," in Casework Papers 1960, pp. 126–50. New York, Family Service Association of America, 1960.

Milt, Harry. Young Adults and Their Parents. New York, Public Affairs Pamphlet, 1964.

Molloy, Julia S. Teaching the Retarded Child to Talk. New York, John Day, 1961.

Morse, William, *et al.* Understanding How Groups Work. New York, Adult Education Association, 1955.

Moscrop, Martha. In-Service Training for Social Agency Practice. Toronto, University of Toronto Press, 1958.

Murphy, Frances Salomon. Runaway Alice. New York, Scholastic Book Services, 1961.

Murphy, Lois Barclay, and collaborators. The Widening World of Childhood. New York, Basic Books, 1962.

National Association of Social Workers. Goals of Public Social Policy. New York, the Association, 1959.

National Social Welfare Assembly. Jobless Youth . . . a Challenge to Community Organizations. New York, the Assembly.

Neisser, Edith C. The Many Faces of Money. New York, Human Relations Aids, 1958.

Neisser, Edith C., and Nina Ridenour. Your Children and Their Gangs. Washington, D.C., U.S. Department of Health, Education, and Welfare, 1960.

Nelson, Calvin C. Developing a Positive Self-Concept in the Mentally Retarded. New York, American Association on Mental Deficiency, 1963.

Neumann, Frederika, *et al.* Primary Behavior Disorders in Children. New York, Family Welfare Association, 1945.

Neustaedter, Eleanor. Relief—a Constructive Tool in Casework Treatment. New York, Charity Organization Society, 1930.

New York City Youth Board. Reaching the Unreached. New York, the Board, 1952.

New York State Council for Children. Good Living for Young Children. New York, the Council, 1960.

New York State Department of Health. The Pre-School Years. New York, the Department, 1957.

New York State Youth Commission. Blueprint for Delinquency Prevention. New York, the Commission.

Nicholds, Elizabeth. A Primer of Social Casework. New York, Columbia University Press, 1960.

Page, Norma Kroll. Protective Services: a Case Illustrating Casework with Parents. New York, Child Welfare League of America, 1955.

Parad, Howard J., ed. Ego Psychology and Dynamic Casework. New York, Family Service Association of America, 1958.

Parad, Howard J., and Roger R. Miller, eds. Ego-oriented Casework: Problems and Perspectives. New York, Family Service Association of America, 1963.

Parker, Beulah, M.D. Psychiatric Consultation for Non-psychiatric Social Workers. Washington, D.C., U.S. Department of Health, Education and Welfare, 1958.

Parkhurst, Helen. Growing Pains. Garden City, N.Y.' Doubleday and Co., 1962.

Perlman, Helen Harris. Social Casework: a Problem-solving Process. Chicago, University of Chicago Press, 1957.

Peters, Mary Overholt. The Caseworker—Person with Value. Chicago, American Public Welfare Association, 1959.

—— Talks with Beginning Social Workers. New York, Family Service Association of America, 1947.

Prugh, Dane, Robert Harlow, *et al.* Deprivation of Maternal Care. Geneva, Switzerland, World Health Organization, 1962.

Rabinow, Mildred, and Oscar Rabinowitz. "The Use of Casework Concepts in Parent Group Education," in Casework Papers 1961, pp. 131–42. New York, Family Service Association of America, 1961.

Rall, Mary E. Casework with Parents of Adolescent Unmarried Mothers and Potential Unmarried Mothers. New York, Child Welfare League of America, 1961.

Rall, Mary E., and Esther Glickman. Working with the Child and His Parents. New York, Child Welfare League of America, 1954.

Redl, Fritz. Pre-Adolescents: What Makes Them Tick? New York, Committee on Mental Hygiene.

Redl, Fritz, and David Wineman. Children Who Hate. Glencoe, Ill., Free Press, 1951.

—— Controls from Within, Glencoe, Ill., Free Press, 1952.

Reik, Theodor. Listening with the Third Ear. New York, Farrar Straus and Co., 1948.

Ribble, Margaret A., M.D. The Personality of the Young Child. New York, Columbia University Press, 1955.

—— The Rights of Infants. New York, Columbia University Press, 1943.

Ridenour, Nina. Some Special Problems of Children, Two to Five. New York, Committee on Mental Hygiene, 1947.

Robinson, Marion. "Community-wide Planning for Family Health and Welfare,"*Marriage and Family Living* (1957).

Roe, Phyllis, Caroline Fell, and Laura Pittman. Families Are for Children. Chicago, American Public Welfare Association, 1962.

Rosenthal, Maurice J., M.D., and Mary E. Sullivan. Psychiatric Consultation in a Public Child Welfare Agency. Washington, D.C., U.S. Department of Health, Education, and Welfare, 1959.

Ross, Helen, and Adelaide H. Johnson, M.D. Psychiatric Interpretation of the Growth Process. New York, Family Service Association of America, 1949.

Rowan, Matille, and Reuben Parmor. Casework with the Unmarried Father. New York, Child Welfare League of America, 1959.

Ruesch, Jurgen, and Weldon Kees. Non-verba Communication. Berkeley, Calif., University of California Press, 1957.

Saunders, Lyle. Cultural Difference and Medical Care. New York, Russell Sage Foundation, 1954.

Savoca, Rose. Home Visiting with the Retarded Child in Cuyahoga County. New York, National Association for Retarded Children, 1962.

Schneiderman, Leonard. "Value Orientation Preferences of Chronic Relief Recipients," *Social Work,* IX, No. 3 (1964), 13-18.

Schorr, Alvin L. Filial Responsibility in the Modern American Family. Washington, D.C., U.S. Department of Health, Education, and Welfare, 1960.

Schottland, Charles I. "The Nature of Services in Public Assistance," in Casework Papers 1959, pp. 5–19. New York, Family Service Association of America, 1959.

Sears, Robert R., Eleanor E. Maccoby, and Harry Levin. Patterns of Child Rearing. Evanston, Ill., Row, Peterson and Co., 1957.

Simcox, Beatrice R., and Irving Kaufman, M.D. Character Disorders in Parents of Delinquents. New York, Family Service Association of America, 1959.

Simon, Anne W. Stepchild in the Family. New York, Odyssey Press. 1964.

Slaughter, Stella. Forgotten Children. New York, National Association for Mental Health.

— The Mentally Retarded Child and His Parent. New York, Harper and Brothers, 1960.

— The Mentally Subnormal Child. World Health Organization Technical Report Series No. 75. New York, Columbia University Press, 1954.

Slavson, Samuel R. Introduction to Group Therapy. New York, Commonwealth Fund, 1943.

Small, S. Mouchly, M.D. Symptoms of Personality Disorder. New York, Family Welfare Association of America, 1945.

Smith, Richard M., M.D. Between One and Five. Boston, Mass., John Hancock Mutual Life Insurance Co., 1950.

Spitz, René. Emotional Growth in the First Year. New York, Child Study Association, 1947.

Spock, Benjamin, M.D. Common Sense Book of Baby and Child Care. New York, Duell, Sloan & Pearce. 1946.

— Problems of Parents, New York, Houghton Mifflin, 1962.

Strain, Frances Bruce. Being Born. New York, Appleton-Century Co., 1942.

Strode, Josephine, and Pauline R. Strode. Introduction to Social Case Work. New York, Harper and Brothers, 1940.

Swanson, Lynn. "Police and Children," *Police Chief* (1958).

Thornhill, Margaret. Problems of Repeated Out-of-Wedlock Pregnancies. New York, Child Welfare League of America, 1959.

Towle, Charlotte. Common Human Needs. New York, National Association of Social Workers, 1945.

Tyler, Inez. Intake in a Public Agency. Chicago, American Public Welfare Association, 1941.

U.S. Department of Health, Education, and Welfare. The Application Process in Public Assistance Administration. Washington, D.C., the Department, 1948.

——Illegitimacy and Its Impact on the ADC Program. Washington, D.C., the Department, 1960.

—— Maine – Guides to Interviewing. "How They Do It." Washington, D.C., the Department, 1960.

—— Maine – Work Simplification. "How They Do It." Washington, D.C., the Department, 1960.

—— Mental Retardation. Washington, D.C., the Department, 1962.

—— Prenatal Care. Washington, D.C., the Department, 1955.

—— Protective Services for Older Persons. Washington, D.C., the Department, 1964.

—— Public Assistance under the Social Security Act. Washington, D.C., the Department, 1961.

—— Understanding Juvenile Delinquency. Washington, D.C., the Department, 1950.

——What's Happening to Delinquent Children in Your Town? Washington, D.C., the Department, 1953.

—— Your Child from One to Six. Washington, D.C., the Department, 1945.

—— Your Child from Six to Twelve. Washington, D.C., the Department, 1949.

Vincent, Clark E. Unmarried Mothers. New York, Free Press of Glencoe, 1961.

Voiland, Alice, and associates. Family Casework Diagnosis. New York, Columbia University Press, 1962.

Voiland, Alice, Martha Gundalach, and Mildred Corner. Developing Insight in Initial Interviews. New York, Family Service Association of America, 1947.

Von Mering, Otto, et al. Significance of the Father. New York Family Service Association of America, 1 59.

Weinstein, Eugene A. The Self-Image of the Foster Child. New York, Russell Sage Foundation, 1960.

Welsch, Exie F., M.D. "Sustaining the Child in His Impaired Home," *Child Welfare*, XXXII, No. 7 (1953), 3–7.

Wexler, Susan Stanhope. The Story of Sandy. New York, Bobbs-Merrill, 1955.

White, Gladys, Alberta Hill, and Edna Amidon. Improving Home and Family Living among Low-Income Families. Washington, D.C., U.S. Department of Health, Education, and Welfare, 1962.

Wilkie, Charlotte. "A Study of Distortions in Recording Interviews," *Social Work,* VIII, No. 3 (1963), 31–36.

Williams, Frankwood. Adolescence: Studies in Mental Hygiene. New York, Farrar and Rinehart, 1921.

Williamson, Margaret. Supervision, Principles and Methods. New York, Woman's Press, 1950.

Wirtz, Willard, *et al.* The Challenge of Jobless Youth. Washington, D.C., U.S. Department of Labor, 1963.

Witmer, Helen. Parents and Delinquency. Washington, D.C., U.S. Department of Health, Education and Welfare, 1954.

Wrieden, Jane. The Unmarried Obstetrical Patient, Washington, D.C., U.S. Department of Health, Education, and Welfare, 1956.

Yarrow, Leon, Mary Ainsworth, and Kurt Glaser. Maternal Deprivation. New York, Child Welfare League of America, 1962.

Young, Leontine, R. Out of Wedlock. New York, McGraw-Hill Book Co., 1954.

—— Wednesday's Children. New York, McGraw-Hill Book Co., 1964.

Zachry, Caroline B., and Margaret Lighty. Emotion and Conduct in Adolescence. New York, Appleton-Century, 1940.

Zimmerman, Carle C. Consumption and Standards of Living. New York, Van Nostrand, 1936.

INDEX